YOUR FIRST YEARS TEACHING ELEMENTARY MATHEMATICS

SUCCESS from the START

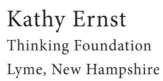

Kathy Ernst
Thinking Foundation
Lyme, New Hampshire

Sarah Ryan
University of Delaware
Newark, Delaware

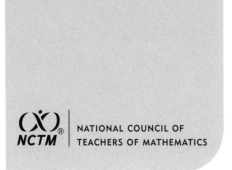

more**4u**
www.nctm.org/more4u
Access code: SSE13954

NCTM® | NATIONAL COUNCIL OF
TEACHERS OF MATHEMATICS

Copyright © 2014 by
The National Council of Teachers of Mathematics, Inc.
1906 Association Drive, Reston, VA 20191-1502
(703) 620-9840; (800) 235-7566; www.nctm.org
All rights reserved

Library of Congress Cataloging-in-Publication Data

Ernst, Kathy.
  Success from the start : your first years teaching elementary mathematics /
Kathy Ernst, Sarah Ryan.
      pages cm
  Includes bibliographical references.
  ISBN 978-0-87353-678-3
  1. Mathematics--Study and teaching (Elementary)--United States. I. Ryan, Sarah,
1966- II. Title.
  QA135.6.E76 2013
  372.7--dc23
                                   2013033470

The National Council of Teachers of Mathematics is the public voice of mathematics education, supporting teachers to ensure equitable mathematics learning of the highest quality for all students through vision, leadership, professional development, and research.

Page 133 (word problem at top of page). From Investigations Curriculum Unit (Teacher Edition) Grade4 Unit 3 by Sussan Jo Russel and Karen Economopoulos, copyright 2008 Pearson Education, Inc. or its affiliates. Used with permission. All rights reserved.

Printed in the United States of America

CONTENTS

ACKNOWLEDGMENTS...V

INTRODUCTION vii

I. MATHEMATICS TEACHING AND LEARNING.................1

1. How Should Elementary Math Class Look and Sound? 3

2. Learning Mathematics with Understanding 17

II. LAYING THE GROUNDWORK.............................33

3. Preparing for a Successful Beginning 35

4. Setting Up Your Classroom 45

5. Building a Supportive Learning Community 53

6. Establishing Routines to Support Mathematics Learning 75

7. Developing Computational Fluency 91

III. THE LESSON CYCLE 113

8. Tasks That Promote Learning Math with Understanding......... 115

9. Lesson Planning...129

10. Lesson Enactment....................................... 151

11. Lesson Reflection..169

IV. ESSENTIAL ELEMENTS OF EFFECTIVE
MATHEMATICS TEACHING...........................193

12. Mathematical Discourse....................................195

13. Assessment and Feedback 215

14. Differentiation: Meeting the Needs of Diverse Learners 235

15. Homework...251

REFERENCES 259

INDEX... 265

TECHNOLOGY
FAMILY ENGAGEMENT

ACKNOWLEDGMENTS

We could not have written this book without help and support. Lucy West believed in us and gave us the opportunity to write this book. Cathy Fosnot taught us about the landscape of learning and how to use contexts, visual models, and number strings to support student learning. Her work has made us better teachers—and teachers of teachers.

Many people directly contributed in different ways, from offering meeting space to opening their classrooms so that we could videotape lessons and gather student work: Fabrizia Adang, William Barton, Julie Broderick, Trina Cassidy, Samara Estroff, Lilliana Ferreira, Sarah Fiarman, Renee Griffith, Ellen McCrum, Elena Megalos, Amy Musto, Michelle Pearson, Annette Raphel, Ray Rissmiller, Kimberly Salvatore, Kelly Toscano, and Debra Taylor. Kristine Reed Woleck, Lucy West, Estrella Lopez, and Meghan Fitzgerald offered feedback to improve the book. Many administrators, teachers, and students have welcomed us into their schools and classrooms over the years, teaching us much about the teaching and learning of mathematics.

Finally, we thank Myrna Jacobs, NCTM's publications manager, for her support and encouragement throughout the development of this book. We also thank Gabe Waggoner, whose skillful editing helped us make the book more concise.

Kathy Ernst

Rachel MacAnallen ignited my passion for math problem solving, inspiring me to join the math reform movement almost thirty years ago. Adrianne Wallace-Bearak, Ellen McCrum, Eric Forman, and teachers in the Harrison Central School District and Colorado Academy Lower School helped me refine explicit frameworks for lesson planning, enactment, and reflection. I thank David Hyerle for his support and for Thinking Maps, tools that have had a vital impact on my teaching, coaching, supervision, and leadership. Dennis Kortright and Julie Broderick's expertise and voices about math teaching and learning have been constant companions.

My deepest gratitude goes to Larry Alper—my husband, colleague, and friend—for his love, support, and incisive thinking. My daughters, Kyla and Molly, have patiently taught me how to be a better teacher as they have grown into adulthood.

Sarah Ryan

Lucy West taught me much as a new teacher, particularly the value of curiosity toward one's teaching. My colleagues from Community District 2 in New York City provided an unparalleled professional learning community. My colleagues at the University of Delaware, Jon Manon, Valerie Maxwell, Jan Parsons, and Janice MacCarthy, were flexible and supportive throughout the writing process and offered valuable insights into teaching and learning.

My parents and sister encouraged me, and I am grateful to my children, Hunter, Eliza, and Henry, for all they have taught me. I marvel at how they think about mathematics. From observing and listening to them, I have learned much about children's capacity to find mathematics intriguing and to make sense of it. My greatest thanks go to my husband, Rob, both a source of astounding support and a remarkably thoughtful and insightful colleague.

INTRODUCTION

When the National Council of Teachers of Mathematics (NCTM) Educational Materials Committee asked us to write a book for beginning elementary math teachers, we were excited and overwhelmed. We were excited to share teaching practices honed through years of experience as classroom teachers, coaches, supervisors, and staff developers—practices we developed by building on others' work and research. Yet this was a daunting challenge: How could we convey the complexities of teaching math without overwhelming new teachers, or make information about math teaching accessible without oversimplifying?

We first thought about goals for students: What is important for students to learn? What does a successful math student look like? To succeed in today's information age, students must interpret, generate, and represent data, and they need to be fluent with numbers and operations to do mental calculations. They also need deep, connected mathematical knowledge to access and transfer to new and complex problems. NCTM (1989, 2000) presents a framework of Process Standards through which students must engage to learn math with understanding. The Common Core State Standards for Mathematics, CCSSM (National Governors Association Center for Best Practices and Council of Chief State School Officers, 2010), incorporates and expands on the NCTM Process Standards in their Standards for Mathematical Practice. Both documents highlight the goals of developing proficiency in problem solving and procedural fluency with conceptual understanding.

NCTM Process Standards	**CCSSM Standards for Mathematical Practice**
• problem solving	• Make sense of problems and persevere in solving them
• reasoning and proof	• Reason abstractly and quantitatively
• representation	• Construct viable arguments and critique the reasoning of others
• communication	• Model with mathematics
• connections	• Use appropriate tools strategically
	• Attend to precision
	• Look for and make use of structure
	• Look for and express regularity in repeated reasoning

The guiding principles and essential practices we share with you in this book align with both the NCTM Process Standards and the CCSSM Standards for Mathematical Practice.

Successful mathematics students also demonstrate the dispositions of effective problem solvers: curiosity, flexibility, persistence, risk taking, and reflection. Such students are curious about patterns and relationships, question why numbers and operations behave the way they do, explore the underlying mathematical structure of problems, and wonder what conjectures they can make. They are flexible as they manipulate numbers in problems to make them easier to solve or as they consider other ways to solve problems. As they grapple with problems, they persist in understanding them, solving them, proving their solutions correct, and seeking to make new connections and generate new problems. They take risks in inventing strategies or considering new strategies or ideas. As they problem solve, successful math students continually reflect on and monitor their thinking and work, asking themselves, "Does this make sense?"

To support math learning, classrooms must be mathematical communities where students work together to solve problems, raise questions, invent procedures, explore patterns and relationships, formulate proofs, and justify their solutions and ideas through classroom discourse. Together with students, teachers create a safe, supportive environment where important mathematical ideas emerge, are debated, and are investigated.

This book presents both the challenges and the opportunities inherent in developing mathematical thinkers. This book will help you transform the challenges into opportunities for rich learning. You might already be asking yourself these questions:

- How can I differentiate my teaching to meet the diverse needs of my students?

- What assessments best advance student learning?

- How can students understand math if I do not show them different strategies and tell them about the underlying mathematical structures and properties?

- What advice do I give parents about how to support their children's math learning?

These questions and more are what beginning math teachers should ask themselves and their colleagues as they revise and refine their practices. This book suggests ways to address such questions as you support your students' development of mathematical ideas.

This is not a book of math activities. Instead, it focuses on how students learn math and on pedagogy. Vignettes, all based on real classroom discussions, illustrate teaching practices to support math learning. Chapters about the lesson cycle come from conversations teachers had when they planned, enacted, and reflected on a lesson. These vignettes model effective mathematics teaching and learning.

Start by taking small steps to improve your teaching, gradually working toward skillful practice. As you read each chapter, try one or two ideas. With more experience, you can return to the chapters to clarify your thinking, delve more deeply, and refine your teaching by trying out more complex ideas. As you revisit this book, we hope that it will support you to make deeper, more meaningful connections between your teaching experience and our model of math practice.

The book comprises four sections. Section I (Mathematics Teaching and Learning) envisions what mathematics learning and teaching look like and the fundamental underpinnings of best practices. Chapter 1 consists of vignettes from a grade 2 classroom followed by important aspects of teaching and learning. Students engage in problem solving with peers, and their teacher facilitates a class discussion in which students analyze different solutions. Chapter 2 describes how children learn math with understanding, and presents guiding principles and brain-engaging practices to maximize math learning. Understanding how students learn—by developing neural connections—can help you appreciate the vitality of the practices that this book, NCTM, and CCSSM recommend. In later chapters you will find "essential practices" that are aligned with the guiding principles and brain engaging practices, but are more specific to the topic of each chapter.

Section II (Laying the Groundwork) focuses on work you can do either before the school year starts or within the first few months to make successful math learning more likely. Chapter 3 identifies important first steps, such as developing relationships with colleagues and establishing support networks in your school. We also explain how you can learn to use your curriculum materials and how to establish productive relationships with families. Chapter 4 offers ideas about classroom arrangements (and sample floor plans) to maximize math learning through class discussions, student access to materials, and group problem solving. Chapter 5 discusses emotional safety and its influence on complex thinking. Learn to establish a supportive math community where students help each other do their best thinking, work, and problem solving. Chapter 6 describes management routines that support math learning, presenting a metacognitive problem-solving routine vital to learning. Chapter 7 describes computational fluency, a key learning goal. The chapter also explains instructional routines to build computational fluency and shows how to engage students in generalizing about underlying mathematical ideas and properties.

Section III (The Lesson Cycle) illustrates through vignettes how two fourth-grade teachers plan, enact, and reflect on a lesson. Chapter 8 describes tasks most likely to yield significant learning and explains how to make curriculum tasks more mathematically engaging. Chapter 9 shows how these teachers adapt a well-known framework to plan a division lesson and how they document their planning to guide enactment and reflection. Chapter 10 illustrates how purposeful planning enabled easier, more effective decisions during teaching. One teacher introduces the lesson, and we see how she and her colleague interact with students as they solve problems. The teacher engages students in sharing their strategies and thinking in a class discussion at the end of the lesson. Chapter 11 shows how the teacher and her colleague reflect on the lesson together and document their reflections. They look for evidence of student learning and analyze student work to identify next instructional steps for students and ways to improve the lesson and the teaching.

Section IV (Essential Elements of Effective Mathematics Teaching) covers classroom discourse, assessment, differentiation, and homework—including background on why each element is important, suggestions to get started, and ways to reflect and improve. Chapter 12 describes productive discourse in classrooms and suggests questions you can ask to elicit student thinking. Learn to foster broad participation in rich discussions, how to make the math thinking visual, and how to engage students in math discussions. Chapter 13 explains how effective assessment starts with setting and communicating clear goals and expectations for learning. We explore assessment, giving students descriptive feedback, and engaging students in assessing their own work and thinking. Chapter 14 introduces differentiation as a necessary practice to ensure classroom equity. We describe how to differentiate instruction, emphasizing ways to engage English language learners and struggling students in developing mathematical thinking. Methods of teaching English language learners and struggling learners are fundamentally similar to ways of effectively teaching all students to learn mathematics with understanding. Chapter 15 explains the purposes and types of homework. We suggest how to ensure that homework is purposeful in supporting student learning and offer ideas to differentiate homework.

Supporting chapters dealing with technology and family engagement are available at this book's More4U website (look on the title page for your access code).

* * *

Just as students need time to develop mathematical understanding, teachers need time to develop expertise in teaching. Becoming an effective teacher is a process, not an event. As with any worthwhile pursuit, you will feel challenged, inspired, and sometimes confused. This is to be expected and even embraced—this is what learning is about. Draw on the same dispositions you want your students to exhibit: curiosity, flexibility, persistence, risk taking, and reflection. We hope that you find this book a supportive and reassuring companion that you can return to throughout your journey.

Mathematics
Teaching and
Learning

Section I presents a vision of mathematics teaching and learning. This vision is based on our beliefs about how students learn and the processes they use to develop mathematical understandings. These beliefs are grounded in research, theory, and our own experiences teaching mathematics.

Skillful teachers are aware of the purposes of their interactions with students. They make instructional decisions designed to maximize student learning. These decisions reflect their beliefs about how students learn, beliefs grounded in an understanding of how they develop mathematical ideas.

As you read these chapters, reflect on your beliefs about mathematics teaching and learning. Consider how these beliefs inform and influence the instructional decisions you make and how you might need to adjust your practice to more closely align it with what we know about how students learn mathematics with understanding.

Chapter 1 illustrates a vision of effective mathematics teaching and learning through a vignette of a second-grade classroom. Chapter 2 draws on research and theory to explain how students learn and how engagement in the NCTM Process Standards supports the neural processing necessary for students to learn mathematics with understanding.

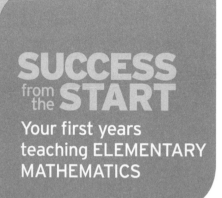

SUCCESS
from the **START**
Your first years
teaching ELEMENTARY
MATHEMATICS

chapter **one**

How Should Elementary Math Class Look and Sound?

Picture a second-grade classroom. It is November, and students are working to make sense of and solve addition story problems. They are involved in doing mathematics, and the teacher is working skillfully and intentionally to support them. Read and reflect on several excerpts from one lesson to examine the work of students and teachers in classrooms where students learn math with understanding.

For the past two weeks, these second-grade students have been solving addition and subtraction story problems with two-digit addends. During each class period, students solve problems on their own, share their solutions with a partner, and engage in a ten- to twenty-minute whole-class discussion of a few student strategies. These students have not been taught particular procedures for adding and subtracting two-digit numbers, nor have they been taught to recognize "key words" for deciding which operations to use to solve story problems. However, these students have studied place value and have been using what they know about two-digit numbers to develop increasingly efficient and sophisticated strategies for addition and subtraction. At the front of the room hang charts of addition and subtraction strategies that the students have developed.

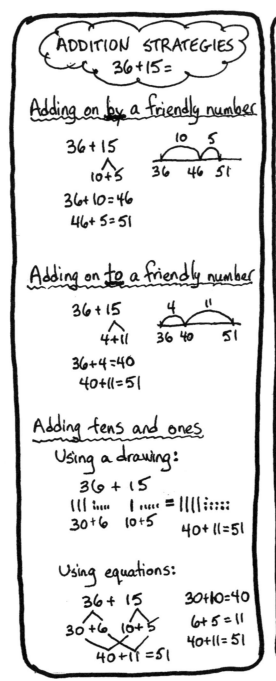

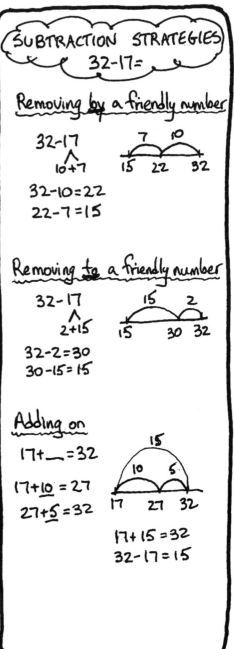

The teacher, Ms. Davis, has assessed her students informally throughout the unit. Each day during class, she circulates as students work, observing what strategies students use, taking notes, and questioning students both to better assess what they know and to support and extend their thinking. Today, she focuses her questioning and instruction on addition strategies. At this point in the unit, many students have developed the strategy of breaking both numbers into tens and ones to add them (adding tens and ones). However, many students still rely on drawings to break the numbers into tens and ones. Ms. Davis wants to encourage more students to try using just equations when solving the problems. But she wants to do so such that the new strategy makes sense to students and that they see the connection between the drawings and the equations.

As you read these vignettes, pay attention to what the students do and say and what that reveals about what they know and are learning about mathematics. Also, pay attention to what the teacher does and says and how her words and actions are likely to support students' learning.

Read through each vignette once, paying attention to the students, and then read it again, paying attention to the teacher. Then read the commentary provided.

INTRODUCING THE LESSON

Ms. Davis has written this problem on the board:

> Sandy had 46 baseball cards. Her brother gave her 37 baseball cards for her birthday. Now how many baseball cards does Sandy have?

Ms. Davis Saya, "Today we are going to work on some more story problems, just like you've been doing for the past few days. We'll begin by thinking about the first problem together. Read the problem to yourself and try to picture what is happening in the story. Then decide what the story is asking you to find out." After about a minute, she says, "Raise your hand if you've had enough time to figure out what is happening in this story problem."

Twenty of the twenty-five students raise their hands.

Ms. Davis says, "I'm going to read the problem out loud, and I want everyone to try to picture what is happening in this problem." She reads the problem. Ms. Davis then turns to Isaiah, who had raised his hand previously, and says, "Isaiah, can you tell us what happens first in this story problem?"

Isaiah slowly responds, "Um . . . first Sandy has 46 baseball cards."

Ms. Davis begins making a flowchart. She writes "Sandy has 46 cards" and draws a rectangle around it. "Then what happens?" She pauses for students to think. "Emma, what happens next?"

"Her brother gives her 37 more baseball cards," Emma says.

Ms. Davis draws an arrow and another rectangle. Inside she writes, "Brother gave her 37 cards." Then she asks, "What happens next?" She calls on Marcus.

Marcus says, "How many cards does she have now?"

Ms. Davis records the following:

Ms. Davis says, "So let's read our problem together." She leads the class in choral reading of the chart sequencing the action of the story. "What do we have to find out?" She calls on Alia.

Alia says, "We have to find out how many cards she has now."

Ms. Davis asks, "How can we find out how many cards Sandy has now?"

"You have to add 37 cards to the 46 because now she has more," Alia answers.

Ms. Davis asks, "Who agrees with what Alia just said?" All hands go up. Ms. Davis writes the numbers 46 and 37 and a question mark under the boxes in the flowchart.

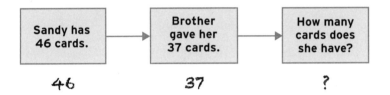

"How can we show that we're adding 37 to the 46? Sam, how do you think we could do that?"

"Put a plus sign?"

"That's right. We use an addition sign to show that we're adding."

Ms. Davis writes "46 + 37 = ?" on the board. She continues, "Let's read this together." The class reads the equation as Ms. Davis points: "46 plus 37 equals something."

Ms. Davis asks, "What's the 'something' you have to find out?"

The students say, "You have to find out how many baseball cards Sandy has now."

"So now we've translated the story problem into an equation, and Alia just told us we have to find out what 46 cards and 37 cards adds up to. Now I'd like you to think of a strategy that you could use to solve this problem. You can look at the chart of addition strategies to help you. Choose a strategy that makes sense to you and that you think is efficient. When you have a strategy, put a hand on your head. When I know you have a strategy, I will call on you to go back to your seat and get started. You will have about twenty-five minutes to work on these problems."

STOP+REFLECT

>> What did Ms. Davis ask the students to do and think about in the lesson introduction?

>> How did Ms. Davis support all students to make sense of the problem?

The lesson begins with a problem, and Ms. Davis does not tell the students how to solve it. Instead she deliberately focuses students on visualizing the sequence of actions in the problem, translating the problem into an equation, determining what the problem asks them to find out, and choosing a strategy to solve it. Instead of telling students key words, Ms. Davis gives them time and focus questions to help them make sense of any problem. Her goal is to have all students leave the meeting area understanding the first problem and with an idea for a strategy they could use to solve it. She is supporting all her students in becoming problem solvers.

TWO STUDENTS AT WORK

Tiffany and Michael tackle Ms. Davis's problem:

> Sandy had 46 baseball cards. Her brother gave her 37 baseball cards for her birthday. Now how many baseball cards does Sandy have?

Tiffany sits down at her desk and writes her name on her paper. She rereads the problem, looks up briefly at the strategy charts, and then writes

$$46 + 37$$
$$40 + 6 \quad 30 + 7$$

in the space under the word problem. Under the 46 she writes 40 and 6, showing that 46 can be split into 40 and 6. Under the 37 she writes 30 and 7, showing that 37 can be split into 30 and 7. Then she writes

$$4 + 3 = 7, \text{ so } 40 + 30 = 70$$
$$6 + 7 = 13$$
$$70 + 13 =$$
$$10 + 3$$

She then writes

$$70 + 10 = 80$$
$$80 + 3 = 83$$

Tiffany moves on to the next problem.

Michael, sitting next to Tiffany, writes

$$46 + 37 =$$

on his paper. He then says "40" as he draws four lines to represent sticks of ten and says "6" as he draws six small dots next to the lines. He writes an addition sign and mouths "30" as he draws three lines and "7" as he draws seven dots. He writes an equals sign and draws four lines, then three more, then a row of six dots and a row of seven dots underneath. His paper now looks like this:

$$46 + 37$$
$$\text{IIII} \ \text{......} + \text{III} \ \text{.......} = \text{IIIIIII} \ \text{::::::.}$$

Michael writes "70" under the sticks of ten, counts the dots by ones, and writes "13" under the dots. He writes "70 + 13 =" and then he pauses, looks intently at the hundred chart on the wall for few moments, and then writes "83." His paper now looks like this:

$$46 + 37$$
$$\text{IIII} \ \text{......} + \text{III} \ \text{.......} = \text{IIIIIII} \ \text{::::::.}$$
$$\qquad\qquad\qquad\qquad\qquad\qquad 70 \qquad 13$$
$$70 + 13 = 83$$

Michael goes on to the next problem.

After about twenty minutes, the teacher stops the class and says, "Now I would like you to share your solutions with your partner. When I finish talking, show your partner your paper and explain how you solved the problem. Then look at your partner's paper and listen to how your partner solved the problem. After that, I want you to discuss ways that your solutions are similar and different. You have three minutes. Please begin."

Tiffany immediately turns to Michael, who does not look up. Michael continues making lines and dots on his paper to represent numbers in the problem he is working on. Tiffany says, "Stop. We need to share."

Michael says, "I know," as he draws four more dots. He then looks up.

Tiffany turns her paper toward Michael and says, "I solved the first one by breaking the 46 into 40 and 6 and the 37 into 30 and 7, and I added the 40 and 30 to get 70 and the 6 and 7 to get 13. Then I added the 70 and 13 and got 83."

Michael says, "I drew sticks of ten. I made four sticks of ten and six ones, and three sticks of ten and seven ones, and then I counted the sticks and counted the ones and added them up. I got 83, too." Michael adds, "We both got the same answer."

Tiffany says, "We both wrote 70 + 13 = 83," and then adds, "But you make sticks of ten and I just used numbers."

STOP + REFLECT

» What is Tiffany doing and thinking about as she solves the problem?

» What is Michael doing and thinking about as he solves the problem?

» How do Tiffany's and Michael's solutions compare?

» What does the teacher ask them to do?

» What is the teacher's role in this vignette?

As the students complete the problem, record their work, and share strategies, they are problem solving, reasoning, representing their thinking on paper, communicating their thinking to each other, and looking for connections. Tiffany reasons about numbers and number relationships when she writes "4 + 3 = 7, so 40 + 30 = 70." Michael uses a base-ten representation when he records 46 as four ten sticks and six ones. Tiffany and Michael communicate their thinking orally and in writing, which helps them become aware of the strategies and mathematical relationships that they are using to solve the problem, helps them see connections between their strategies, and will let the teacher assess what each student knows and can do.

The teacher's role here may seem minimal. However, this level of student work and conversation is possible only because the teacher has established a safe and intellectually rigorous classroom environment in which students are expected to solve problems, record their thinking, and communicate clearly and respectfully with one another.

THE TEACHER SUPPORTS A STUDENT HAVING DIFFICULTY

Timmy is sitting at his desk staring at his paper, not writing anything. Ms. Davis walks by and stops. She waits a few minutes, watching Timmy. Timmy writes "46 + 37" on his paper. Then he stops. Ms. Davis squats down at eye level with Timmy and says, "Tell me about this equation that you just wrote down." Ms. Davis points to the 46. "What does the 46 represent?"

Timmy pauses, glancing up at the flowchart Ms. Davis constructed with the class during the lesson launch. "That's how many baseball cards Sandy had."

"And what does the 37 represent?"

"That's the cards her brother gave her for her birthday."

"What is the problem asking you to find out?"

"Um . . . how many baseball cards she has now?"

"How can you figure that out?"

"By adding the 46 cards and the 37 cards."

"What strategy can you use to help you add all the cards?"

[*Pause.*] "I could draw sticks of ten?"

"OK. Why don't you draw sticks of ten? I'll come back in a few minutes to see what you've done."

When Ms. Davis returns, Timmy has drawn a picture similar to Michael's: four sticks of ten and six dots, and three sticks of ten and seven dots. He is counting the dots. She sees him point to the last few dots and say, "180, 190, 200, 300." He writes "300" on his paper and circles it.

IIII ...... + III ....
(300)

Ms. Davis gently asks, "Timmy, can you explain to me how you solved this problem?"

"Um . . . I drew four tens and six ones for 46 and I drew three tens and seven ones for 37. Then I counted the tens: 10, 20, 30, 40, 50, 60, 70. Then I counted the ones: 80, 90 . . . no . . . I mean, 71, 72, 73, 74, 75, 76, 77, 78, 79, 80, 81, 82, 83."

STOP+ REFLECT

>> What does Timmy understand about the baseball cards problem?

>> What does he understand about the numbers 46 and 37?

>> What mistake does Timmy make in solving the problem?

>> How does the teacher interact with Timmy after she notices him staring at his paper? After she sees him write an equation? After she observes him counting incorrectly?

>> How does the teacher support Timmy in problem solving?

Ms. Davis asks, "So how many baseball cards do you think Sandy now has?"

Timmy answers, "83."

Ms. Davis asks, "Why 83 and not 300?"

"Because I counted wrong before."

Ms. Davis says, "Good work! You found your mistake by checking your thinking," and she leaves to observe other students solving the problems.

Timmy is slow to start solving the problem and then makes a common counting mistake. He initially continues counting by tens when he moves from counting the sticks of ten to the ones. However, Timmy does realize that the problem is an addition problem, and he represents 46 as four tens and six ones and 37 as three tens and seven ones. Ms. Davis first observes Timmy staring at his paper but says nothing. Then she asks him about the meaning of his equation and how he plans to solve the problem, and she tells him she will return to check on his progress. Later, after observing him make a mistake, she asks him to explain his thinking, during which he realizes his mistake and fixes it.

Asking students to record their work and explain their solutions helps them become more aware of their own thought processes. Here, explaining how he got his answer enables Timmy to find and fix his own mistake. Ms. Davis supports Timmy in problem solving by initially assessing whether he understands the problem and has a way to solve it, by monitoring and assessing his progress in solving the problem, and by asking him to explain his thinking. Ms. Davis also supports Timmy in problem solving through what she does not do: She does not step in and do any work for him, either to help him fix his mistake or to help him get more work done.

SHARING STUDENT SOLUTIONS WITH THE WHOLE GROUP

Ms. Davis asks students to bring their papers but not their pencils to the meeting area. The students sit in a circle on the rug. Ms. Davis asks them to place their papers on the floor in front of them so that she can see their different solutions. Ms. Davis has already circulated as students worked, so she is aware of most strategies students used and has jotted down names of some students who used each strategy. However, because she talked for ten minutes with Timmy, she could not observe what strategies all students used. Ms. Davis takes a minute to scan the papers, as the students wait patiently.

Ms. Davis says, "We'll discuss solutions to the first problem about the baseball cards and then compare two different ways to solve that problem. Who would like to remind us of the problem? Maya, can you please read it loudly enough for all of us to hear?"

Maya reads, "Sandy had 46 baseball cards. Her brother gave her 37 baseball cards for her birthday. Now how many baseball cards does Sandy have?"

Ms. Davis says, "I first want us to look at Michael's solution. Michael, would you come up and show us how you solved the problem?"

Michael carries his paper with him to the front of the room. "First, I knew it was addition, so I wrote '46 + 37.'" He writes

$$46 + 37 =$$

He looks at his paper. "Then I drew tens and ones." Michael draws four tens sticks and six dots, and three tens sticks and seven dots, under the 46 and 37. "Then I added them." Michael writes on the board what is on his paper.

$$46 + 37$$
|||| ...... + ||| .... = |||||| :::::.
$$70 \qquad 13$$
$$70 + 13 = 83$$

Ms. Davis asks the class, "What do you notice about Michael's solution?" She calls on a few students:

One says, "He used tens and ones."

Another says, "He made drawings."

Someone else says, "He did addition."

Ms. Davis says, "Michael, I have a question. How did you add the 70 and 13 to get 83?"

Michael answers, "I used the hundred chart."

"How did you use the hundred chart—can you show us?"

Michael walks to the hundred chart and points. "I started at 70. I went down one." He moves his finger to 80. "And then I went 81, 82, 83."

Ms. Davis asks, "Why did you 'go down one'?"

"To add 10."

Ms. Davis waits and then asks, "Where did the 10 come from?"

"The 13."

Ms. Davis summarizes, "So it looks like Michael broke this 13 into a 10 and 3." She writes "10" and "3" below Michael's equation.

$$70 + 13 =$$
$$\overset{\displaystyle\diagup\diagdown}{10 \; + \; 3}$$

"Michael made a jump of ten on the hundred chart to add the 10, and then he moved three spaces horizontally—one, two, three [*pointing to the 81, 82, and 83 on the chart*]—to add the 3." She writes

$$70 + 10 = 80$$
$$80 + 3 = 83$$

Ms. Davis continues, "Let's look at our chart of addition strategies. What strategy did Michael use?" She pauses to let students think. "Ally, what strategy do you think he used?"

"He added tens and ones . . . and he did drawings."

Ms. Davis writes "Michael" and "Add tens and ones (using drawings)" above Michael's solution.

She then says, "Next I would like Tiffany to share her solution. Tiffany, can you write your solution on the board next to Michael's?" Tiffany carries her paper to the front of the room. First she writes. Then she stops to explain, "I split 46 into 40 and 6 and 37 into 30 and 7." She pauses briefly and then continues: "I added 30 plus 40 and got 70, and I added 6 plus 7 and got 13." She clarifies, "I knew that 6 plus 6 was 12, so one more was 13," but does not record that part. "Then I added 70 plus 13. I split the 13 into 10 and 3, like Michael. I just knew that 70 plus 10 was 80 and then I knew that 80 plus 3 was 83."

The board now has both students' strategies side by side:

Michael
Adding tens and ones
(using drawings)

$$46 \quad + \quad 37$$
|||| ...... + |||....... = ||||||| :::::.
$$\qquad\qquad\qquad\qquad 70 \qquad 13$$

$$70 + 13 =$$
$$\qquad \diagdown$$
$$10 + 3$$

$$70 + 10 = 80$$
$$80 + 3 = 83$$

Tiffany

$$46 \quad + \quad 37$$
$$\diagup\diagdown \qquad \diagup\diagdown$$
$$40 + 6 \quad 30 + 7$$

$$40 + 30 = 70$$
$$6 + 7 = 13$$

$$70 + 13 =$$
$$\qquad \diagdown$$
$$10 + 3$$

$$70 + 10 = 80$$
$$80 + 3 = 83$$

Ms. Davis says, "Thank you, Tiffany. You can go back to your seat now." Then Ms. Davis says to the group, "I'd like everyone to look carefully at Tiffany's solution and see whether you understand what she did. Once you understand it, please raise your hand." Ms. Davis waits for one whole minute. By then eighteen hands have gone up. "Explain to your partner what you think Tiffany did to solve the problem."

Students turn and talk. Ms. Davis leans in and listens to a few different pairs. "Now stop talking. I have another question for you. How is Tiffany's solution similar to Michael's? Think about it first. Then talk to your neighbor about how they are similar."

Ms. Davis again listens in as students talk. Crystal says, "They both did tens and ones. Tiffany used numbers and Michael used pictures."

After giving students another minute to talk, Ms. Davis asks them to stop and calls on Crystal. "Crystal, can you share how you think what Tiffany did is similar to what Michael did?"

Crystal replies, "They both did tens and ones."

"Can you say more about how they both used tens and ones?"

Crystal continues, "They both split numbers into tens and ones. Tiffany wrote 40 and 6 and 30 and 7. Michael drew four ten sticks and six ones and three ten sticks and seven ones."

"How else are the solutions similar? Thomas?"

Thomas answers, "They both used addition."

"Are they similar in any other ways? Andre?"

Andre replies, "I know a way they are different."

"How are they different?"

"Michael used the hundred chart and Tiffany didn't."

"That's true, but let's keep talking about how these are the same. Hannah? How do you think these strategies are the same?"

Hannah responds, "Most of it is the same. They mostly have the same numbers. But Michael drew tens and ones and Tiffany just did numbers."

Ms. Davis asks, "Who heard what Hannah just said?" Ten hands go up. "Hannah, can you say what you just said again? And come show us the parts that you think are mostly the same."

Hannah says, "This part is mostly the same." She waves her hand around the equations under Michael's drawings and the same equations in Tiffany's solution. "Michael just made drawings at the top, and Tiffany didn't."

Ms. Davis says, "This is interesting. Crystal, you said the first part of their solutions were similar. You said that they both broke their numbers into tens and ones. Now Hannah is saying that the next part of their solutions are similar. It sounds like these two solutions are pretty similar. They both used the adding-tens-and-ones strategy. They both split 46 into 40 and 6 and 37 into 30 and 7, and they both added 70 plus 13 to get 83.

"I'm curious, who solved the problem in a way similar to Tiffany's?" Eight hands go up. "Who solved the problem in a way similar to Michael's?" Nine hands go up. "Who solved the problem in a different way?" Six hands go up. Ms. Davis says, "We've been talking about choosing efficient ways to solve problems—ways that make it easy for you to keep track of the problem and all the steps. Which solution was more efficient, adding tens and ones by using drawings or by using equations? [*She points to the two solutions on the board.*] Think, and then talk to your partner about which one you think is most efficient and why."

Ms. Davis listens to conversations the students have with each other. She notices that as they justify their reasoning, all are looking at Michael's and Tiffany's solutions. She hears Somo and Andre discussing the number of steps in each strategy. After three minutes, she says, "I heard Somo say something interesting. Andre, can you tell us what Somo said?"

Andre says, "Somo said that using equations is more efficient because it has fewer steps."

Ms. Davis asked, "Do you know what Somo means about fewer steps?"

"Yeah, you don't have to make the drawings and count the dots. You just have to write the numbers. You can add 6 and 7 in your head instead of counting."

Ms. Davis checks with Somo, "Is that what you said?"

Somo replies, "Uh-huh . . . and . . . I think you might make a mistake when you are drawing. You might draw the wrong number . . . like you might draw eight dots when you were supposed to do seven."

Ms. Davis summarizes, "So you thought of two reasons why using equations is more efficient than using drawings. You said that it has fewer steps. You also said if you use equations you might be less likely to make a mistake."

She tells the class, "I want you to think about whether you agree with what Andre and Somo just said, disagree with it, or are not sure." She gives them time to think. "OK, put a thumb up if you agree with what Andre and Somo said." Most show a thumbs-up sign. "OK, now put your thumb up if you disagree with what Andre and Somo said." Nobody puts a thumb up. "Now put your thumb up if you are not sure about what Andre and Somo said." Three students show thumbs-up. She looks at those students and says, "That's OK if you are not sure. We are going to keep thinking and talking about this."

Then Ms. Davis ends the lesson by saying, "It seems that most of you think that adding tens and ones by using equations is more efficient. But remember, it's efficient for you only if it makes sense and you practice using it. If you've used only drawings, I'd like you to try using equations tomorrow when you solve problems."

STOP + REFLECT

» Why does Ms. Davis ask Michael and Tiffany to share their solutions?

» How does Ms. Davis engage students in thinking and talking about Michael's and Tiffany's solutions? Find specific things that she does.

» Why does Ms. Davis spend class time discussing two solutions, instead of sharing many different solutions or going over the answers to all the problems?

» What might students learn from this discussion? How might they solve future problems differently because of this discussion?

Ms. Davis chooses two students to share their solutions after observing students solving the problems and after scanning papers that students brought to the rug. Ms. Davis chooses these two students because she has a learning goal in mind: to move students from drawing pictures of tens and ones to using equations.

She knows that not all students are ready to stop using drawings. Timmy may continue using them for some time. But other students, like Michael, are probably ready. She wants those students to realize that Tiffany's approach is not so different from theirs. So Ms. Davis focuses on the similarities between the solutions and asks the students to look for connections.

Ms. Davis's decisions support students in understanding representations, making connections, and communicating their thinking and reasoning: She makes room on the board for two solutions to be written side by side. She periodically asks clarifying questions, such as where the 10 came from. She asks students to show their thinking, as when she asks Michael to show how he added the 13 with the hundred chart or when she asked Hannah to show the parts of the solutions that are "mostly the same." Ms. Davis gives wait time after her questions. She asks students to talk to further process their ideas, and she calls on a range of students, not just the first ones to raise their hands. Finally, Ms. Davis asks students to think about which solution is more efficient and why. Through all these means, Ms. Davis supports broad participation in a mathematically focused discussion.

CONCLUSION

The National Council of Teachers of Mathematics (2000) identified five Process Standards that "highlight ways of acquiring and using content knowledge": problem solving, reasoning and proving, making and using representations, communicating mathematical thinking, and making connections (p. 29). They are similar to the Common Core State Standards for Mathematical Practice. In classrooms such as Ms. Davis's, the teacher engages all students in these processes.

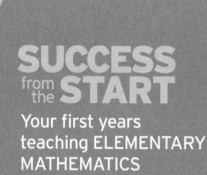

chapter two

Learning Mathematics with Understanding

Guiding Principles

LEARNING IS MAXIMIZED WHEN STUDENTS—

>> interact in a safe, supportive learning community;

>> activate and build on prior knowledge;

>> process information both visually and linguistically;

>> solve problems with meaningful contexts;

>> engage in reflection, self-monitoring, and metacognition; and

>> engage in complex thinking.

Y ou probably recognized in chapter 1 some features of standards-based mathematics instruction that you have observed, learned about, or used. Students in Ms. Davis's class solved problems in cooperative groups, used models and a variety of ways to solve and represent problems, explained and proved their reasoning, communicated their approaches and strategies in a class discussion, and made connections between different approaches and strategies.

These features are necessary but not sufficient. Students in a math class can do all these things and yet still learn mathematics only superficially. Students may engage in "math talk," but if the talk does not focus on questioning, explaining, and justifying strategies and ideas, it will not help students understand math. Students may use manipulatives to solve problems, but if learners do not connect their use of manipulatives to mathematical ideas, the manipulatives will not deepen mathematical understanding. Students may share different strategies for solving problems, but if they do not analyze, compare, and evaluate them, they will not learn that some strategies are better for solving particular types of problems than others. Your challenge is to incorporate these features of standards-based math teaching in a way that develops students' mathematical thinking and sense making.

To teach for understanding, it is important to understand how students learn. Knowing the basics of how the brain makes meaning optimally and efficiently lets you maximize students' learning by being more intentional and purposeful in your teaching. Your use of manipulatives, classroom discourse, and group problem solving will advance a deep, rather than superficial, understanding of mathematics. In this chapter, we will draw upon research and theory from a variety of disciplines to help you understand—

- how the brain makes meaning;

- learning mathematics with understanding versus by rote;

- why developing computational fluency is important;

- brain-engaging practices to maximize learning with understanding; and

- how the National Council of Teachers of Mathematics (NCTM) Process Standards engage the brain in learning with understanding.

HOW THE BRAIN MAKES MEANING

To understand how children learn mathematics, it's important to have a basic knowledge of how the brain transforms information into knowledge (Jensen, 2008). Although neuroscientists continue learning about how the brain functions, the following view is widely accepted:

The brain is a pattern detector, constantly processing information from the senses: sight, hearing, taste, touch, and smell. The brain searches for meaning—looking for similarities between incoming patterns of information and information stored in memory. If no connection is made between prior knowledge and new information, the information is most likely discarded. If the input activates stored networks of knowledge, pattern recognition occurs, the brain pays attention, and possibilities for new learning abound.

When new information makes sense but conflicts with prior knowledge, cognitive dissonance occurs. Take the example of a first grader, who once believed that 10 represented only ten things. Now the child is counting the number of animal books in his class library, keeping track of how many by bundling them into groups of ten. When he counts how many all together, he grapples with the new idea that 10 can simultaneously represent ten books and one bundle of ten (unitizing). Through his struggle of making sense about why the 1 in 10 represents one bundle of ten, he sheds his old conception that 10 can represent only ten things. His brain changes as he connects this new knowledge to other related prior knowledge and organizes it around the big idea of unitizing. This process changes, expands, and enhances his network of neural patterns, and learning has occurred.

Students build continually growing networks of connected mathematical ideas as they solve challenging mathematical problems, explain and justify their reasoning, get feedback from their peers and teachers, and revise their thinking. Continued problem solving, discourse, and practice expands and strengthens their networks of connected ideas. The deepest understanding of mathematics occurs when students accurately organize information around related big ideas and concepts. Such networks of deeply connected knowledge increase the likelihood that information will be robustly stored in memory and effectively accessed and transferred to new problems and situations. This is what we mean by learning mathematics with understanding.

LEARNING MATHEMATICS WITH UNDERSTANDING VERSUS BY ROTE

Let's look more closely at how building networks of connected knowledge can yield robust understanding of mathematics. We will compare the mathematical knowledge that two students, Tiffany and Sam, call upon as they solve 46 + 37. Tiffany and Sam have similar backgrounds, learning profiles, dispositions, and abilities, but they were taught math differently.

Tiffany: Taught with NCTM Process Standards

Tiffany learned addition by developing her own strategies as she solved problems. She also engaged in focused discourse in which she developed complex mathematical thinking. This discourse, which Ms. Davis carefully scaffolded and facilitated, allowed Tiffany to see and hear the strategies of her classmates, compare several strategies, evaluate strategies for accuracy and efficiency, adjust her thinking, and connect this knowledge to concepts of addition.

Let's revisit the evidence of Tiffany's thinking as she solved 46 + 37. What has she learned so far about addition with two-digit numbers? Tiffany has developed the following mathematical connections and relationships:

- Story problems about getting more of something (not the key word *more* but the action of getting more) can be represented with addition equations.

- Numbers can be decomposed (broken apart) and recomposed (put back together) in any order (commutative property) or in any grouping (associative property) without changing the total.

- Two-digit numbers are composed of tens and ones: 46 = 4 tens + 6 ones = 40 + 6; 37 = 3 tens + 7 ones = 30 + 7. Tiffany can also tell from the digits in any two-digit number how many tens and ones are in the number.

- Addition combinations can be used to solve related problems. For example, 6 + 7 is one more than 6 + 6. Tiffany can also use number combinations to solve related two-digit problems. For example, 3 + 4 = 7 can be used to reason that 30 + 40 = 70.

- Two-digit numbers can be represented by base-ten materials. However, Tiffany no longer needs to use those concrete models to help her decompose and recompose numbers because she has developed a mental model of tens and ones and an understanding of place value.

Fosnot and Dolk (2001a, b) describe developmental frameworks for number and operations in which students construct landmarks of learning—big ideas, strategies, and ways of modeling—along developmental trajectories, or landscapes of learning. Figure 2.1 illustrates the key categories of mathematical knowledge that Tiffany calls on.

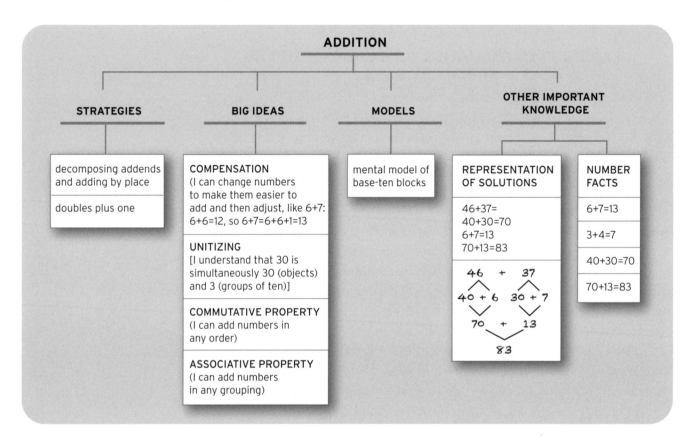

Fig. 2.1. *Categories of mathematical knowledge Tiffany uses to solve 46 + 37*

By calling on and using this knowledge each time she solves a problem and discusses it, Tiffany strengthens and solidifies the connections among the various related mathematical ideas. Because Tiffany's web of connected knowledge is so complex and organized around overarching ideas such as unitizing and the place-value structure of the number system, she experiences math as making sense. She understands math. For Tiffany, math is not a jumble of isolated facts and procedures, but a web of connected ideas and relationships.

Sam: Taught by rote

Sam has a learning profile similar to Tiffany's. The main difference between Sam and Tiffany is how they have been taught.

Sam's teacher showed how to add two-digit numbers by using the conventional algorithm. Sam and his peers had no chance to explore and develop, on their own, the different ways they could add. Sam followed the teacher's procedure, applied it to many problems, and through practice became quite fluent in adding. However, Sam operates on the digits in the addends without understanding the value of the numbers in the tens and ones places. Because he learned to add by using only a procedure the teacher showed him, he lacks experience in thinking flexibly about operations and decomposing and recomposing numbers. He also lacks knowledge about how to solve problems more efficiently.

Figure 2.2 shows the key categories of mathematical knowledge that Sam calls on as he solves 46 + 37.

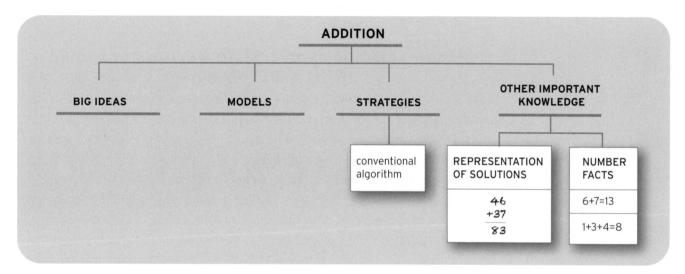

Fig. 2.2. *Categories of mathematical knowledge Sam uses to solve 46 + 37*

Sam's mathematical knowledge contrasts sharply with Tiffany's. His procedural knowledge and knowledge of facts lack connection to the big ideas underlying addition. Although Sam, like Tiffany, has the ability to develop webs of deeply connected knowledge, his teacher has not given him opportunities to do so. His understanding of addition is thus superficial and weak.

Some students in classrooms where math is taught procedurally do learn math with understanding. However, these students make mathematical connections and organize their knowledge around overarching concepts largely on their own, without teacher or peer support. They learn math with understanding not as a result of being taught procedurally, but despite it.

WHY DEVELOPING COMPUTATIONAL FLUENCY IS IMPORTANT

Tiffany is developing computational fluency—procedural fluency with conceptual understanding. Computationally fluent students deeply understand the structure of the base-ten system and properties of the operations. They apply this understanding flexibly, using and inventing strategies that make sense for the numbers in the problems they solve.

Computational fluency has three main components: efficiency, accuracy, and flexibility (Russell, 2000). Efficiency involves using a strategy in which the steps are easy to keep track of and carry out. Accuracy applies to the whole problem-solving process, including knowing and using number facts and important relationships, monitoring thinking and work, and checking answers. Flexibility involves knowing more than one way to solve a problem and choosing a strategy that works best with the numbers in the problem. People often refer to students who are computationally fluent as having number sense.

When students learn computation together with the underlying structures and properties of arithmetic, they build webs of neural connections among the facts, models, strategies, and big ideas of the operations. They see the operations as related to each other rather than as separate, isolated procedures.

BRAIN-ENGAGING PRACTICES TO MAXIMIZE LEARNING WITH UNDERSTANDING

Seven brain-engaging teaching practices support students' learning math with understanding. They are based on guiding principles, which offer a rationale and purpose for the recommendations in this book.

Teaching all students to develop deeply understood mathematical knowledge that they can access and flexibly transfer to new problems is a complex endeavor. Let's take a closer look at how teachers like Ms. Davis apply the guiding principles to develop students' mathematical thinking and dispositions. As you read these practices, think about how problem solving and making sense of mathematics is important work for all students, including English language learners and struggling students.

Build a safe, supportive learning community

Children develop mathematical ideas as they struggle with problems, monitor their work and thinking, try alternative strategies, justify and defend their reasoning, make and test conjectures, and wonder about connections. Interacting with peers as they solve problems and engage in mathematical discourse strengthens and expands children's neural connections among related mathematical ideas. As evidenced by the students in Ms. Davis's math class, children learn best within a social community of interaction and discourse. However, complex mathematical learning can happen only in a safe, supportive learning environment—one that nurtures a low-threat, high-challenge state of mind (Caine and Caine, 1991).

Emotional safety opens the door to complex learning. When processing information from the senses, the brain first filters it for emotional safety and relevance—it feels before it thinks. If the incoming information or classroom environment causes fear, anxiety, stress, embarrassment, or other perceived threat, a neural response is triggered. This neural response, sometimes referred to as an amygdala hijack (Goleman, 1995), or "shutdown," inhibits complex thinking. Be aware of situations that can cause a student to shut down in math class, such as the following:

- Peers ridicule a student's idea or mistake.

- A student hears someone say, "That's so easy!" and she feels dumb because she is struggling to solve it.

- A student cannot make sense of a problem because he has difficulty reading.

- A peer or teacher "jumps in" to correct a student's mistake.
- A student feels the pressure of time constraints.

The following basic actions are essential to establishing a safe, supportive mathematics learning community. Chapter 5, Building a Supportive Learning Community, explores this topic further.

Set clear, explicit expectations

Clear and explicit expectations can guide students to help each other do their best thinking, work, and problem solving. You can do this by—

- explicitly teaching students the problem-solving dispositions—curiosity, flexibility, persistence, risk taking, and reflection—and scaffolding students' transfer of these dispositions to their problem solving; and
- developing math class norms with your students that invest them in creating a supportive math community.

Students in Ms. Davis's class respectfully listened to one another in the discussion, and Tiffany and Michael shared their solution approaches with each other and the class. Both are evidence that Ms. Davis had developed such clear expectations with her students.

Give wait time

Ms. Davis gave her students time to think after she asked questions. Wait time not only gives all students time to think but also eliminates the anxiety that many feel when expected to find an answer quickly. Using wait time shows that you value your students' thinking, which motivates them to take their time to think more deeply about math.

Treat mistakes as learning opportunities

Using mistakes as opportunities to learn nurtures risk taking, a necessary disposition for new learning and a hallmark of supportive math communities. Ms. Davis could have caused Timmy to shut down if she had corrected his mistake in counting. Instead, she asked him to explain his thinking. He found and corrected his own mistake, an empowering experience. Ms. Davis supplied the emotional safety Timmy needed to build understanding and self-efficacy—confidence in his mathematical competence. When students feel successful and competent, they are more likely to exert effort in future challenges. Their motivation to learn also tends to increase when they have mutually trusting and respectful relationships with their teachers.

Reduce math anxiety

Often caused by prior negative experiences or influences at home or in school, math anxiety inhibits student success in math learning. Students may have heard their parents or teachers say, "I was never good in math," and are led to believe that they missed out on the "math gene." If students believe that intelligence is fixed, they may believe that no matter how hard they try, they will never be good in math.

You can dispel the faulty notion of a math gene by praising effort, not ability (Dweck, 2006). Praising students' ability—for example, "You're so smart at math!"—shows that we expect students to always be smart. When this happens, many students focus on maintaining their status of being correct and smart. As a result, they tend to avoid challenging problems or trying new strategies for fear of making mistakes. Praising effort, however, with comments such as "You did a great job of checking your work and finding your own mistake," or "You remembered to estimate your answer before solving the problem," offers descriptive feedback that reinforces effective problem solving. Such feedback builds student success and self-efficacy and can motivate students to take risks in their thinking and engage more rigorously in their math work.

Assess and build on what students know, understand, and can do

Every student enters your class with mathematical knowledge uniquely shaped by family and school experiences, culture, background, strengths, and learning needs. Students' brains are uniquely organized and develop in different ways and at different rates. Because the brain connects new information to prior knowledge, you must assess the math your students know, understand, and can do so that you can plan instruction that builds on and advances their learning. Also find out what misconceptions students may have, so you can plan instruction that addresses misconceptions and builds on accurate mathematical knowledge.

For each main content topic in mathematics, research-based frameworks exist that describe students' mathematical development. In the framework of Fosnot and Dolk (2001a, b), students construct progressively sophisticated big ideas, strategies, and models along a landscape of learning, or developmental trajectory. As they progress through the landscape of learning, students develop understandings of predictable landmarks—the big ideas, strategies, and models. They may also develop common misconceptions as they construct these mathematical ideas. However, because learning is not linear and students' brains are unique, they take different pathways to reach the landmarks. Students also reach those landmarks at different times. Therefore, you must find out what your students understand so you will have an idea of what they need to learn next. Questions such as the following can guide you:

- What do my students know and understand about this math topic?
- Where are my students on the landscape of learning?
- What do my students need to learn next, and how can I build on their understanding?

Teachers first assess where the student is on the landscape of learning. Giving assessments before a new unit is one way to get information about what students know and understand. Another way is to observe students as they problem solve.

By continuously observing her students at work and prompting them to reveal their thinking as they solved problems, Ms. Davis accurately assessed her students' prior knowledge of addition strategies. She asked open-ended questions to find out how students were thinking rather than impose her own ideas by guiding them to say what she wanted them to say. Her question to Timmy is an example of an open-ended question: "Timmy, can you explain to me how you solved this problem?" As Timmy explained, Ms. Davis listened with a focus on how he was thinking.

As you observe your students, ask them to show you and tell you how they are thinking. Here are some things to observe as students problem solve and communicate their reasoning:

- What tools (including models) are students using?

- What strategies are students using?

- What big ideas are students drawing on?

- How are students representing their work and thinking?

- What mistakes are students making, and what might those mistakes tell you about what they know or do not know?

- Do students need more challenge?

After you assess what students know and understand, plan instruction to build on their mathematical knowledge. Interacting with and getting scaffolding or support from more knowledgeable peers and teachers strengthens, expands, and revises students' neural connections of math knowledge and ideas. Therefore, giving students opportunities to solve problems together and engage in mathematical discourse is essential to the scaffolding and development of new learning.

When you select partnerships, group children with comparable readiness levels. Ms. Davis facilitated such scaffolding for Michael by pairing him with Tiffany, whose readiness level was beyond—but not too far beyond—Michael's. Ms. Davis based her decision on her assessment of Michael's and Tiffany's development along the landscape of learning and her knowledge about what Michael needed to learn next. She gave them opportunities to discuss and justify their reasoning so that Michael could see and understand Tiffany's more sophisticated way of using equations to model the decomposition and recomposition of addends.

Activate students' prior knowledge

When the brain recognizes a pattern and makes a connection, it pays attention. The purpose of activating prior knowledge is to engage students in connecting what they already know to what they will need to learn. You should begin lessons by activating students' prior knowledge in a way that purposefully connects the new task to what they already know.

Ms. Davis began her lesson by activating the students' prior experiences with story problems: "Today we are going to work on some more story problems, just like you've been doing for the past few days." The students were familiar with the routine of solving story problems, representing their work, and discussing and comparing solutions with a partner. Ms. Davis's prompt activated their connection to this routine, including their memory of her expectations of how they should interact with each other and what their finished work should look like.

Another way to effectively activate prior knowledge at the beginning of a lesson is to discuss or review the strategies and math vocabulary central to the lesson's learning goals. When strategies and math vocabulary are charted and prominently displayed, students can readily refer to them and make powerful visual connections to their prior knowledge. Activating prior knowledge and making it accessible in this way benefits all learners but is especially important for English language learners and struggling learners.

Make mathematics and mathematical thinking visual

You might have heard people say, "I'm a visual learner—I need to see things before I understand them," or "He's such a visual learner." Actually, the brain for all sighted people is dominantly visual. According to Jensen (1998), up to 90 percent of all information that comes into the brain is visual, which makes us wonder the following:

- If the brain is primarily a visual pattern detector and mathematics is the science of patterns and relationships, how can teachers maximize students' potential to see and understand the patterns and relationships that exist in mathematics?

- What visual models most powerfully enable students to construct mental models of mathematics—to progress from concrete to pictorial to abstract levels of understanding?

- How can teachers maximize students' understanding of mathematics by making the mathematical thinking and discourse visual?

These questions guide the decision making of teachers who build on the brain's strength as a visual processor and pattern detector. Such teachers plan lessons to make the mathematics and the mathematics thinking visual in several ways.

Use nonlinguistic representations

Dual-coding theory informs us that information is more likely to be transformed into knowledge and remembered when it is processed both linguistically and non-linguistically. When information is processed through multiple senses, a more complex network of connected knowledge is constructed. This is why graphic organizers and other visual tools, when effectively used to organize and chunk information in ways that the brain can detect patterns, advance learning for all students (Marzano, Pickering, and Pollock, 2001). When Ms. Davis used a flowchart to guide students through the sequence of the story actions and map it to the addition equation, she enabled students to visualize and understand the problem.

Use models to make the mathematics visual

Ms. Davis used models of base-ten blocks to supports students' developing understanding of place value. The structure of the blocks helped students see patterns and relationships in our number system. As you can see from her class strategy chart, Ms. Davis also developed the students' understanding and use of the number line. This powerful visual tool invites flexible and sophisticated thinking about addition and subtraction because it enables students to decompose numbers in ways other than by place. When teachers effectively scaffold students' use of models, students move from using concrete representations (modeling the problem with objects) to pictorial representations (modeling the problem with drawings) to mental models and abstract representations (using abstract symbols to model problems).

Powerful visual models to help students detect patterns and relationships in number and number operations

- Math racks
- Ten frames
- Money
- Hundred chart
- Number line
- Open number line
- Ratio table
- Array
- Open array

Create strategy charts and math vocabulary walls

In class discussions, Ms. Davis recorded students' different approaches to problems on strategy charts. Students could readily see similarities and differences between the strategies and the ways they could be represented. Ms. Davis and the class also developed a vocabulary wall of math words organized into related categories. These visual anchor charts hung prominently in the classroom along with a hundred chart and number line. Such representations and models should be clearly visible and accessible so that students can refer to them in problem solving and discourse.

Make student discourse and thinking visual

Finally, Ms. Davis maximized her students' learning by making student math talk and thinking visual in the class discussion. As Michael and Tiffany explained their thinking, they represented their solutions on the board. Before the discussion, Ms. Davis set up the board so that the solutions could be recorded side by side, enabling students to readily compare the two. This visual documentation of Michael's and Tiffany's thinking allowed students to simultaneously see and hear the information, enabling them to more deeply connect ideas and understand the strategies. If discussions lack visual representations of thinking and shared ideas, many children will tune out because they cannot follow or make sense of what they hear.

Engage students in solving problems with meaningful contexts

Learners are motivated to engage in tasks that are appropriately challenging, relevant, and personally meaningful. When presented with a task, the brain tries to make sense of it, seeking connections to prior knowledge stored in memory. Memories are contextual, embedded in experiences. The more meaningful and relevant the experience, the more likely the knowledge learned from the experience will be remembered.

Interesting and relevant problem contexts that support mathematical thinking invite students to engage meaningfully. By engaging in such problems, students are more likely to build robust networks of connected mathematical knowledge. The following questions guide teachers like Ms. Davis, who strive to maximize students' learning by using contexts meaningful to their students:

- What mathematics do I want my students to learn?

- What problem contexts invite rich mathematical exploration of those ideas?

- How can I connect the mathematics to events and situations in and out of school that are meaningful and relevant to my students?

Designing tasks that have meaningful contexts can be as simple as using students' names, interests, cultures, or experiences in story problems, as Ms. Davis did. However, the problem must demand and develop important mathematical thinking. Ms. Davis had a clear learning goal in mind: to advance students from using pictorial representations to using abstract representations when adding. Her grade 2 students had been excited about trading baseball cards during their free time, so she integrated the baseball card context into a discussion about representations that she wanted students to more deeply learn about and remember. When one of her students solves an addition problem in the future, she might well say, "Oh, this is just like the baseball card problem!"

The mathematics must be the focus of the learning experience and should not get lost in the context. If students plan a budget for a field trip, for example, they should remember not only the trip but also the problem solving and reasoning they engaged in to plan the budget.

Contexts can help students construct mathematical models to support developing important mathematical ideas, relationships, and strategies. Examples include the following:

- Contexts about things in rows. When students are challenged to find all the candy box sizes to arrange twenty-four candies in rows, most students model the problem with arrays. Using array contexts supports students' development of the array as a tool to understand the commutative, associative, and distributive properties of multiplication. Thinking about division as arrays also helps students understand the relationship between multiplication and division.

- Contexts about distances. When students are asked to find the distance between the third floor and the fortieth floor of a building, most students model the problem with a number line. Using number-line contexts supports students' development of the number line as a tool to understand such ideas as part–whole relationships and how addition and subtraction are related. Flexible use of the open number line gives students opportunities to explore different ways to add and subtract, multiply, and divide whole numbers and fractions.

Engage students in reflection, self-monitoring, and metacognition

Metacognitive students are aware of their thinking as they solve problems. Throughout their problem-solving process, they conduct an internal dialogue, consciously calling on prior knowledge and reflecting on and analyzing their thinking. They might ask themselves: *What's this problem about? Is it similar to other problems I've solved? What do I know that will help me solve it? What's the best way to solve it? Does my solution path and answer make sense? How can I check my answer by solving it a different way?* As they struggle with problems and engage more consciously with the mathematics on a metacognitive level, students construct more and stronger connections among related facts, procedures, models, strategies, big ideas, and concepts.

Even young students can learn to think metacognitively. When students learn the internal dialogue of effective problem solvers—how they think and what they do as they problem solve—they have the potential to independently and successfully transfer these metacognitive skills to new problems. Teachers like Ms. Davis scaffold students' development of metacognition by first making the internal dialogue explicit. Figure 2.3 shows a version of that internal dialogue that we have used in our math teaching. It is a sequence of questions that guides students' thinking and development of metacognition as they solve problems. This internal dialogue also challenges students to attend to communicating their thinking with precision.

In her lesson launch, Ms. Davis sent a clear message that taking time to understand the problem is the first thing a successful problem solver does. She then prompted the students to think about strategies they knew that might help them solve the problem. Her prior work in visually charting the students' addition strategies played an essential role in their ability to think metacognitively—they could readily access the strategies they knew and consider which ones made the most sense.

As Ms. Davis's students later worked in pairs to communicate and justify their reasoning, get feedback from each other, and compare approaches, they became more aware of their thinking about addition strategies, models, representations, and other ideas. This awareness enabled them to focus more deeply on connections between those mathematical ideas. Thinking metacognitively was essential to the students' ability to organize this connected knowledge around the concept of efficiency in their class discussion.

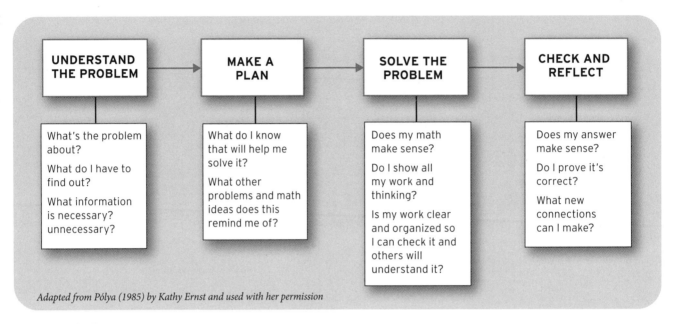

Adapted from Pólya (1985) by Kathy Ernst and used with her permission

Fig. 2.3. *Thinking Through a Math Problem*

When students think metacognitively, they are also more likely to monitor and make adjustments in their own learning. When teachers set landmarks of learning so that students can see where they are in relation to what they need to learn, students can more purposefully reflect on and monitor their thinking and work. With teacher encouragement and support, they also tend to take more ownership in assessing their progress and setting goals. Ms. Davis established such landmarks at the end of the lesson—some students were adding with drawings and others were adding with numbers. She ended the discussion by suggesting that students who used drawings try solving the problem just with equations. She set a goal for students but left it up to them to decide whether they were ready to try it.

Engage students in complex thinking

Mathematical understanding deepens with more and stronger neural connections. Students do not make such connections by simply solving more problems. They develop connected knowledge about mathematics when they solve fewer problems in greater depth—engaging in complex thinking about their problem solving and the mathematics related to the problem solving.

Students develop complex thinking through problems and activities that engage them in mathematical reasoning and proof: exploring patterns and relationships; looking for similarities and differences; evaluating solutions to problems; and generating, testing, and evaluating mathematical conjectures or ideas. Ms. Davis engaged her students in such complex thinking at the end of the lesson when she prompted them to compare Tiffany's and Michael's solutions. Such comparison invites students to look for patterns and notice relationships between numbers and operations, strategies, models, and problem types. When Ms. Davis asked her students to evaluate which strategy was most efficient, she challenged them to think in even more complex ways. They had to generate criteria for efficiency, analyze each strategy with greater precision to determine how it met the criteria, judge which strategy was most efficient, and justify their reasoning.

Students engage in complex thinking when they organize their networks of knowledge around related big ideas or concepts. They do this through active processing, consciously connecting the key ideas and concepts of their learning experience to prior knowledge. Most students do not do this thinking on their own; they require the support of a teacher who effectively prompts them to capture and explore key ideas and concepts by challenging them to summarize the main idea of a lesson or unit of study. This usually happens at the end of a lesson or investigation in which students discuss the problems or task they have worked on, as in Ms. Davis's class.

Ms. Davis's lesson goal was to move a large group of students from using a pictorial representation (drawing of tens and ones) to using an abstract representation (decomposing and recomposing tens and ones with equations) to solve an addition problem. By facilitating their analysis and evaluation of these two approaches, Ms. Davis enabled the students to capture the main idea of the lesson: "In the future, we should try using a more efficient approach to solving addition problems."

Although Ms. Davis wanted the students to connect the idea of efficiency to the more sophisticated addition approach, she knew that some students, like Timmy, might not be ready for such a leap. However, she knew that if Timmy participated in a class discussion in which a variety of ideas and representations were shared, he would have an opportunity to make connections between new information (splitting tens and ones by using equations) and what he already knew (splitting tens and ones with a drawing).

Children also engage in complex thinking about mathematics when they are explicitly challenged to make and prove generalizations. A generalization is a rule about how numbers and operations behave. Although many children implicitly apply generalizations as they solve problems, they must explore and apply generalizations to construct deeply connected math knowledge. To engage children in complex thinking about numbers and operations, it's important to explicitly bring forth and explore generalizations in classroom discourse through guided inquiry. For example, if you wanted children to construct an understanding of the commutative property, you can ask them to solve $2 + 3$ and $3 + 2$ and prompt: "How are these problems the same? Different?" and "Does switching the numbers in an addition problem always work? Why or why not?" These questions prompt students to make and prove many kinds of generalizations about math. For example, in a future lesson, Ms. Davis might ask her students, "Can you always split two-digit numbers into tens and ones and add them in any order?"

HOW THE PROCESS STANDARDS ENGAGE THE BRAIN IN LEARNING WITH UNDERSTANDING

When we reflect on how the brain constructs related networks of knowledge that are robustly understood, remembered, accessed, and flexibly transferred, we discover that the NCTM processes—problem solving, reasoning and proof, representing, communicating, and making connections—are integral to learning mathematics with understanding. When students have time to formulate their own strategies as they grapple with mathematically rich problems, they do what the brain is innately inclined to do: they seek to make sense of the mathematics as they seek a solution to the problem. They engage in complex thinking that challenges them to make connections to related prior math knowledge and experiences; use concrete, pictorial, or abstract representations to model and visualize problems; explore and analyze patterns and relationships; and generate, test, and evaluate solutions and conjectures (reason and prove). As students problem solve, they expand and strengthen neural connections among related networks of facts, procedures, and concepts.

When students communicate their thinking and problem solving through focused, effectively facilitated discourse that engages them in active processing of important mathematics, they develop increasingly sophisticated strategies and deepen their understanding of mathematical ideas. They increase and strengthen the connections they have made among related types of mathematics knowledge as they justify their reasoning, get feedback from their peers, analyze and evaluate a variety of representations and strategies, make and prove generalizations, and summarize main ideas. Engagement in all NCTM processes supports the neural processing essential to learn and understand mathematics.

CONCLUSION

Your goal is to engage all your students in using their brains optimally and efficiently to learn mathematics in a way that is deeply understood and remembered, readily accessed, and flexibly transferred to a variety of settings and problems. When you reflect on how the brain makes meaning and how children learn, you can more deeply appreciate why using brain-engaging teaching practices is essential to learning mathematics with and for understanding.

Just as students need time to develop mathematical understanding by constructing networks of connected knowledge grounded in mathematical concepts, teachers need time to construct webs of connected knowledge grounded in teaching mathematics with and for understanding. There is so much to learn—about mathematics, general pedagogy, and how students learn mathematics—that it can feel overwhelming to a new teacher. No one expects you to know it all. Developing expertise in teaching takes years, and expert teachers never stop reflecting on their practice and constructing new knowledge about how to maximize their students' mathematics learning.

II Laying the Groundwork

Teaching in the ways that we describe is complex and cannot be accomplished without also developing a well-organized and well-functioning classroom community. Section II offers five chapters devoted to what you can do before school starts and in the first months of school to develop relationships, classroom spaces, norms, and routines to support you and your students in your year of learning together.

Chapter 3 focuses on developing relationships with colleagues and families and learning to use curriculum materials. Chapter 4 explains how to set up your classroom to facilitate both independent and cooperative learning and classroom discourse. Chapter 5 offers suggestions for how to transform your classroom of students into a supportive learning community. Chapter 6 describes management routines and a metacognitive problem-solving routine that support student math learning. Chapter 7 explains computational fluency and describes instructional routines to support your students' development of computational fluency and their understanding of mathematical generalizations.

SUCCESS
from the START
Your first years
teaching ELEMENTARY
MATHEMATICS

chapter three

Preparing for a Successful Beginning

Guiding Principles

LEARNING IS MAXIMIZED WHEN STUDENTS—

>> interact in a safe, supportive learning community;

>> activate and build on prior knowledge;

>> process information both visually and linguistically;

>> solve problems with meaningful contexts;

>> engage in reflection, self-monitoring, and metacognition; and

>> engage in complex thinking.

Good teaching may appear spontaneous. You probably have images of teachers from movies or childhood who seemed to know exactly what to do or say in response to almost any classroom situation. In reality, successful teaching develops over time and is supported by both careful planning and a willingness to seek help from others.

Essential Practices

>> Find teachers to help you assess what your students already know and understand about math.

>> Find colleagues for ongoing support with classroom culture, lesson planning and reflection, and assessment.

>> Familiarize yourself with your curriculum materials.

>> Develop positive relationships with the families of your students.

As a new teacher, you can learn a lot from the wisdom and knowledge of others: mentors, colleagues, and the families of the students you teach. You can also learn from your curriculum materials.

FIND TEACHERS TO HELP YOU ASSESS WHAT YOUR STUDENTS ALREADY KNOW AND UNDERSTAND ABOUT MATH

Teachers are expected to hit the ground running each year. For example, you may be asked to formally or informally assess your students within the first six weeks of school. This can be a daunting task for new teachers who do not yet have a sense of what students coming to their grade are likely to already know or how students are likely to demonstrate their knowledge.

One way to prepare yourself is to have a conversation with someone who has taught or student-taught children at the previous grade level. If you will be teaching fourth grade, find a third-grade teacher to talk to. Try to find someone from the school where you will teach, someone with considerable experience teaching that grade level, or someone who has used the same curriculum materials that you will use. Ask questions like these:

- What did your students learn in math last year? What topics did you spend the most time on? How did students' thinking about those topics change over the year?

- What strategies did your students use to [add, subtract, multiply, or divide]? What materials or models did they use to help them? By the end of the year, what strategies were most students using?

- Near the end of last year, did students play games that they especially liked? Could you teach them to me so that I can begin the year by having students play those games?

- When I observe my students in September to assess what they know and how they are thinking about math, what should I look for?

If the answers that you get the first time do not help, ask someone else. Such conversations should help you to both gather useful information for assessing your students and find people who can offer support throughout the year.

FIND COLLEAGUES FOR ONGOING SUPPORT WITH CLASSROOM CULTURE, LESSON PLANNING AND REFLECTION, AND ASSESSMENT

All teachers, not just new teachers, benefit from developing networks of supportive colleagues. Sometimes schools offer new teachers mentors, math coaches, or math specialists to help them. Other times teachers must find their own support communities. New teachers often need support in these areas:

- Establishing and maintaining a classroom culture in which students work respectfully and productively with others, persevere in solving problems, and share their thinking

- Identifying the mathematical goals of lessons and planning with those goals in mind

- Anticipating and understanding students' mathematical thinking

- Figuring out why a lesson did not go as planned

- Understanding the assessments students need to take and how to interpret the data

- Understanding local, state, or national standards on which the assessments are based

Sometimes assigned mentors do not provide all the kinds of support listed above (or do not provide that support often enough), and teachers need to seek it out elsewhere. Feel free to ask for the help you need. The more assertive you can be in requesting support, and the more specific you can be about the types of support that you would like, the better.

Finding knowledgeable and helpful people

Teachers in general tend to be knowledgeable and helpful people, but they also tend to be modest and busy. Experienced teachers also know that new teachers have lots to figure out and make sense of, and they may give you space rather than foist their accumulated wisdom upon you. However, that does not mean that they are not willing to give you their time when asked. Many experienced teachers would love to have colleagues with whom to discuss the topics above.

Let the principal know that you are interested in opportunities to learn more about teaching math and to work with a mentor or math coach if one is available. Ask the principal to recommend teachers especially good at or interested in teaching math who might offer you support. Finally, let your principal know that you are interested in attending any professional development in mathematics.

Let teachers know that you want to talk about math teaching

Let other teachers know that you want to talk about math teaching with them and that you want help from them in the ways listed above. Meeting with and learning from teachers on your grade level is often easiest, but sometimes the most knowledgeable or open teachers teach other grade levels. Look for teachers who—

- have set up their classrooms in ways that support students working together and sharing ideas;

- listen to and learn from their students and colleagues;

- read through their curriculum materials carefully;

- reflect on their teaching and continually try to improve; and
- have participated in professional development in mathematics.

Approach these teachers and ask them whether—

- they would help you learn to teach students to work together and share their thinking in mathematics;
- they would help you figure out why a lesson did not go as planned;
- you can ask them questions about the lessons in your curriculum materials; and
- teachers meet regularly to plan lessons and if you may join them.

Although you may feel like you are impinging on other teachers' time, the work of establishing and maintaining a respectful and productive classroom culture, analyzing student work and thinking, and identifying important mathematical goals for lessons never ends. A mentor or experienced teacher may do this work more quickly or easily than you can. However, he or she probably welcomes the opportunity to talk with you about these topics and is likely to benefit from the conversations as well.

FAMILIARIZE YOURSELF WITH YOUR CURRICULUM MATERIALS

Most school districts have chosen particular curriculum materials, or math programs, for teachers to use. In many districts, teachers must use these materials as their sole or primary resource for teaching students. As a result, one of the first challenges that teachers face is figuring out how to understand and use their curriculum materials.

Before 1990, most math programs consisted of textbooks with explanations and exercises. The focus was on skills and procedures, and teacher materials consisted mainly of answer keys. In the early 1990s, the National Science Foundation funded the development of new math programs designed to support students in developing conceptual understanding of mathematics, as well as procedural fluency. These math programs supplied more problems with meaningful contexts and multiple entry points for students to solve. They also offered support materials designed to help teachers—

- understand elementary mathematics more deeply;
- understand how students develop mathematical understanding over time;
- support students in problem solving, reasoning and proving, communicating mathematical thinking, using representations, and making connections; and
- formatively assess students as they work.

Elementary math programs now typically include at least some problems with meaningful contexts and multiple entry points, recommend the use of manipulatives and mathematical representations, and explain the value of strategies other than the traditional algorithms. Current math programs also include large amounts of information designed to help teachers support students in various ways.

Familiarize yourself with the materials for teachers that are part of your math program. Math programs often include the following:

- In-depth information about the math you are expected to teach

- Information about the types of problems, activities, and games that appear in the program and suggestions for how to manage them

- Information about computational strategies that students tend to develop or that are explicitly taught in the program, and how these strategies compare with more traditional algorithms

- Information about mathematical models used in the program, such as ten-frames, base-ten materials, number lines, arrays, and fraction bars, and how these models support students' thinking

- Suggestions for how to formatively assess students

- Samples of student work with commentary about whether the work meets expectations and why or why not

- Information about how to work with various populations of students such as English language learners, struggling students, and students ready for more challenge

- Letters that you can send to families (often in Spanish and English) to inform them of what math students will be learning in each unit and how families can support their child's math learning at home

- Sample dialogue or video clips of students and teachers from real classrooms

Use the time before school starts to read or skim through the different materials to find out what they contain. Then carefully read information about the math topics that you will be teaching this year, the strategies and representations that students are likely to use, and how to formatively assess students and keep track of that information.

Finally, read through some initial lessons in your teacher's guide with the following lesson-planning questions in mind:

- What are the mathematical goals of the lesson?

- What mathematical vocabulary are students expected to use and understand?

- If students were allowed to solve the problems in any way that made sense to them, what strategies and representations might they use?

- What could I look for and listen for that would tell me how students were solving the problems?

DEVELOP POSITIVE RELATIONSHIPS WITH FAMILIES

Establishing positive relationships with families is crucial. Positive relationships enhance student learning, give you access to important information about your students, and make it more likely that families will work with you to resolve learning or discipline issues. What you communicate and how you communicate with parents early in the year will affect how comfortable parents feel engaging with you.

Ask families about their knowledge of and hopes for their children

Asking families about their children is a great way to begin a relationship. If you give families an opportunity to tell you what their children already know about various subjects and any hopes or concerns they have about their children's learning, you show that you value their input. You may also learn crucial information about their child that will help you in your teaching.

In the first days or weeks of school, send out a survey to parents—in whatever languages they speak. This survey could not only cover math but also include questions about other subjects and about the child's interests outside school. Here are some sample questions, written in simple and direct language:

- How does your child feel about math?

- What are your child's strengths in math?

- What concerns, if any, do you have about your child in math?

- What do you hope your child will learn this year in math class?

- Does your family play any math-related games at home (math games on computer, Sudoku, board games, card games, or chess)? If so, which ones?

Back-to-school night

In addition to gathering information from families, you will need to give them information about what math their child will learn from you and how they can support their child in doing mathematics, especially for homework. Most schools hold a back-to-school night during which you can give parents this information. This event is also a good time to distribute a survey if you have not done so already, and to ask families about their preferred ways of communicating with you.

The most important thing you can do during back-to-school night is to establish a welcoming environment that makes all families feel included and valued. Also, be clear and organized about the information you present and focus on the essential information that parents want and need to know. Presenting this information in a electronic presentation or handout, as well as explaining it, is helpful. Strive to communicate the following about mathematics:

- Topics students will study in math this year.

- That problem solving will be an important part of math class and that students will solve problems in ways that make sense to them. This may mean that students solve problems differently from how adults solve problems.

- How often you plan to give math homework and about how much time you expect students to spend completing it.

- How parents can help students with homework. (See the following letter. It is also available on More4U.)

Homework is a more complicated issue than it appears. Parents usually want children to have some homework and generally want that homework to be somewhat challenging (otherwise they worry that their child is not learning in school.) However, homework is often completed near the end of the day, when both children and adults are tired. Sometimes students get stuck doing their homework, and parents need clear, concrete ideas for how to help their children without doing the homework for them. Below is a sample letter that you can give parents at back-to-school night with suggestions for how to help children with homework. Chapter 15 has more about homework.

Also use back-to-school night to gather information from families about how best to communicate with them. Place a sign-in sheet on a desk near the door, and ask for information such as what languages family members speak, phone numbers and e-mail addresses where they can be reached, preferred means of communication, and times when it is easiest for them to speak on the phone. As busy as you are, the adults in your students' families are also busy. They may work more than one job or work at odd hours. You will save time and minimize frustration for everyone if you respect their needs and preferences around communication. Send home a summary of the information presented at back-to-school night to families who could not attend.

{ more**4U**

See More4U for the Family Engagement chapter about communicating with parents.

Dear Families,

A goal of homework is for children to figure out problems on their own. Children learn about important math ideas by struggling with problems and trying to figure them out. If your child continues to struggle and asks for help, help your child think about how to solve the problem without showing or telling him or her how to solve it.

Here are some things you can say if your child is stuck:
- What is the problem about?

- What is the problem asking you to find out?

- What do you know that might help you solve it?

- What have you thought about so far?

- Does this problem remind you of any other problems you've done? How is it the same?

- What tools (drawings, equations, models) or strategies have you used in school to solve problems like this? (If your child has difficulty answering this, let me know.)

Another goal of homework is for children to think about whether their answers make sense, to prove the accuracy of their answers, and to discover and correct any mistakes on their own. (Don't tell them they're wrong or correct their answers—let them figure it out.)

Here's what you can say to help your child think about their answers and discover any mistakes he or she may have made:

- How did you figure that out?
- Does your answer make sense? Why?
- Did you double-check?

If your child doesn't understand part or all of the homework, and can't do it independently, let your child know that it's OK not to finish it. Please let me know if your child needs help.

Sincerely,

See the Family Engagement chapter for more information about math orientation workshops.

Math orientation workshop

Many parents do not understand how math is currently taught and why. They may have trouble supporting their children with math at home. Schools should give families in-depth opportunities both to experience math in the ways that their children experience math at school and to hear clear explanations of why current math instruction emphasizes problem solving and learning with understanding. Work with your principal and your colleagues to host a math orientation workshop. Your school should hold such a night within the first few months of school.

Foster ongoing communication with families

Here are a few additional things you can do to nurture positive relationships with families and foster ongoing communication:

- Send home any family letters that come with your math program.
- Send weekly or monthly newsletters letting parents know what your students have been learning and how they have been demonstrating that learning. (If you communicate by e-mail, make sure that all families have Internet access.)
- Set up a class website with links to websites that have math games or challenging problems.
- Communicate something positive about each student through a phone call, e-mail, text message, or postcard within the first two months of school. Families often hear from schools only when a problem arises.

Make the first communication with parents about their child a positive one. Praise students' effort or problem-solving dispositions. This practice will model the encouragement that you would like parents to give.

CONCLUSION

Your ability to build productive, collaborative relationships with your colleagues and with the families of your students is critical for a successful beginning.

As you seek support from your colleagues about the math curriculum and ways to plan and reflect on lessons together, keep an open and inquiring mind. Don't be afraid to ask questions. Taking the stance of a learner is a quality of highly effective teachers. Your colleagues can be an invaluable source of information about your students' past knowledge and experiences in math. Identifying a mentor or group of colleagues to provide ongoing support and feedback to you throughout the year will serve to sustain your professional and personal growth and well-being.

Finally, developing productive relationships with families is essential to maximizing student success in school; welcoming your families with equity and inclusion is an important way to start your year. Throughout this book, we define "family" as those who are a student's primary caregivers, such as parents, guardians, grandparents, or an older sibling. We use "family engagement" and "parent engagement" interchangeably. Other people who are significant influencers, like ministers or coaches, may be in the sphere of family if they are the child's primary providers of support and encouragement. It's important for you to identify and build relationships with your students' influencers.

SUCCESS
from
the START

Your first years
teaching ELEMENTARY
MATHEMATICS

chapter **four**

Setting Up Your Classroom

Guiding Principles

LEARNING IS MAXIMIZED WHEN STUDENTS—

>> interact in a safe, supportive learning community;

>> activate and build on prior knowledge;

>> process information both visually and linguistically;

>> solve problems with meaningful contexts;

>> engage in reflection, self-monitoring, and metacognition; and

>> engage in complex thinking.

When you set up your classroom for the first time, think carefully about your room design. The decisions you make as you prepare your classroom will influence how comfortable students feel as they work, how easily they can access the materials and information they need, and how well they can learn from one another. Create a classroom where students can—

- work productively for sustained periods without being cramped or jostled;

- communicate ideas and share materials with partners at tables or desks;

- independently access math materials;

- refer to class charts and other visuals for information; and

- fully participate in class discussions of important ideas.

A fourth-grade teacher we know has an extremely inviting and well-designed classroom. Desks are arranged in groups of four, and the room has an empty area near the whiteboard where the class can gather on the carpet to discuss ideas. Enough space is between the desks for students to move around comfortably, and students can independently get up to get a new book off the shelf during reading time, get math materials in easy-to-reach bins during math time, and sign themselves out to go to the bathroom as needed.

The teacher displays completed student work in various parts of the room. The classroom has student-created maps of Africa across the top of one wall, final drafts of student narratives at eye level where peers can read them, and student-generated math puzzles on a bulletin board with an invitation to solve them. At the front of the room, near the whiteboard, are a few clearly written class charts, summarizing key ideas discussed or explored in the past few days in various subjects. This area also includes a math vocabulary wall and charts of computation strategies, neatly presented and organized.

Classrooms designed to support mathematical learning should have the following:

- Tables or desks arranged so that students can work with partners regularly

- Generous quantities of frequently used math materials stored in easy-to-reach places

- Space for whole-class discussions in which students can easily see and hear one another

- Enough board space for teachers and students to record more than one mathematical strategy at a time

- Displays of important models such as hundred charts and number lines, where students can easily see and use them

- Class-generated charts of computation strategies and mathematical vocabulary hung where students can see and refer to them

---

Classroom Features That Support Learning

Design a classroom space with the following components:

- A meeting area for whole-class discussions

- Desk arrangements that allow individual, partner, and small-group work

- Math materials accessible to students

- Wall space to hang visual models and charts

You will also need to take into account the unique constraints of your own physical space. Your classroom may be small or oddly shaped or contain built-in shelves or cubbies in awkward places. Do your best to creatively work around these constraints to design a classroom that supports learning.

A MEETING AREA FOR WHOLE-CLASS DISCUSSIONS

Each day will have times when you will need to gather your entire class and focus each student on the same task, routine, or idea. Students gather for—

- morning meetings that focus on routines such as taking attendance, going over the schedule, and discussing important events of the day;

- introductions to activities at the beginning of lessons; and

- whole-class discussions in which students' solutions and ideas are shared and explored.

Design a separate area in your classroom (away from students' desks) for these gatherings. A meeting area offers a space where students' attention can be focused on discourse and thinking that supports learning. When seating arrangements allow students to see and hear each of their classmates when they speak, they are more likely to attend to what is being said. They can more deeply engage with ideas being shared and are more likely to respond directly to their peers. Many elementary students have difficulty projecting their voices when they speak, particularly when they are tentative in their thinking. This makes communicating across the length of a classroom difficult. It is even more difficult when background noise from the hallway, the playground, or a heater distracts listeners. Also, when students are seated near you, you can better assess their engagement level and more easily keep students on task.

An ideal meeting area has several characteristics. First, all students and the teacher should be able to see and hear one another. Meeting areas are often defined by a rug where students sit. They can also include chairs or benches around the periphery. Providing seating at two different levels makes seeing one another and the board easier for all students.

All students must have visual access to the board and to other information related to the discussion. Most whole-class conversations involve visual learning. When gathering in a meeting area, all students are close enough to the board and to the teacher to see what is written or modeled. A U-shape arrangement, as opposed to a full circle of students, generally ensures that all students can see what is on the board.

The meeting area should have enough space for students to sit comfortably so they can attend to what is being discussed. Some teachers use mats, tape, or other physical markers to indicate where on the rug students should sit. When seating is clearly marked, you waste no time seating students where they can participate productively.

Finally, students are more likely to stay focused if the meeting area is free of distracting materials. If students need to write during a discussion, they can bring a notebook or clipboard to the rug. Similarly, if you want students to share work that they have done, ask them to bring just their papers from that day to the meeting area.

The best place for a meeting area is near a large amount of open board space. Mathematical discussions of strategies and representations require lots of space for you to record what different students contribute. Comparing two strategies is hard if the first strategy must be erased to make room for the next. If you are planning to use technology such as an overhead projector, document camera, or interactive whiteboard, the meeting area must accommodate the tool. If this technology requires outlets and electrical cords, run cords under the rug or tape them to the floor to minimize tripping.

If you have a small room and absolutely cannot figure out a way to create a meeting area, think creatively about how you arrange student desks so that all students can see the board and can see and hear one another during class discussions.

DESK ARRANGEMENTS THAT ALLOW INDIVIDUAL, PARTNER, AND SMALL-GROUP WORK

After establishing where to place the meeting area, decide how to set up desks or tables. Many teachers place desks in groups of four, allowing students to work individually, in pairs, or as a foursome. Other teachers create groups of six or eight desks.

Leave enough space around each table or group of desks for you and the students to move around easily. You need space to circulate around the room during lessons to assess and work with students. Students need space to walk between tables or groups of desks to get supplies or go to the bathroom. If you have a small classroom, consider creating more space to walk by making groups of six or eight desks or pushing two tables together. You might also consider giving up your desk to create more room. Teachers who do this keep their files in a separate filing cabinet and keep supplies such as pens, staplers, and paper clips on a shelf or in a closet.

Arrange desks and other furniture such as shelves in ways that allow you to easily see and monitor your students from any place in the classroom. You should be able to look up from any place in your classroom and check whether all students are on task. Place tall furniture against a wall so that it will not block your sightlines. Figure 4.1 shows two examples of classroom arrangements. In each floor plan, the meeting area is prominently placed in front of the board. Both have tables or desks arranged so that students can sit in groups of four or six. In both classrooms the teachers have decided to forgo their desks to make more space. In the second floor plan, the teacher has a small table for working with groups of students. This small table is placed so that the teacher can see the entire classroom and even monitor students coming in and out.

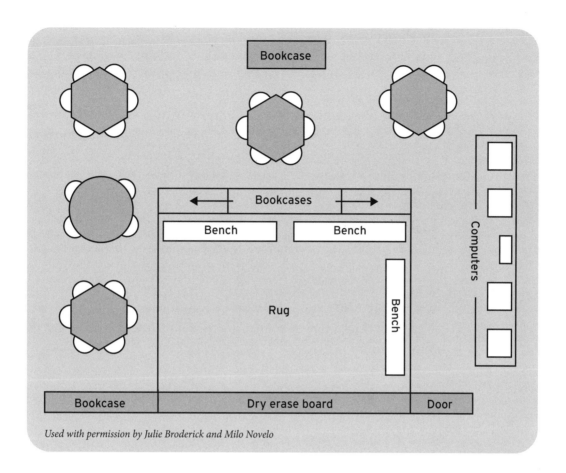

Used with permission by Julie Broderick and Milo Novelo

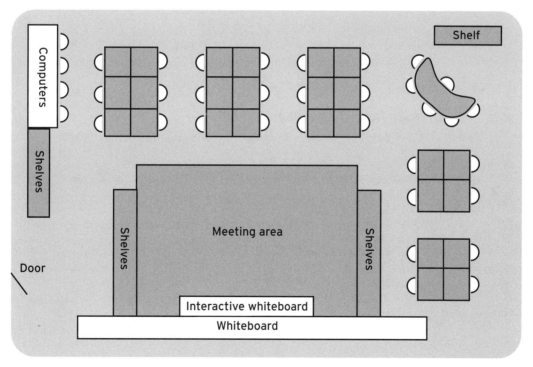

Fig. 4.1. *Two possible classroom configurations*

Small-group instruction

On many days you will want to gather a small group of students for focused instruction. Many teachers have a small table for this purpose. A table that can fit up to six students and a teacher is ideal. A configuration of six desks can also work. Recording should be a feature of most small-group discussions, so make sure that you have a way to record students' thinking. You can use chart paper and an easel, a portable whiteboard, or chart paper taped to the wall. Be creative. You can also work with small groups in the meeting area, which has more board space and helpful visuals such as the number line and the hundred chart.

Space for computers

Most classrooms have two to four desktop computers. To maximize students' use of the computers, teachers often have two students at a time work together on a computer. Some teachers cycle students through computer activities while the rest of the class works on other tasks. Try to set up your computers so that two students can sit side by side at one computer, and place the computers where they will not distract other students.

MATH MATERIALS ACCESSIBLE TO STUDENTS

After you arrange desks or tables, think about where and how you will store math materials. Students at every grade level should have access to math materials such as interlocking cubes, pattern blocks, real or play coins, number lines, and rulers. These materials help students solve problems, create visual representations of their thinking, and communicate ideas and solutions to others. You should have enough for your whole class to use them at one time. Store these materials so that you and your students can get them when needed, carry them to tables and desks to use, and return them in an orderly and timely fashion.

Math materials students need

Many teachers inherit boxes of materials and are not sure which ones will be most useful. Check your curriculum guides to see what materials you will be asked to use most often. The following are some of the most useful math materials:

- Interlocking cubes
- Base-ten blocks
- Pattern blocks
- Real and play coins
- Hundred charts and number lines
- Dice, playing cards, and other game materials
- Rulers
- Calculators

Descriptions of each set of materials are available on More4U.

Making materials accessible to students

Organize your materials by how often you plan to use them, available storage room, and your tolerance for individual students moving around your room during lessons.

Bins on shelves in designated "math areas"

Keeping bins of common math materials on shelves in one or two math areas of the room allows materials to be stored neatly where all students can see and access them. Label bins with words or pictures that match labels on shelves so students can easily put materials away in appropriate places. Labeling also builds vocabulary and reading skills for young students, struggling students, and English language learners.

When all students at one table or group of desks need the same material, one student can bring a bin to the table for the group to share. When different students want to use different materials to solve problems, they can individually get the materials they prefer. This approach allows for differentiated learning.

Consider the size of the bins that you store materials in. Some cubes, for example, may come in large bins, but these bins are not useful for easily distributing an appropriate amount of materials to several groups of students. Shoebox-sized bins for materials are preferred. Plastic bins this size are available at dollar stores.

Large bins of different materials on shelves in one math area

An organized second-grade teacher wanted to give students a choice of math materials for solving problems while minimizing student movement around the room. She created large bins for each group of four students. In each bin, she placed a bag of interlocking cubes, 4 hundred charts, 4 number lines, 2 rulers, and a bag of coins. One student from each group would get the bin of materials and place it in the center of the four desks at the beginning of each period. Each student had a range of tools without needing to get up.

Where and when to place materials

Store math materials in a central area of your classroom reachable from more than one direction. When math materials are located in a back corner of the classroom, students trying to get materials end up jammed in a line or clump, and students who have just picked up materials cannot get back to their seats.

Some teachers place all these materials on shelves before the beginning of the school year. Other teachers gradually introduce materials over the first two months of school, to ensure that they are used and cared for properly. Either way, set clear expectations for how students handle and store math materials and routines for obtaining materials and putting them away. (See chapters 5 and 6 for more about establishing norms and routines.)

WALL SPACE TO HANG VISUAL MODELS AND CHARTS

After setting up desks and math materials, think about what to post on your walls to support students in staying focused and thinking productively during math lessons.

Place visual models such as a hundred or two hundred wall chart and a number line (placed low enough for students to touch) near the meeting area so that the whole class can see and use these materials during class discussions. You can place small analog clocks next to your class schedule to show what time each subject starts. You can also make a place for the calendar and any math activities related to it. These visuals should not cover most of your board space: Have plenty of free board space during lessons to record students' strategies and ideas.

Use room around the board to hang charts that you will create with students to remind them of rules and expectations, as well as charts for subject-specific information. In math you will need charts of both vocabulary and students' strategies, but create these with students as you introduce vocabulary and as students begin to use various computation strategies.

In general, you want enough visual reminders in the room to cue students to the things you are studying and to give them tools and vocabulary to solve problems and communicate their ideas. However, too much visual information can be distracting. A few clear, neat charts that relate to topics being studied are better than a scattered collection of every chart your class has created all year. Some teachers pin charts related to each subject area neatly on top of one another; students see only the most recent charts but have access to the others by flipping the pages. For example, from the view of a student, your whiteboard area might look like this:

STOP+REFLECT

>> This is an example of a whiteboard area for a K-1 classroom.

>> What would be important to include on a whiteboard area for grade K? 1? 2? 3? 4? 5?

CONCLUSION

Be intentional about how you set up your classroom. A well-designed classroom supports learning in many different ways. Create a meeting area in your own classroom. Arrange desks or tables so that four, six, or eight students can sit together. Organize your math materials so that students can easily get the materials they need. Hang visual models and charts where students can see and use them. Enjoy setting up your room and the anticipation of working productively with your students once they arrive.

chapter **five**

Building a Supportive Mathematics Learning Community

Guiding Principles

LEARNING IS MAXIMIZED WHEN STUDENTS—

>> interact in a safe, supportive learning community;

>>activate and build on prior knowledge;

>> process information both visually and linguistically;

>> solve problems with meaningful contexts;

>> engage in reflection, self-monitoring, and metacognition; and

>> engage in complex thinking.

One of the most important tasks on your first day of school is to begin building a supportive mathematics learning community. As students enter your classroom, they feel emotions ranging from eager anticipation to anxiety and fear. They wonder: *Will my teacher be fair and kind? Will the kids in my class like me? Accept me? Will the work be too hard? Too easy? Will I like it here?* Your most important job begins today: building relationships with every student and establishing a climate of safety and respect.

Emotions play a vital role in learning. If students feel threatened or overly stressed, they cannot engage in complex mathematical thinking. Your challenge is to build a safe, secure classroom environment in which the guiding rule is "We will help each other do our best thinking, work, and problem solving." Establishing such a climate involves teaching your students about the dispositions, or habits of mind, of effective problem solvers and why they are important to develop. It also requires establishing clear expectations about how students should interact with each other to maximize everyone's learning. When your students understand why a supportive classroom environment is essential for learning math, and you engage them in developing class norms that nurture such a climate, they will take ownership of those norms and responsibility for carrying them out.

Developing a supportive mathematics learning community requires purposeful planning and teaching. To frame your thinking about supportive math communities, you must examine your beliefs and attitudes about mathematics and envision a supportive mathematics community.

EXAMINE YOUR BELIEFS AND ATTITUDES ABOUT MATHEMATICS

It is important to reflect on and examine your beliefs and attitudes about math because they can affect your students' attitudes and math learning. Ultimately, how students feel about math influences the classroom environment. You can start by reflecting on questions such as these: What was my experience as a math student? Did I do well in elementary math but have difficulty with more complex math in high school or college? Was math engaging and did it make sense throughout my years as a student? How do I feel about math? Do I believe it is a difficult subject to learn? Easy? Do I enjoy math or am I anxious about it?

Unfortunately, many elementary math teachers have math anxiety. Children are perceptive. If you dislike math or have math anxiety, you will unwittingly communicate to your students that math is difficult to learn and a subject to be feared. If you have math anxiety, that is probably because math did not make sense to you. If so, join a group of colleagues to discover the joy and beauty of math by solving problems together and exploring the underlying structures and properties of numbers and operations.

Meanwhile, pay attention to how your words and actions can influence students' attitudes toward math. If you say to your students, "Subtraction is hard to learn," they will probably believe you. (Subtraction is hard to learn only when presented in a way that students cannot make sense of it.) Keep an open and inquiring mind, and focus on practicing and modeling the dispositions of effective problem solvers. If a question arises in math class that you cannot answer, you can model curiosity by asking, "What do you think?" or you can say, "I'm not sure about that. How can we find out?"

PICTURE A SUPPORTIVE MATHEMATICS LEARNING COMMUNITY

In a supportive mathematics learning community, students respect each other's unique experiences, culture, knowledge, needs, and ways of thinking. Students view everyone in their class—students and teachers alike—as learners, teachers, and problem solvers. When assuming the role of "teacher," students help each other discover mistakes and give hints rather than correct each other or give solutions to problems. They value learning as a lifelong endeavor because in this classroom, they see their teacher engaged in inquiry and learning throughout the school day.

In a supportive mathematics learning community, curiosity drives students to wonder about and explore patterns, relationships, and ideas. Students persist as they grapple with problems because they are motivated to explore solutions, and they believe that they can succeed. Flexibility is routinely practiced as students discuss multiple ideas and solutions to problems. Students take risks in generating, testing, and sharing ideas and solutions without fear of uncertainty, ridicule, or failure. Students respectfully listen to, elaborate on, and sometimes challenge each other's thinking and ideas. Students are motivated to make sense of math, and to that end, they continually reflect on their thinking and that of their peers. Students help each other develop their problem-solving dispositions: curiosity, flexibility, persistence, risk taking, and reflection.

Most important, students understand and value the purpose of a supportive mathematics learning community. They communicate their reasoning and solutions with clarity and precision to deepen their understanding of mathematics, to get feedback from their teacher and peers, and, ultimately, to contribute to the collective learning of the class. They are clear about the explicit actions they can take to support each other, and they invest in helping each other do their best thinking, work, and problem solving.

Finally, by creating such an environment, and by teaching, modeling, and reinforcing these community norms and habits of mind, you help students become metacognitive—to become aware of and monitor their thinking as they solve problems—which is vital to learning math with understanding.

Essential Practices

To develop a supportive climate in which students engage rigorously in developing their thinking and problem-solving skills, several practices are essential:

Laying the Groundwork

>> **On day one, establish high expectations for learning together in respectful, supportive ways.**

>> **Guide students in exploring the dispositions of effective problem solvers and why developing them is important.**

>> **Help students understand why a supportive classroom community is vital for their brains to do their best thinking, work, and problem solving.**

>> **Invest students in developing and practicing class norms of behavior that support productive thinking, work, and problem solving.**

Building and Sustaining a Supportive Learning Community

>> **Give consistent, descriptive feedback emphasizing students' success in developing problem-solving dispositions and enacting class norms.**

>> **Engage students in—**

  - **monitoring and assessing the development and transfer of their problem-solving dispositions;**
  - **reflecting on, monitoring, and assessing their progress in carrying out group norms; and**
  - **periodic reflection on the norms.**

Building a supportive mathematics learning community is a complex, long-term process that requires treating every child with fairness and respect, knowing how children learn, and believing that every child can make meaning of mathematics.

This chapter gives you an instructional model that grades K–5 teachers have used to develop a supportive math-learning community. The model breaks the essential practices above into an instructional sequence with two major stages: "Laying the Groundwork" and "Building and Sustaining a Supportive Learning Community."

Details about how teachers have implemented these important practices should give you ideas about how to engage your students in developing class norms that support them to do their best thinking and problem solving. This is not a recipe. Modify these suggestions and make them your own. Incorporate your own voice and expertise and adjust the pacing and contexts to accommodate the needs, experiences, and interests of your students. As you teach students the essential ideas in laying the groundwork, do the following:

- Give students opportunities to connect their experiences to new ideas that you introduce—so students see that building a supportive community makes sense.

- Create neat, visually appealing charts with linguistic and nonlinguistic representations of important ideas that you introduce to students—so that all students can access and learn them.

- Engage students in purposeful decision making—so they are motivated to enact behaviors and norms of a supportive math learning community.

LAYING THE GROUNDWORK

Laying the groundwork introduces students to the fundamental knowledge about supportive mathematics learning communities. You can implement this model in four to seven sessions, depending on scheduling constraints and the grade level, needs, and experiences of your students.

Establish high expectations for learning together in respectful, supportive ways

You can introduce these ideas on the first day of school. This session can last twenty to thirty minutes, depending on the age and experience of your students.

Goals
Students begin to understand and recognize that—

- everyone in the class is a learner, teacher, and problem solver;

- their classroom is a safe and supportive place; and

- their classroom has high expectations for thinking, work, and problem solving.

You can begin to build a supportive culture by introducing your students to the idea that your classroom is a learning community and that members of a learning community alternate between being learners, teachers, and problem solvers. Most children have no trouble seeing themselves as learners and problem solvers, but identifying themselves as teachers, or their teacher as a learner and a problem solver, is a challenge. These are big and important ideas to convey to students, because you want them to share their thinking, strategies, and solutions and to teach, and learn from, each other. And they need to view you, their teacher, as one who engages with problems and who delights in and models continual learning. When you take this stance, students view you not only as their teacher but also as a member of their learning community.

Setup

1 Create a neat, visually appealing chart on poster board or paper (posted permanently in class so children and visitors can refer to it—not on an interactive board).

> Each of us is a learner.
>
> Each of us is a teacher.
>
> Each of us is a problem solver.
>
> We will help each other do our best thinking, work, and problem solving.

2 Cover each sentence with a strip of construction paper. Students will eagerly anticipate and wonder about what is hidden. Uncover one sentence at a time as you introduce it.

3 Earlier in the day, teach your students the talk move called think, turn, and talk.

Introducing the lesson

Mr. Garcia, a third-grade teacher, introduces his students to these ideas.

Mr. Garcia:	This year we're going to learn many things together in our class. Let's read this together. [*Mr. Garcia removes the paper strip covering the sentence, and the children join in a choral reading.*]
All students:	Each of us is a learner.
Mr. Garcia:	Think about something you learned to do. What was hard about learning it? Turn and talk to your partner about what you learned and what was hard about learning it.

As the children talk, Mr. Garcia listens to what they say. He asks students to briefly share a few stories with the class, showing challenges students faced when learning something new. He shares a story about how he learned how to use a new app to keep track of all the phone numbers and birthdays of his friends and family.

STOP+REFLECT

>> What story about something you learned can you share with your students?

Mr. Garcia continues to lay the groundwork:

Mr. Garcia:	All people in our class have their own special ways of thinking, special things they've seen or done, and things they know that no one else knows. There are things we can learn from each person in our class, so each of us is a teacher [*Mr. Garcia removes the next paper strip as he speaks*]. Let's read this together.
All students:	Each of us is a teacher.
Mr. Garcia:	Think about a time you taught someone something . . . maybe you taught a little sister or brother, or maybe you taught something to your mom or dad or a friend. What was hard about teaching it? Think, and then turn and talk to your partner about what you taught, and what was hard about it.

(Although many students initially express surprise at hearing that each of them is a teacher, even kindergarteners recall experiences in which they taught something to another person.)

Mr. Garcia continues to engage his students in this inquiry process as he introduces "Each of us is a problem solver." He makes a point to model his own problem solving by sharing the experience when his subway train broke down and he had to figure out a different way to get to school.

As Mr. Garcia listens to his students share their stories, he notes any in which they demonstrated curiosity, persistence, flexibility, risk taking, or reflection (dispositions of effective problem solvers). When he introduces students to these dispositions in the next session, he plans to use these stories to help students make explicit connections between the dispositions and their experiences.

Next, Mr. Garcia uncovers the guiding rule for the class: We will help each other do our best thinking, work, and problem solving. "This is our guiding rule for our class this year." He explains to students that in the coming days, weeks, and months, they will learn more about how to do this, but for now, he asks all students to commit to helping others do their best thinking, work, and problem solving. He does a "go-around" in the circle, asking each child to say, "I agree to help each other," or "I disagree."

At the end of this lesson, Mr. Garcia's students have all orally committed to carrying out the guiding rule. He is on his way to building a supportive learning community. His students begin to—

- feel valued for their unique experiences, knowledge, and ways of thinking;

- expect that they will learn from and teach each other;

- trust that in this classroom, they will be supported to do their best thinking, work, and problem solving.

Guide students in exploring the dispositions of effective problem solvers and why developing them is important

You can begin to introduce the five dispositions of effective problem solvers in the first week of school. Teaching each disposition can take thirty to forty-five minutes, depending on the age and experience of your students. Young children should be introduced to no more than one disposition each day (five dispositions = five sessions). In some classrooms, teachers of older students have effectively introduced more than one disposition per day. However, their students have learned and applied the dispositions because their teachers have given consistent and frequent feedback and support.

Goals

- Students become familiar with the qualities of a good problem solver—curious, persistent, flexible, risk taking, and reflective—and begin to understand why developing them is important.

- Students connect problem-solving dispositions to their experiences and those of literary characters.

- Students begin to understand why developing problem-solving dispositions is important.

This next step in laying the groundwork for a supportive mathematics learning community builds on students' basic understanding that in this classroom, everyone is a problem solver. Effective mathematical problem solvers reflect on what they already know that might help them solve a problem, and they periodically reflect on their thinking to see whether it makes sense along the way. They persist in working on a problem even in the face of struggle, and their curiosity prompts them to wonder whether a better way to solve it, prove it, or represent it might exist. They think flexibly as they seek other solution paths and perhaps take a risk by trying an approach or strategy they have never succeeded with before. At the end, they reflect again on the reasonableness of their answer and check their work. When the dispositions and actions of effective problem solvers are explicit and make sense to students, they understand why practicing them is important for members of a mathematical learning community.

A Good Problem Solver Is . . .

Curious: Wonder about things, ask questions, and explore to find out more.

Flexible: Look for different ways to solve a problem.

Persistent: Keep on trying and don't give up . . . you can take a break and come back to it later.

Risk taking: Try new or challenging things . . . don't be afraid of mistakes; you can learn from them.

Reflective: Take time to think about what you are doing, why you are doing it, whether it makes sense, and how you can do it better.

Used with permission from Kathy Ernst

Setup

1 Create a neat, visually appealing chart on poster board or paper (posted permanently in class so children and visitors can refer to it—not on an interactive board).

2 Cover each disposition and description with a strip of construction paper. Students will eagerly anticipate and wonder about what is hidden. You can uncover dispositions one at a time as you introduce them to students.

3 Select a picture book or short story in which a character(s) demonstrates the disposition you plan to teach.

Introducing the lesson

As we noted, you should introduce these dispositions to the whole class, one at a time, followed by a sequence of prompts to reinforce the meaning of each. Below is a suggested protocol of prompts for introducing curiosity to your class. You can use this protocol as a model for teaching the other problem-solving dispositions:

- (Uncover the word *curious* in the chart.) "Let's read this together: 'A good problem solver is curious.' What do you know about the word *curious*?'" Solicit and record ideas from students and then uncover your definition. Read it together with the class, and briefly discuss its meaning. Make connections between your definition and dispositions children revealed in their stories about learning, teaching, and problem solving in the first day's session.

- "Think of a time when you were curious about something. What were you curious about? What made you so curious? Think, turn, and talk to your partner." Ask students to share a few stories with the whole group.

- "Now I'm going to read you a story. As I read, see whether you notice anyone in the story who is curious. What is he or she doing or saying that tells you the person is curious?" (Or with older students: "Try to identify any characters in the story who you think are curious. What evidence can you find to support your inference that they are curious?") After reading the story, have a class discussion about the characters that are curious, and identify actions that show their curiosity.

- Engage your students in identifying an icon or simple picture to represent curiosity. Draw the icon on the chart next to the word to serve as a visual anchor.

- Give each student a written prompt to reflect on, illustrate, and write about: "A good problem solver is curious. He or she wonders about things, asks questions, and explores to find out more. I was curious when I _____." You can give younger students a sheet with space for a drawing and the story prompt. They can complete this in class, with nonwriters dictating their stories. Older students can write a brief paragraph in school or at home. As students share their completed prompts in small groups, you can observe their understandings and misconceptions about the meanings of the terms. (This activity enables students to more powerfully connect their experiences to the new vocabulary and meaning of problem-solving dispositions. This is an important part of their learning and can be completed during their writing time later in the day.)

Teach the Problem-Solving Dispositions by Setting an Example

Modeling the problem-solving dispositions in your interactions with students is important. For example, when students hear you wondering aloud whether another way to solve a problem exists, whether an answer makes sense, or whether a procedure always works, they will learn that successful mathematicians are curious about numbers and how the operations behave.

Explore why a supportive classroom community is essential for our brains to do our best thinking and problem solving

This session lasts twenty to thirty minutes, depending on the age and experience of your students.

Goals

- Students begin to understand what causes their brains to do their best thinking.

- Students begin to understand what causes their brains to "shut down" their thinking.

See "How to Develop Students' Problem-Solving Dispositions" for suggestions about supporting students' development of curiosity, persistence, flexibility, risk taking, and reflection.

- Students identify and reflect on experiences that cause them to shut down their thinking.

After introducing the last of the problem-solving dispositions to your students, explore how the brain works to help students understand why and how specific actions help or hinder each person's ability to do his or her best thinking. Students with this understanding see the purpose of a safe and respectful environment and usually demonstrate increased motivation to interact with each other in productive, supportive ways. When students, especially those in the older grades, realize what happens in their brains to cause them to "shut down" when nervous, scared, embarrassed, angry, or upset, they seem relieved to know that this phenomenon has real, not imagined, causes. Students are also more open to exploring coping strategies they can use when stress or threat compromises their thinking.

Setup

1 Familiarize yourself with the Neocortex Story.

We include a simple version of the Neocortex Story here; a detailed version with illustrations is available online. Choose the one that best suits your students' level of readiness.

Neocortex Story

"I'm going to tell you a story about the neocortex. The neocortex is the part of our brain that we use to do our best thinking. All the information coming into our brain goes to our amygdala, our brain's feeling center. If the information makes us feel angry, scared, nervous, upset, or embarrassed, the amygdala sends a danger signal to another part of our brain. When that happens, our muscles tighten, sometimes our heart beats faster, and our brain feels like it freezes—we can't think clearly. Our neocortex can't do its best thinking. Some people call this an 'amygdala hijack.' It's like our brain just shuts down—it doesn't really shut down, but it feels that way. Our neocortex can't do its best thinking until we relax our body and mind and let go of those unsafe feelings."

2 Get chart paper to record students' responses to "What do you know about the brain?"

3 Use the diagram of the brain available on More4U (if you choose to use it to illustrate the Neocortex Story).

4 Get chart paper to record students' responses to "What shuts down my thinking?"

Introducing the lesson

- Activate students' prior knowledge about the brain by asking, "What do you know about the brain?" You can chart students' responses, using pictures and words to illustrate the ideas of young children. Even young students have many ideas about the brain, and most know that it is connected to thinking.

- Tell a version of the Neocortex Story, about how our emotions control our ability to do our best thinking and problem solving. (If you use the diagram of the brain [available on More4U], students can see that the distance from the thalamus [intake site] to the amygdala [emotional center] is shorter than the path from the thalamus to the neocortex [complex thought], and then it makes sense to students why all information coming into the brain is filtered first for emotional safety—and why having an emotionally safe classroom is important.)

- Give students an example of what a shutdown can look like: "I'll tell you a story about a time my neocortex felt like it shut down. One day when I was driving on a road, a dog leaped in front of my car and I hit it. I stopped the car. Luckily the dog was OK. But I was so upset that when the dog's owner came out of her house and asked me where I lived, I couldn't remember. I was so upset that my brain 'shut down,' and for a moment, I couldn't even think about where I lived. Can you imagine that?"

STOP+REFLECT

» What "shutdown" story can you share with your students?

- Ask students to think about and discuss a time when their emotions caused a shutdown. You can say, "Now, I'd like each of you to think about a time when you might have been so scared, angry, upset, nervous, or embarrassed that your neocortex felt like it had a shutdown. It could be a time in school or a time outside school." Ask students to think, turn, and talk, and then listen to their conversations. Call on students to share stories with the class.

Young children tend to recall experiences in which they were frightened or angry. When students in grades 3–5 are asked what has caused them to experience a shutdown in school, they say such things as the following:

- "When I gave an answer and everyone shouted, 'That's wrong!' I was so embarrassed I couldn't think of how to get it right."

- "When I went up to the board to show how I solved a problem, I got so nervous that I couldn't think."

- "When I'm doing work that's hard for me and the kid next to me says, 'That's so easy!' I feel so dumb that I can't think."

- "When I take mad-minute tests, I'm so nervous that my mind shuts down."

- Connect what children just learned about how the brain works to their guiding rule. You can say, "Let's look at our class guiding rule and read it together: 'We will help each other do our best work, thinking, and problem solving.'" You can continue, "Our goal is to do and say things that help everyone's brain do its best thinking. We just discovered that our brains can't do their best thinking and problem solving when we're angry, afraid, nervous, upset, or embarrassed. So tomorrow, we'll figure out what we can do and say to help each other do our best thinking and problem solving."

* * *

By now, students who have engaged in the preceding learning experiences—

- understand that they will assume the roles of learners, teachers, and problem solvers;

- committed to abide by the guiding rule of the classroom;

- begin to understand the dispositions of effective problem solvers and why developing them is important;

- understand that threat or stress inhibits learning; and

- identified comments and actions that can inhibit their learning in class.

Students are now ready to apply this knowledge to developing class norms—defining actions that support each other in doing their best thinking and problem solving.

Engage students in constructing class norms

This session takes thirty to forty-five minutes. With older students, some teachers have conducted this session immediately after the previous session or later in the day.

Goals

- Students develop class norms that help them do their best thinking and problem solving in math class.

- Students commit to carrying out the class norms.

In this final step of laying the groundwork for a supportive mathematics learning community, students are guided to generate norms of behavior that advance productive interactions and learning. When students are invested in creating norms, they carry them out with purpose and ownership. Your challenge is to find a way in which everyone participates in developing and committing to the norms.

Setup

Prepare a two-column chart in which you can list students' responses to "How Can We Help Each Other Do Our Best Thinking and Problem Solving?" (Cover up the writing as was done on the first day.)

How Can We Help Each Other Do Our Best Thinking, Work, and Problem Solving?	
We Say (It Sounds Like)	**We Do (It Looks Like)**

Introducing the lesson

Let's look at how Mr. Garcia engages his students in developing class norms. First, he asks his students to activate their prior knowledge about building a supportive learning community. He draws their attention to the two class charts hanging in the meeting area:

{ more**4U**

See More4U for Mr. Garcia's handouts.

> Each of us is a learner.
> Each of us is a teacher.
> Each of us is a problem solver.
> We will help each other do our best thinking, work, and problem solving.

A Good Problem Solver Is . . .

Curious: Wonder about things, ask questions, and explore to find out more.

Flexible: Look for different ways to solve a problem.

Persistent: Keep on trying and don't give up . . . you can take a break and come back to it later.

Risk taking: Try new or challenging things . . . don't be afraid of mistakes; you can learn from them.

Reflective: Take time to think about what you are doing, why you are doing it, whether it makes sense, and how you can do it better.

Mr. Garcia: What do you remember about these charts? Think, and then turn and talk to your partner. [*He listens, invites comments from students, and continues.*]

Mr. Garcia:	We've talked about things that shut down our thinking. [*Uncovering the tree chart*] So now, we're going to talk about this: "How can we help each other do our best thinking and problem solving?" Let's read that together:
All students:	How can we help each other do our best thinking and problem solving?
Mr. Garcia:	What can we say or do to help people do their best thinking when they've been working really hard and it seems like they're about to give up? [*He waits until many thumbs go up.*] James, what do you think?
James:	You could say, "You're smart; you can do it."

Mr. Garcia wants his students to praise effort, not ability, so he rephrases his question to guide students to describe behaviors that make someone smart.

Mr. Garcia:	If someone is working really hard and she is about to give up, but she's a good problem solver, what might she do?
Sean:	She wouldn't give up.
Mr. Garcia:	What problem-solving disposition does that remind you of?
Melinda:	[*She reads the chart.*] Be persistent. Keep on trying and don't give up.
Mr. Garcia:	So you can say, "You can do it!" or "You're being really persistent." [*Mr. Garcia records the suggestions on the chart.*]

Mr. Garcia continues the discussion, asking students what they can do or say—

- if they are playing a game and their partner doesn't know the answer right away;
- to help their partner be flexible;
- when their partner is explaining their thinking; and
- to help their partner be reflective.

He records student responses to each question. Most essential to a productive mathematics learning community is the norm of responding to incorrect answers in a manner that advances student learning. Mistakes are learning opportunities only if everyone in the class responds in a way that helps learners do their best thinking—in a way that empowers them to discover their mistakes and figure out the problems on their own. Many students, as well as many parents and teachers, believe that helping means giving someone the answer. Discuss this misconception with your students. They probably will not know how to appropriately respond to someone who gives an incorrect answer, so you will need to take a direct approach. Mr. Garcia intentionally brings up this issue with his students:

Mr. Garcia:	Suppose your partner gave a wrong answer. What could you do or say to help her do her best thinking?
Tawanda:	You could give them the answer.
Mr. Garcia:	If you give your partner the answer, does that help him or her do his or her best thinking?
All students:	[*spontaneously*] No!
Mr. Garcia:	Does anyone else have an idea of how you could help your partner do his or her best thinking if he or she gave a wrong answer?
John:	You could just say "That's not right."
Mr. Garcia:	If your partner told you that you were wrong, how would you feel?
All students:	[*various responses*] I'd feel sad/bad/dumb/like I don't know anything/I'm not smart.
Mr. Garcia:	What happens in your brain when you're feeling bad, or dumb, or sad?
All students:	[*various responses*] You can't think/It feels like your brain shuts down.
Mr. Garcia:	When someone gives a wrong answer, the way to help him do his best thinking is to say, "How did you figure that out?" or "How do you know that?"

Mr. Garcia also wants his students to ask questions like "How did you figure that out?" when they don't understand someone's thinking so that whenever students hear this question, they don't think they've made a mistake.

Mr. Garcia:	Suppose someone explains or shows you a solution and you don't understand it. What could you do or say so that you can understand and do your best thinking?

The students pause to think.

Mr. Garcia:	Umesh, what do you think?
Umesh:	You can ask the same thing . . . "How do you know that?"
Mr. Garcia:	That's an excellent suggestion. Our goal is to help each other do our best math thinking, and when we share our ideas, we learn from each other. If we don't understand each other, we need to say, "How do you know that?" or "How did you figure that out?" What else can you do or say to help each other do our best thinking, work, and problem solving?

As students make suggestions and Mr. Garcia facilitates the discussion, more ideas emerge, and Mr. Garcia adds them to the chart. Next, Mr. Garcia brings up a norm he believes is important: Give each other time to think.

Mr. Garcia: When people explain how they got an answer, they can usually discover their own mistake and figure it out. So it's important after you ask one of these questions to give each other time to think. If you agree with that, put your thumb up. [*All students gesture with a thumbs-up, and Mr. Garcia adds this norm to the chart:*]

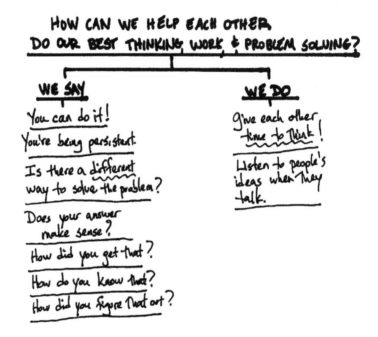

Mr. Garcia: Let's read these together. [*All students read the norms aloud as Mr. Garcia points to each.*]

Mr. Garcia asks the students whether they disagree with anything on the chart or whether anything is missing. They indicate that they agree with all the norms and have no further ideas to add.

Mr. Garcia: I want to add two important things to this list: (1) Give help or a hint only if the learner asks for it. (2) Ask an adult or other group a question only when everyone in your group has the same question. Why do you think these are important? Think, and then turn and talk to your partner.

Mr. Garcia listens to his students' ideas as they talk with each other. He then summarizes.

Mr. Garcia: Many of you had the same idea about why it's important to give the learner help or a hint only if he wants it. Sometimes, the learner might not need or want help, and if we give him ideas, we could distract him from figuring out problems on his own.

Why do I want you to ask an adult or other group for help only when everyone in your group has the same question? Because I want you to work as a team. Good team members help each other by answering each other's questions. If no one in your group knows the answer, then you can go to another group or to me for help.

Mr. Garcia ends the lesson by engaging students in committing to carrying out the norms they have just constructed.

Mr. Garcia: How many of you agree that these are the ways we all should work with each other? [*All thumbs go up.*]

Mr. Garcia: We'll keep adding to this chart. These behaviors—things we do and say—are what we call class norms. Norms are like rules. People make rules and norms for a purpose. What's the purpose of our norms?

Mr. Garcia asks this question to see whether his students understand that the purpose of math norms is to guide them to help each other do their best thinking, work, and problem solving.

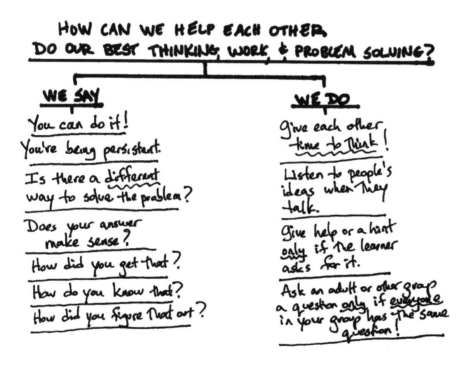

Follow-up

The next day, Mr. Garcia posts a chart summarizing the norms most important for students to learn and carry out. He facilitates a brief discussion in which the students see how this abbreviated list of norms connects to everything they discussed and agreed on the day before:

Norms for Our Math Class

1. Help each other do our best thinking. (Look at our chart: We Say/We Do)

2. Give each other time to think.

3. Give help or a hint only if the learner wants it. Ask, "Would you like help?"

4. If you don't understand someone's thinking or answer, ask, "How do you know that?" or "How did you get that?"

5. If you disagree with someone's thinking or answer, ask, "How do you know that?" or "How did you get that?"

6. You can ask an adult or other group a question only if everyone in your group has the same question. (Norm 6 is from Burns [1991], "Rules for Groups of Four.")

Used with permission by Kathy Ernst

Mr. Garcia made copies of the class roles and guiding rule (from the day one session), dispositions of a good problem solver, and class norms for students to affix to the inside cover of their math binders. These visual tools support students in developing their problem-solving dispositions and productive group interactions.

BUILDING AND SUSTAINING A SUPPORTIVE LEARNING COMMUNITY

After you have laid the groundwork of developing a supportive learning community, your work has just begun. Now you must continue to build and sustain, throughout the year, a productive and supportive community of mathematicians. To do so, students need consistent practice in developing problem-solving dispositions and enacting the class norms, and they need feedback that informs them about what they're doing well and how they can improve.

This section suggests teaching and coaching moves that support your students' development of productive dispositions and ways of interacting in math class that they can transfer to other situations both in and out of school.

Give consistent, descriptive feedback emphasizing students' success in developing problem-solving dispositions and enacting class norms

When you acknowledge what students are doing successfully, you reinforce positive behaviors and motivate students to continue to apply them. When you do it publicly, as in a whole-class discussion, students can see what the expected behaviors and norms look like. The more explicit and descriptive your comments, the easier it is for students to see and understand what you expect. Here are some examples of descriptive feedback acknowledging effort and productive work on tasks:

- "You were flexible when you looked for a different way to represent the data."

- "Marissa was reflective when she stopped in the middle of her problem and realized that her strategy wasn't working."

- "Tina and Ari figured out how to work together to connect the triangle faces in their icosahedron construction."

- "You did a great job of letting your partner take his time to solve that problem by himself."

- "Shawn elaborated on Keisha's thinking because he was listening carefully to how she solved it."

Giving students feedback that helps them understand what they need to improve and how they can improve is empowering and advances learning. Consider the example of two fifth graders, Malik and Yvette. Yvette has just corrected Malik's answer. The teacher, who has been observing the interaction, asks Yvette in a non-threatening tone, "Instead of correcting Malik, what can you say to him to help him do his best thinking and discover his mistake?" This feedback helps Yvette think about what she needs to improve and how she can improve. Sometimes students need a simple reminder of what language to use. If Yvette were unsure of how to respond, her teacher could give her two or three suggestions, such as "Malik, show me how you figured that out" or "How do you know that?" and let Yvette choose her preferred response. Giving students choice in this way shows that you respect their autonomy and value their participation. It also motivates students to engage meaningfully in their learning.

Engage students in monitoring and assessing the development and transfer of their problem-solving dispositions

Journal writing offers a way for students to regularly reflect on, discuss, and write about examples of how they applied curiosity, persistence, flexibility, risk taking, or reflection to their mathematics work and problem solving. Ask students to write, once every week or two, about situations in or out of school where they applied these habits of mind. Even kindergarteners have written in journals, drawing and writing about (or dictating) problem-solving experiences, correctly identifying the dispositions they demonstrated. Such reflections give students an opportunity to develop their metacognitive skills—to develop an awareness of how these essential habits of mind contribute to their thinking and work, and how they can be transferred to all domains of problem solving. Notable reflections can be shared in class discussions.

You can also periodically ask your students to assess their problem-solving dispositions after they have done class work. They can assess their demonstration of one or two dispositions, but they should also identify another they want to further develop. You can help students identify actions they can take to improve.

Engage students in reflecting on, monitoring, and assessing their performance in carrying out group norms

From time to time, ask your students to assess how they worked with their math partners or groups. You can pose open-ended questions such as these: What did we do or say to help each other do our best thinking, work, and problem solving? How could we work better next time?

See "How to Develop Students' Problem-Solving Dispositions."

Periodically engage the class in reflecting on the norms

Periodically revisit classroom norms to see whether any changes are needed. The system is flexible and adaptive. Is something missing that we all believe should be added? Which norms seem most important? Identifying the most important norms gives the class, individually and collectively, an explicit focus for setting goals and assessing progress. What are we doing well? How can we improve to help each other do our best thinking? How can we improve in our roles as teachers, learners, and problem solvers? Students can engage in rich, productive discussions about how to continue to build a supportive classroom culture if you have given them an understanding of the essential elements and language of a mathematical learning community.

CONCLUSION

Students' brains can engage in complex math thinking only in a safe, nonthreatening environment. Developing an emotionally safe and supportive classroom environment is essential, not optional. You can lay the groundwork for a supportive mathematics learning community on the first day of school by sending the message that each person has unique ways of thinking about math and that everyone's ideas have value.

When you teach students to develop and be cognizant of their problem-solving dispositions, they engage more deeply with math. If you give consistent and effective feedback, students will transfer these dispositions not only to their math problem solving but also to their problem solving in other domains in and out of school.

When you give students a basic understanding of how emotions affect the brain's ability to engage in complex thinking, they can understand why having a safe, supportive environment is important. Engaging students in establishing productive math norms of behavior will invest them in enacting the norms and supporting each other in doing so. Building a supportive mathematics learning community takes time and planning. However, taking the time to develop a classroom environment where all students have access to complex thinking is vital.

chapter **six**

Establishing Routines to Support Mathematics Learning

Guiding Principles

LEARNING IS MAXIMIZED WHEN STUDENTS—

>> interact in a safe, supportive learning community;

>> activate and build on prior knowledge;

>> process information both visually and linguistically;

>> solve problems with meaningful contexts;

>> engage in reflection, self-monitoring, and metacognition; and

>> engage in complex thinking.

A well-managed classroom is essential to student learning, and routines are key to a well-managed classroom. Routines allow you and your students to use time, space, and resources efficiently and effectively. Well-designed routines build in supports for engaging students in productive mathematical discourse and reasoning, which in turn maximize mathematics learning. During the first days and weeks of school, establish routines that will influence student success in learning. Some of these routines are procedures such as entering or leaving class, handing in homework, cleaning up, and using materials. In general, well-established routines have the following outcomes:

- Students feel secure knowing what to expect and what is expected of them.
- Students take responsibility for their own behavior and their own learning.
- Student confusion, disruption, and off-task behavior are minimized, and instructional time is maximized.

This chapter introduces two types of routines that maximize student learning: Management routines support student autonomy in using materials and engaging in games and activities during math work time. A metacognitive problem-solving routine based on the work of Pólya (1985) supports students' development of metacognition, habits of self-monitoring, and problem-solving dispositions as they learn to become independent problem solvers. The following essential practices will guide you in planning and implementing effective routines.

Essential Practices

>> Develop routines that are purposeful, explicit, and implemented consistently

>> Follow a general protocol to establish routines.

>> Develop routines to manage math games and math materials.

>> Teach students a metacognitive problem-solving routine.

DEVELOP ROUTINES THAT ARE PURPOSEFUL, EXPLICIT, AND IMPLEMENTED CONSISTENTLY

The purpose of any routine you establish should support learning and make sense to students. Without understanding the point of a routine, students may comply blindly, without thinking about what they are doing or why. Some students may resent you or resist complying if they view the routine as a way to control their behavior.

To avoid these pitfalls, engage your students in exploring the purpose of each routine you introduce. One approach is to activate students' prior experiences related to the routine. For example, to establish a routine that guides students to independently organize and put away math materials, you might present the following analogy: "What happens if you have such a messy room that you can't find something important, such as your comb or a favorite shirt?" Students might discuss the following effects: wasting time, making more of a mess, or getting frustrated. To help students explicitly connect the need for an organized bedroom to the need for an organized math area, you could ask, "What do you think would happen if our cubes were mixed up with our pattern blocks, and math bins were mixed up with the art bins?" Exploring the connection more deeply can surface the purpose of the routine. When they understand why a routine is important, students are more likely to assume ownership of the routine and be motivated to carry it out responsibly. When students can explain the routine to visitors and to each other—and describe why it is important—you know that you have effectively communicated its purpose.

Effective routines are also explicit, communicated in language that students understand. As chapter 2 discussed, students make meaning of and remember information best when it is presented both linguistically and nonlinguistically. When you present routines with words, graphic representations, and direct modeling, the routine will be more explicitly understood. For example, role-playing common events of noncompliance or confusions about routines can give students an even more explicit understanding of their expectations. When students are clear about procedures, expected behaviors, and boundaries, they tend to feel secure in knowing what to expect. As a result, they are likely to engage confidently in classroom activities, decreasing their reliance on teachers and increasing their autonomy as learners.

Finally, routines must be implemented with fidelity and frequency for students to learn and use them independently. This means that procedures in the routines are implemented consistently and reinforced often. To effectively learn the routines, students need repeated practice and frequent descriptive feedback that emphasize students' successful behaviors. When students hear your feedback about what success looks like and sounds like, they gain more clarity about their expectations and confidence in working autonomously. When children learn the procedures and can implement them independently, they become routine.

FOLLOW A GENERAL PROTOCOL TO ESTABLISH ROUTINES

Planning to introduce a routine through oral instruction, direct modeling, and graphic representation is your first step in establishing an effective routine. If the routine is a procedure, such as a math game or activity, first define the major steps. Then chart the steps with succinct words and graphics. Set up a meeting space and materials for modeling the routine. The general protocol (fig. 6.1) for establishing routines incorporates planning, introducing the routine to your class, and supporting your students in learning the routine.

Keep the language clear and succinct in both your oral directions and your chart to make the procedure accessible to all students. You can use this protocol to introduce routines with multiple steps, such as math games and activities. To introduce routines for care and use of math materials, oral instructions and modeling might be enough, making a visual chart unnecessary. Use your judgment about when students need the support of visual charts to learn the routine.

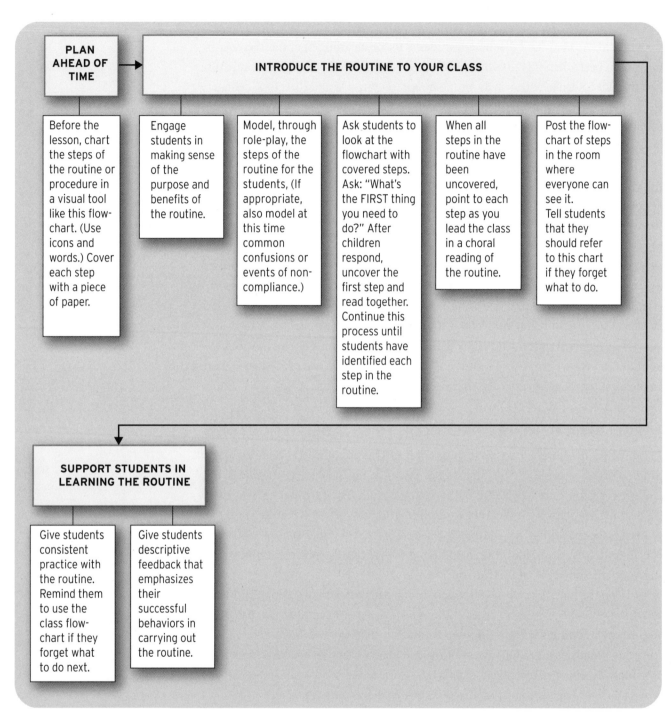

PLAN AHEAD OF TIME

INTRODUCE THE ROUTINE TO YOUR CLASS

Before the lesson, chart the steps of the routine or procedure in a visual tool like this flowchart. (Use icons and words.) Cover each step with a piece of paper.

Engage students in making sense of the purpose and benefits of the routine.

Model, through role-play, the steps of the routine for the students, (If appropriate, also model at this time common confusions or events of non-compliance.)

Ask students to look at the flowchart with covered steps. Ask: "What's the FIRST thing you need to do?" After children respond, uncover the first step and read together. Continue this process until students have identified each step in the routine.

When all steps in the routine have been uncovered, point to each step as you lead the class in a choral reading of the routine.

Post the flow-chart of steps in the room where everyone can see it. Tell students that they should refer to this chart if they forget what to do.

SUPPORT STUDENTS IN LEARNING THE ROUTINE

Give students consistent practice with the routine. Remind them to use the class flow-chart if they forget what to do next.

Give students descriptive feedback that emphasizes their successful behaviors in carrying out the routine.

Fig. 6.1. *A general protocol to establish routines*

DEVELOP ROUTINES TO MANAGE MATH GAMES AND MATH MATERIALS

To learn mathematics with understanding, students must engage effectively with games, activities, and materials during math workshop. When you establish routines that minimize the time for students to learn procedures for games and activities, you maximize time for math work and thinking. You also maximize learning time by establishing routines that enable students to use and store materials appropriately and independently.

Procedures for math games and activities

Many teachers effectively model procedures for games and activities. However, when it is time for students to play the game on their own, many forget what to do and ask for help. Teachers spend much of math time reteaching the rules of the game or the procedure of the activity. Why? When teachers introduce multistep procedures, they typically give oral instructions and model but do not visually represent the steps that reinforce the routine.

Let's look at how a teacher introduces a game to first graders by using this protocol. The two-player game is called "Double Peace" (similar to "War"). The teacher constructed a flowchart (fig. 6.2) of the procedure ahead of time. This chart is posted in the meeting area, but a piece of paper covers each step in the sequence. The teacher models the game with a parent volunteer (you can model with a para-professional, another teacher, or a student if you have time to teach him or her the game before the lesson). The students sit in a U; so that they all can see the modeling.

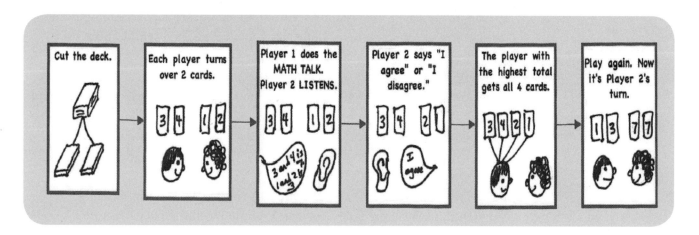

This routine engages students in math talk and reasoning to maximize opportunities to develop deeper understandings. The teacher also embeds her class norms (see chapter 5) and the principle of equity into the game rules:

Fig. 6.2. *Procedure for the math game "Double Peace"*

- Players take turns figuring out and communicating the answers.
- Players listen to and verify each other's answers.
- Players who disagree respectfully ask for each other's reasoning.

Observe how a teacher introduces the routine for playing "Double Peace."

Establishing the purpose

To establish the purpose of the routine, the teacher says, "Today we're going to learn a game that will help you practice adding two numbers. It's called 'Double Peace.' You and a partner will play the game with a deck of cards, like this one."

Modeling the steps

Now the teacher models the steps for the students. "First, one player cuts the deck in half, and the other player gets to choose a half." (The teacher models the step as she talks. Students already know this alternative to dealing out cards one at a time. This method is faster and one that children find fair.)

"Next, each player turns over two cards." (The teacher and her partner model.)

"Then, player 1 finds each person's total number and does the math talk. Player 2 listens to see whether she agrees with the math. I'll be player 1: I do the math talk and my partner has to listen." (The partner listens attentively as the teacher speaks.) "I have 4 and 3; that's 7. You have 5 and 5; that's 10. Ten is more than 7, so you get the cards."

"Now, my partner has to agree or disagree." (Player 2 says, "I agree.")

"Next, my partner gets to take all the cards because she had the highest total." (Player 2 takes the cards as the teacher talks.)

"Now it's player 2's turn to find the totals and do the math talk. What's player 1 supposed to do?" (This question scaffolds students' learning of the routine. The teacher engages students in recalling player 1's role: Listen carefully and agree or disagree.)

As they play another round, player 2 intentionally gets a wrong answer to model what to say when you disagree with your partner: "Five and 4 is 8, and 6 and 5 is 11."

Player 1, looking puzzled, says, "I disagree; how did you get that?"

Player 2 says, pointing to the pictures on the cards, "Five and 4 is 8 because 5, 6, 7, 8—oh no, I mean 5 and 4 is 9!"

The teacher stops the action: "Our class rule is, We will help each other do our best thinking and problem solving. How did I just help my partner do his best thinking?"

The students respond, "You helped him think. You didn't tell him the answer. When he counted he knew 5 and 4 wasn't 8; it was really 9."

Retelling the sequence of steps

The teacher reinforces learning of the steps by engaging students in retelling them. "Now, I want you to look up here." (The teacher points to the chart with covered steps.) The students are excited because they know they will have to find out what is hidden.

The teacher continues, "What did we do first?"

"Cut the deck." After the students name the first step, the teacher uncovers it.

The teacher responds, "What did we do next?" She repeats this process until all steps have been revealed. "Now let's read the steps for playing 'Double Peace' together." The teacher leads the class in reading each step. They read the sequence two more times to reinforce the routine.

The teacher shows miniature replicas of the class flowchart, which she has created and laminated. "When you play with your partner, you can look at our big chart of the steps or look at these small charts that will be at your table groups. If you forget how to play, the chart can help you remember."

When students play the game, some point to the desk charts to keep track of what to do next. Because the teacher introduced the game orally, through direct modeling, with a visual representation, students have received maximum support in learning and remembering the procedure. They play independently and successfully.

Figure 6.3 is an example of a flowchart Kim Salvatore, a kindergarten teacher, created for a counting activity. The simplicity and clarity of the words and graphics makes learning and remembering the routine easy for students.

Developed by Kimberly Salvatore

Fig. 6.3. Steps of a counting activity, which students will use over time

Care, use, and storage of math materials

Because children use manipulatives and materials to model mathematics and develop mathematical ideas, you must explicitly model routines for the storage, care, and use of materials. The time you spend modeling depends on the age and experience of your students. You might say, "This is how you roll two dice [*demonstrate*]. What do you notice about how I just rolled them?" In this way, students name appropriate ways to care for and use materials.

Following up with "Why do you think I rolled them that way?" engages students in grasping the purpose of caring for and using materials in a particular way. Modeling noncompliance, such as how materials should not be used or cared for, clarifies student expectations, especially when you ask students to explain why the behavior is problematic. When students participate in defining routines and understand their purpose, they invest in carrying them out.

How you introduce new math materials can significantly affect the quality and length of your instructional time. Introducing new math materials such as pattern blocks, geoboards, or base-ten blocks will naturally arouse students' curiosity. Children are inherently drawn to explore materials, play with them, manipulate them in various ways, and discover their attributes. Before students use new materials in their problem solving, give them time to explore and play with them. This way, when they use the materials to problem solve, students will focus on the mathematics of the task rather than on discovery of the material. During the exploratory stage, you can prompt students with questions such as these: How can you describe these pattern blocks? What do you notice about these cubes? What do these geoboards remind you of? How are these two blocks (unit and tens blocks) the same and different?

TEACH STUDENTS A METACOGNITIVE PROBLEM-SOLVING ROUTINE

The most successful math students are reflective and metacognitive and can monitor their thinking and work throughout the problem-solving process. Learning how to think independently and effectively as they problem solve is one of the most essential routines you can teach. How do effective problem-solvers think as they approach and solve problems? What do they do? Although problem solving is not a linear process, a basic sequence of thinking and actions guides effective problem-solving (fig. 6.4). This framework incorporates habits of metacognition and self-monitoring. It also incorporates the NCTM process standards and the Common Core State Standard for Mathematical Practice.

Fig. 6.4. *Thinking Through a Math Problem*

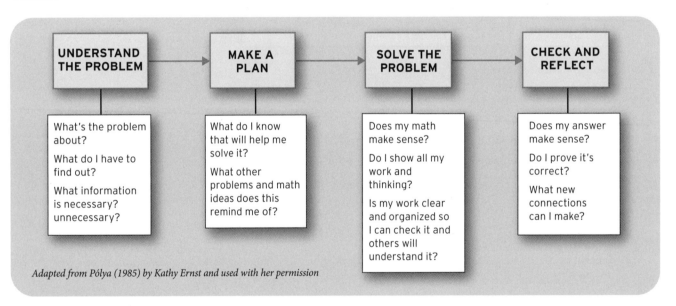

Adapted from Pólya (1985) by Kathy Ernst and used with her permission

STOP+REFLECT

>> What problem-solving dispositions—curiosity, flexibility, persistence, risk taking, and reflection—would students need to answer these questions?

At any point in their problem solving, students may reflect on their work and realize that they need to change course. They may even go back to the beginning and reexamine their understanding of the problem. They carry out their problem solving with curiosity, flexibility, persistence, and risk taking because they have learned to continually ask themselves, *Does this make sense?*

When students learn and consistently apply this sequence of thinking to their problem solving, it becomes routine. Learning how to think like a problem solver takes time—it requires explicit instruction, consistent practice, and scaffolding. How can you teach your students this routine? Just as you guide your students to learn to write by teaching them steps of the writing process, you can guide your students to learn to problem solve by teaching them how to think and what to do as they problem solve.

The following model introduces the metacognitive problem-solving routine and suggests how to teach for transfer. Consider how you might adapt it to your own teaching style and student needs.

Setup of the metacognitive problem-solving routine

- Prepare a flowchart of the problem-solving steps and subquestions, like the chart above or the more detailed one in Figure 6.5 for older students.

- For young students, you can also create a flowchart with pictures:

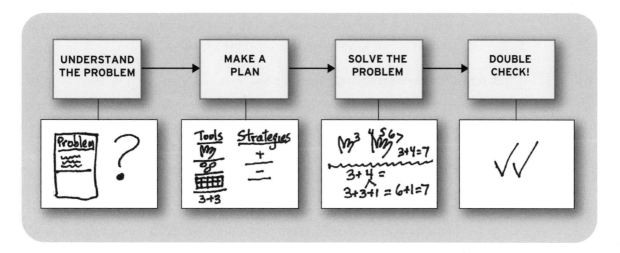

- Cover steps with paper so you can go over them one at a time.

- Prepare individual copies of the flowchart to support students in learning the routine. They can put them in their math notebooks. For some students, you can laminate the flowcharts to put on their desks.

- Prepare a simple story problem to put on the board, one that all students will know how to solve. Why? When introducing new and complex content such as this problem-solving routine, teach it through content that students already know. Doing so reduces the cognitive demand and puts the focus of the learning on the new content. Here is an example of a problem you can use with first graders: Janelle saw 4 ducks in the pond. Then 3 more ducks fly into the pond. How many ducks were in the pond?

Introducing the metacognitive problem-solving routine

1. Explain the purpose of the routine.

- Tell the students, "I'm going to teach you a thinking routine that successful mathematicians use when they solve problems. It teaches you how to think and what to do as you solve problems. The routine has four steps that you will learn as we solve math problems. I have the steps covered up, and we'll learn them, one at a time as we solve this problem together."

- Post the problem and read it together with the whole class.

2. Introduce the first step: Understand the problem.

- Uncover the first step and say, "The first thing a good problem-solver does is understand the problem." Have students read the step aloud with you.

- Prompt with the first subquestion: "The first thing you have to think about is: What's this problem about?" Give students time to think and respond.

- Prompt with the second subquestion: "What's the problem asking you to find out?" Give students time to think and respond.

- Prompt with the third subquestion: "Is there any unnecessary information?" For younger students, you can omit this question if they are just learning how to solve and represent problems.

3. Introduce the second step: Make a plan.

- Uncover the second step and say, "The next thing a good problem-solver does is make a plan." Have students read the step aloud with you.

- Prompt with the first subquestion: "To make a plan, you first have to think: What do I know that will help me solve this? So, think—what do you know that will help you solve this problem?" Don't ask for responses; immediately follow up with the next subquestion: "What other problems and math ideas does this remind you of? Think, and then turn and talk to your partner." As you listen to the students, you will notice that they have many ideas about how to solve the problem because they are making connections to math they know or other problems they have done. Mr. Jackson, a first-grade teacher, has just introduced his students to these steps and the duck problem. Below he continues to teach students about the second step, make a plan.

Mr. Jackson:	I heard Carla say this problem reminded her of an adding problem. Carla, why would you add?
Carla:	Because there were 4 ducks in the pond—and 3 more came, so you have to add 4 and 3.
Mr. Jackson:	How many of you agree with that? [*All students raise their hands.*]
Mr. Jackson:	So Carla has decided to use an adding strategy.

Mr. Jackson recently engaged his students in brainstorming and identifying all the math tools that they use in their problem solving. He has also introduced the terms *addition strategy* and *subtraction strategy*. He wants his students to learn that thinking intentionally about what tools and strategies they might use to solve problems is what they do as they make a plan.

Mr. Jackson:	Carla, what tool would you use to solve this problem—your fingers, cubes, a drawing, or an equation?
Carla:	I'd use my fingers.
Mr. Jackson:	So Carla has made a plan. This problem reminds her of addition, so she will use an adding strategy. She has also planned what tool to use to solve it—her fingers.

4. Introduce the third step: Solve the problem.

Now Mr. Jackson walks students through the third step in the problem-solving process.

Mr. Jackson:	So far, we've understood the problem [*points to step in flow-chart*] and we've made a plan [*points to step in flowchart*]. Now, the next thing we have to do is [*uncovering the third step*] solve the problem. Let's read that together.
All students:	Solve the problem.
Mr. Jackson:	Carla, you said you'd add the 4 ducks and the 3 ducks, and you'd use your fingers. How would you solve it?
Carla:	[*Counts out 4 fingers on one hand and 3 on the other. Then she counts all 7.*]
Mr. Jackson:	[*To the class*] So the next thing a problem-solver does is to ask, Does this make sense? So, does Carla's solution make sense?
All students:	Yes!
Mr. Jackson:	[*To the class*] When you solve a problem, you have to show all your work and thinking. It has to be neat so that other people can understand it and so you can understand it to double-check your work. Let's see whether I can show how Carla solved this problem in a neat and organized way.
Mr. Jackson:	[*Starts to represent Carla's solution, thinking aloud as he writes*] Carla started with the 4 ducks in the pond, so she counted 4 fingers on one hand. Then 3 more ducks flew into the pond, so she counted 3 fingers on her other hand.

1, 2, 3, 4, 5, 6, 7

Mr. Jackson:	Does my drawing match Carla's thinking so far?

All students:	Yes!
Mr. Jackson:	Carla, what equation can I write to show that you added 4 ducks and 3 ducks?
Carla:	Four and then the plus sign. And then the 3 and the equals 7.
Mr. Jackson:	[*Records as he rephrases*] Four plus 3 equals 7.
Mr. Jackson:	Does this solution show all Carla's work and thinking?
All students:	Yes!
Mr. Jackson:	Is it clear and organized so that other people can understand it? Devon, what do you think?
Devon:	Yes.
Mr. Jackson:	How many of you agree that it's clear and organized? [*All students raise their hands.*]

5. Introduce the last step: Check and reflect.

Mr. Jackson continues to walk his students through the last step in the problem-solving process.

Mr. Jackson:	Let's look at all the steps in problem solving we've done so far.
All students:	[*As Mr. Jackson points to each step*] Understand the problem, make a plan, and solve the problem.
Mr. Jackson:	A good problem-solver does one more thing after solving a problem. Do you know what that might be? [*Several hands are raised. Mr. Jackson calls on one student, Kira.*]
Kira:	You have to double-check your answer!
Mr. Jackson:	How many of you agree? [*Many hands go up.*]
Mr. Jackson:	Let's see whether you're right. [*Students watch in eager anticipation as Mr. Jackson uncovers the last step, double-check.*]
All students:	We were right!

Mr. Jackson walks the students through checking the solution and answer.

6. Reinforce the steps and thinking in the routine.

- After you have introduced all the steps and questions in the routine through the guided inquiry process above, engage students in a choral reading of the steps. Point to each step as the students read it. With young students, read the routine at least twice.

- To reinforce the thinking embedded in each step, point to each step while asking students what questions they ask themselves when they—

  — try to understand the problem;

— make a plan;

— solve the problem; and

— check their work.

7 . Make expectations for learning the routine explicit.

- Remind students of the routine's purpose: This routine guides mathematicians about what to do and how to think as they solve problems. Tell students that you expect them to learn the steps and the questions so they can solve problems on their own—and solve them successfully.

- Tell students that learning the steps and the questions they need to ask themselves will take much practice. Let them know you will help them.

- Give students their individual flowcharts of the steps and questions and tell them that they can use these charts to remind them of what to do and how to think as they solve problems. Students can tape them into their notebooks. You can also laminate them and tape them to students' desks or store them in a math bin.

Teaching the routine for transfer through gradual release of support

Eventually, you want students to internalize the routine so they can independently solve problems without your prompts or even the flowchart as reminders. You can accomplish this by gradually releasing your support as students increase their proficiency with the routine and begin to independently transfer it to their own problem solving. At first students will rely on your questions and the flowcharts as supports. Here are suggestions for how to gradually release your support:

- You can move from "The first thing you need to do is understand the problem" to a level of shared responsibility: "What's the first thing you need to do when solving a problem?"

- You can move from "When you try to understand the problem, you have to ask yourself, 'What is the problem about?' and 'What do I have to find out?'" to a level of shared responsibility: "What do you have to ask yourself when you're trying to understand the problem?"

You can also cover parts of the class flowchart (fig. 6.5) to increase students' responsibility for their learning or encourage students to use the flowcharts only for those steps they have difficulty remembering. With consistent practice, students will learn the steps and what to ask themselves without having to use the flowchart as a support.

For students in grades 3–5 and younger students who are ready for more challenge, you can add more refined questions to support development of metacognition, habits of self-monitoring, and problem-solving dispositions. You can teach and scaffold these additional questions in the same way as with the simpler version.

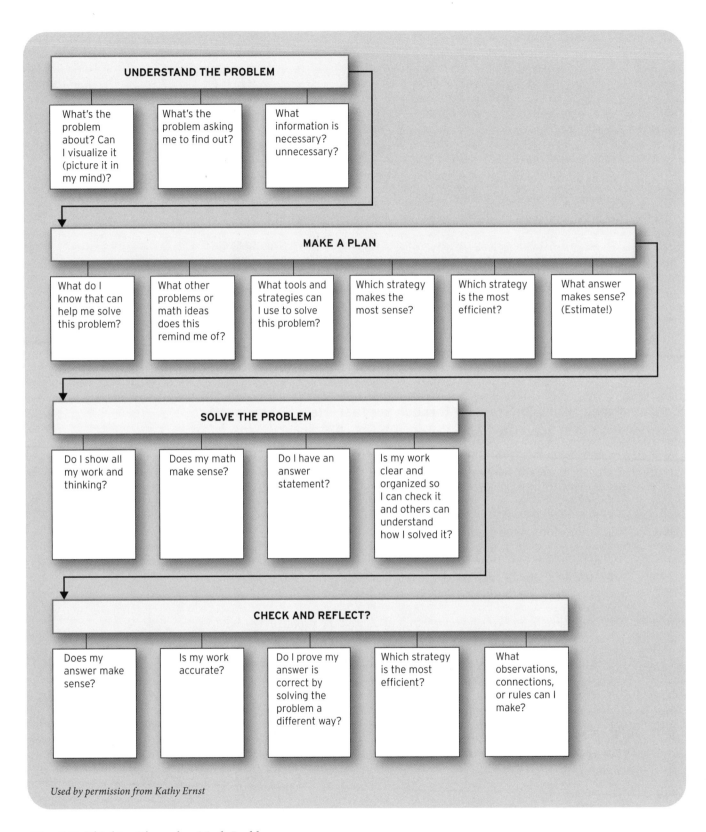

Used by permission from Kathy Ernst

Fig. 6.5. *Thinking Through a Math Problem*

CONCLUSION

Well-managed, smoothly run classrooms are essential to student learning. Effectively teaching students routines takes time. It requires thoughtful planning and teaching through modeling, use of visual aids, scaffolding, and consistent feedback. However, the investment in teaching routines thoughtfully and comprehensively at the beginning of the year will ultimately save you time. Well-established, effective routines not only support student learning but also contribute to a positive, productive classroom environment.

One of the most important routines you can teach your students is the metacognitive problem-solving routine. Especially important for English language learners and struggling students, this routine gives students tools to independently think through problems and monitor their work throughout the problem-solving process. Students who learn to think metacognitively develop confidence in knowing what to do and how to access and transfer knowledge as they solve problems.

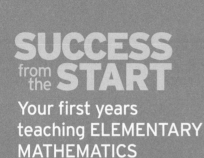

SUCCESS
from the START
Your first years
teaching ELEMENTARY
MATHEMATICS

chapter seven

Developing Computational Fluency

Guiding Principles

LEARNING IS MAXIMIZED WHEN STUDENTS—

>> interact in a safe, supportive learning community;

>> activate and build on prior knowledge;

>> process information both visually and linguistically;

>> solve problems with meaningful contexts;

>> engage in reflection, self-monitoring, and metacognition; and

>> engage in complex thinking.

When you were in elementary school, how did you learn to compute? Did your teacher model procedures that you mimicked and practiced but may never have understood? Or did you have a teacher, like Ms. Davis in chapter 1, who encouraged you to invent computation procedures and explore their underlying structures and properties? If you learned to compute like students in Ms. Davis's class, you probably developed computational fluency—procedural fluency with conceptual understanding.

What Is Computational Fluency?

Computational fluency has three main components: efficiency, accuracy, and flexibility (Russell, 2000). Efficiency involves using a strategy in which the steps are easy to keep track of and carry out. Accuracy applies to the whole problem-solving process, including knowing and using number facts and important relationships, monitoring thinking and work, and checking answers. Flexibility involves knowing more than one way to solve a problem and choosing a strategy that works best for the numbers in the problem. People often refer to computationally fluent students as having number sense.

Your challenge as a math teacher is to develop computationally fluent students, who not only know a variety of procedures to add, subtract, multiply, and divide but also understand why the procedures work. Computationally fluent students can explain the underlying mathematical structures and properties of operations—how numbers and operations behave.

If you are not computationally fluent, developing students who are is difficult. If this is the case, learn along with your students—many teachers do. You can always learn more and make new connections. Developing computational fluency is an ongoing process.

Essential Practices

>> Develop computational fluency through solving problems.

>> Use models that support developing computational fluency.

>> Develop instructional routines that support computational fluency.

>> Make generalizations explicit to develop computational fluency.

DEVELOP COMPUTATIONAL FLUENCY THROUGH SOLVING PROBLEMS

To better understand computational fluency, solve and explore these problems. First remind yourself of the dispositions of effective problem-solvers—curiosity, flexibility, persistence, risk taking, and reflection. Try on each of these dispositions as you attempt to solve the following problems in more than one way.

1 $1 + 2 + 3 + 4 + 5 + 6 + 7 + 8 + 9 = $ _____

2 $2000 - 298 = $ _____

3 $25 \times 46 = $ _____

Although multiple ways exist to solve these problems, this chapter will explore just a few strategies to give you an idea of what computational fluency means.

Problem 1: 1 + 2 + 3 + 4 + 5 + 6 + 7 + 8 + 9 = _____

One strategy is to add the numbers from left to right: $1 + 2 = \mathbf{3}$; $3 + 3 = \mathbf{6}$; $6 + 4 = \mathbf{10}$; $10 + 5 = \mathbf{15}$; $15 + 6 = \mathbf{21}$; $21 + 7 = \mathbf{28}$; $28 + 8 = \mathbf{36}$; $36 + 9 = \mathbf{45}$.

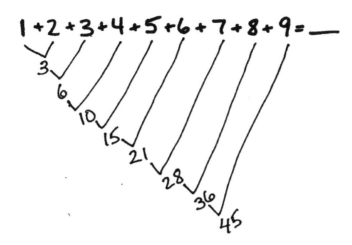

Another strategy is to look for combinations of ten and add the tens by counting: 10, 20, 30, 40 . . . + 5 = 45.

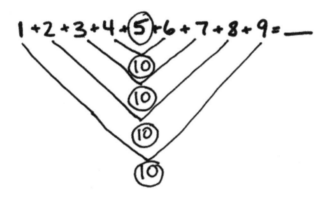

The first strategy is viable, requiring accurate use of known number facts. The second strategy also evidences accuracy, knowledge of the sums of ten. However, because it uses combinations of ten that are easy to add and keep track of, the second strategy is more efficient. Not only does the second strategy offer less chance for mistakes, but the answer is also easier to double-check. The second strategy shows evidence of flexibility—knowledge of different ways to add numbers.

Applying flexibility means changing the numbers in the problem, breaking numbers apart, and/or changing the order and grouping of numbers to make the problem easier to solve. The second strategy relies on the commutative and associative properties of addition, which are the ideas that addends can be combined in any order or any grouping and the sum will remain the same. These understandings are examples of generalizations, rules about how numbers and operations behave.

Problem 2: 2000 − 298 = _____

One strategy is to use the conventional algorithm:

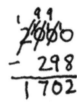

Another strategy is to make the problem easier and adjust, by using an open number line (left) or equations (right):

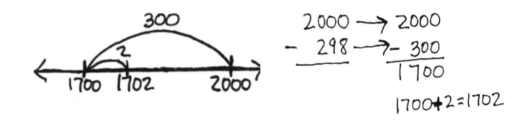

STOP + REFLECT

» Which strategy activates and engages your brain in making sense of the numbers in the problems?

» Which strategy is most efficient?

The first strategy, often referred to as the conventional subtraction algorithm, is a procedure that works. However, most people who use it tend to operate on the digits, losing sight of the magnitude of the numbers in the problem and their relationship to each other. The minuend in this problem also has so many zeros that keeping track of all the steps involved in regrouping can be difficult.

The second strategy, represented on a number line and with equations, shows evidence of flexibility—of looking at the numbers in the problem and thinking about which strategy is most efficient. The strategy, changing 298 to the landmark number 300, requires thinking flexibly about changing the numbers in the problem to make it easier to solve. However, solving this problem accurately also requires knowing how to adjust, or compensate for the 2 added to the 298. Compensation is a big mathematical idea underlying this strategy.

USE MODELS THAT SUPPORT DEVELOPING COMPUTATIONAL FLUENCY

Models, such as hundred charts, ten-frames, math racks, base-ten materials, arrays, number lines, and fraction bars, highlight particular mathematical relationships. Ten-frames can help students see the relationship between 5 and 10 (two rows of 5 make 10) or between other numbers, such as 5 and 7 (7 is 2 more than 5) and 7 and 10 (7 is 3 less than 10). Models can also highlight relationships central to particular operations. Ten-frames can help students think about part–whole relationships for addition and subtraction, and arrays can help students think about relationships between multiplication and division.

Models can be powerful tools to develop computational fluency. Frequent use and discussion of models helps students develop deep, connected knowledge of our number system and the four operations, which supports students in being accurate, efficient, and flexible in their computation.

Models can be incorporated into many instructional routines in this chapter. Some routines already have models built into them. For example, a blank hundred chart is part of the "How Many Days of School?" routine. You can show and discuss images of ten-frames, math racks, arrays, and base-ten materials during "Quick Images." Models can enhance other routines—for example, you can use open arrays and open number lines to record students' strategies during "Number Strings" and "Today's Number."

Open number lines do not show all the numbers in a given interval (see the earlier example of 2000 − 298). They show only the numbers students use and the size of the jumps students make as they add or remove. Open number lines may also show the direction of jumps (adding as a jump forward and removing as a jump back).

Open arrays are rectangular arrays without all the interior squares. They are powerful area models to represent visually the ways numbers are broken apart or changed in multiplication problems, as in the following two ways to solve 25 × 46:

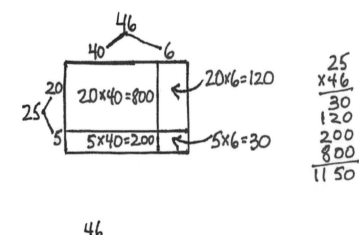

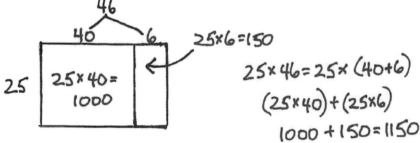

In both models, the factors are broken into parts, and each part of one factor is multiplied by each part of the other, yielding partial products. The open array lets students keep track of how the factors are broken apart. If they can also see that combining the areas of all partial products yields the total area of the large rectangle, they develop an understanding of the distributive property, a big idea underlying multiplication and division.

Representing students' strategies with these models supports the development of computational fluency only if students understand the models. Though explaining how to introduce and use open number lines and open arrays with your students is beyond the scope of this book, there are resources to help you do so.

DEVELOP INSTRUCTIONAL ROUTINES THAT SUPPORT COMPUTATIONAL FLUENCY

Teachers can manage instructional routines because they are brief (ten to twenty minutes) and predictable. Although instructional routines can support the development of any mathematical idea, this chapter focuses on routines that support computational fluency. The routines in this chapter are also available for download at More4U. Implemented effectively, these instructional routines give students opportunities to—

- explore the structure of the base-ten system;

- use powerful mathematical models;

- change numbers in problems to make them easier to solve;

- explore patterns and relationships in numbers and operations; and

- make and prove generalizations about the properties of numbers and operations.

Most routines we recommend are designed to convey relationships and patterns visually, capitalizing on the brain's innate ability to process visual information and to detect patterns. When the routines are presented in a clear and organized way, the patterns and relationships visually pop, enabling students to more readily make connections among related ideas and make generalizations about how numbers and operations behave.

You may have access to curriculum materials with routines like these. However, all teachers should use routines like these in their classrooms several times each week. If your curriculum does not have routines that engage students in thinking deeply about number and operations and communicating their ideas, incorporating them into your daily schedule is even more important.

You may carry out these routines with students at any point during the day— right after students arrive in the morning, before or after math class, before or after lunch, or before dismissal. It's important to schedule time for these routines. Establishing a predictable schedule increases the likelihood that students will transition smoothly into the routine. Consider the following powerful routines:

How Many Days Have We Been in School? (K–1)

Mathematical goals

- Using a chart to record data (the number of days we have been in school)
- Counting to 100 by 1s, 5s, and 10s
- Using the 5 and 10 structure to visualize the quantities 1–10 (subitizing)
- Recognizing 5 and 10 as important numbers in our number system
- Visualizing how the quantities 11–100 can be decomposed into 5s and 10s

Setup

Create and laminate a blank hundred chart in a 10×10 arrangement and place it near your numerical hundred chart in the meeting area:

1	2	3	4	5	6	7	8	9	10
11	12	13	14	15	16	17	18	19	20
21	22	23	24	25	26	27	28	29	30
31	32	33	34	35	36	37	38	39	40
41	42	43	44	45	46	47	48	49	50
51	52	53	54	55	56	57	58	59	60
61	62	63	64	65	66	67	68	69	70
71	72	73	74	75	76	77	78	79	80
81	82	83	84	85	86	87	88	89	90
91	92	93	94	95	96	97	98	99	100

Some teachers create blank hundreds charts using ten-frames

The blank hundred chart above indicates that children have been in school forty days. The first five stickers in the row are one color, and the second set of five are a different color, enabling the 5 structure to visually stand out for children.

Introducing the routine

1 Sometime during the first ten days of school, show your students the blank hundred chart. Ask, "What do you notice about this chart?" Follow up with "How many squares do you see

in the top row?" (Run your finger across the top row to indicate what you mean by row.) Invite a student up to count the squares in the top row to verify.

2 Continue by asking, "How many rows do you see?" (Run your finger across the next few rows.) Ask a student to count all ten rows to verify for the class.

3 Ask, "How many squares do you think there are altogether?" After eliciting responses, you can check by counting up to 100 with the class. This choral counting verifies that the hundred chart has 100 squares. If your students do not know enough of the count sequence to stay engaged, you can say in an excited voice, "This chart has 100 squares!"

4 Explain that this year the class will use the hundred chart to keep track of the number of days they have been in school and that you will celebrate the hundredth day in a special way. (As you near day 100, students can help decide how to celebrate.)

5 Ask students whether they know how many days they have been in school so far. You can use your calendar to help students count the days. Ask students to help you place the appropriate number of stickers on the first row of ten. Show students how to fill in the first row from left to right. Then ask, "In how many more days will it be the tenth day of school?"

Continuing the routine

Each day ask one student from the class to place one sticker in the next square of the blank hundred chart. After the student has placed the day's sticker, ask questions such as these:

- How many days have we been in school? How do you know?
- Does anyone have a different way to count the number of days?
- How many filled rows do you see?
- Do you see more or fewer than ten days? Twenty days? How do you know?
- Point to the partially filled row and ask, "How many stickers are in this row? How do you know?"
- How many more days until we to get to day 20? 50? 100? How do you know?
- Are we halfway, less than halfway, or more than halfway to day 100? How do you know?

Changing the routine over time

In kindergarten, after the hundredth day of school, you can create a second chart that you use more flexibly. Laminate the second chart and use removable stickers or magnets. Each day, place a certain number of stickers/magnets on the chart and ask students to figure out how many there are. Or you can say, "I have 32 stickers to place on the chart. How much of the chart do you think we will fill with 32 stickers?" With kindergarteners, you can begin to develop ways of determining the number of stickers without counting every sticker by ones. In first grade, you can create a second hundred chart and continue counting and keeping track of the days until the end of the year.

Number of the Day (1–5)

Mathematical goals

- Decomposing and recomposing numbers
- Exploring the properties of operations
- Using patterns to generate multiple equations with the same answer
- Using one equation to generate another
- Making generalizations (example: When you add and subtract the same number in an equation, such as $27 + 10 - 10 = 27$, the total does not change)

Setup

- Prepare open board space to record equations that students generate.
- Give students journals or paper to record their equations.
- Choose a number that would be appropriate for your students to work with and some operations that you would like students to explore. In first grade, begin with numbers 6–15 and allow students to use any operation. In fifth grade, begin with three-digit numbers and narrow the operations to subtraction, multiplication, or division.

Introducing the routine

1 Tell students that you will give them a number and that you would like them to come up with different equations that equal that number. Tell the class that you will begin by doing this routine together.

2 Write a number on the board. In fourth grade, this number might be 48, because it has many factors. Ask students to think of (or write down on a whiteboard) one or more equations that equal 48. Tell students that the equation could use addition, subtraction, multiplication, division, or some combination of these operations.

3 Give students wait time. When most students indicate that they have an answer, call on students for equations.

4 Record the equations neatly on the board. Students might think of equations such as $50 - 2 = 48$, $100 - 52 = 48$, $58 - 10 = 48$, or $24 \times 2 = 48$.

Do this routine several times over the next few weeks as described above.

Continuing the routine

- Once all students understand what you expect during this routine, ask them to individually record several different equations for that day's number before you share equations as a class. You can ask first-grade students to record at least five equations and older students to generate at least eight. Generating more equations opens up opportunities for students to create and explore interesting patterns.

- Give students three to five minutes to think of equations and ask students to circle the equation that they think is the most interesting.

- Call on five to six students to share their most interesting equation, recording them neatly on the board for the whole class to see.

- Turn to the class and say, "Take a minute to look at all the equations on the board. Choose one that you think is interesting and decide why it's interesting. Then tell your partner which equation you think is interesting and why."

Over time, students will learn from one another and their equations will become more sophisticated and incorporate multiple operations. First-grade students might write the following equations for the number 17: $20 - 3 = 17$, $10 + 10 - 3 = 17$, $5 + 5 + 5 + 2 = 17$, or $(3 \times 5) + 2 = 17$.

Fourth- and fifth-grade students can work with fractions or decimals. If given the fraction $\frac{3}{4}$, students might write $\frac{1}{2} + \frac{1}{4} = \frac{3}{4}$, $0.25 + 0.25 + 0.25 = \frac{3}{4}$, $3 \times \frac{1}{4} = \frac{3}{4}$, or $\frac{5}{10} + \frac{3}{12} = \frac{3}{4}$. You can also build in constraints to develop students' proficiency with specific mathematical ideas. If students are learning about doubles, you might say, "Today, I want you to use at least one double."

"Number of the Day" can also serve as a differentiated homework assignment.

Quick Images (K–3)

Mathematical goals

- Visualizing how quantities can be decomposed

- Using visual patterns to describe number relationships

- Using previous, related representations to reason about how many are in the next representation

- Developing efficient strategies to recognize quantities

- Making generalizations (for example, multiplication is commutative: $3 \times 4 = 4 \times 3$)

Setup

- Decide on the mathematics you want to focus on and what mathematical model to use.

- Prepare three to four related images to present to students. For example, in kindergarten or grade 1 you might choose a ten-frame or math rack to support using doubles to solve near doubles. You might prepare the following three related quick images to show one at a time:

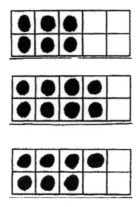

In first grade you might use ten-frames to support students' development of unitizing and decomposing numbers by using the five and ten structures. Here is one such image:

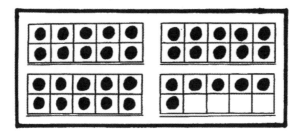

In third grade you might use arrays to encourage students to find the total by adding or multiplying instead of counting. Here is an array you might use:

- Prepare to show students the images you have chosen. You can project the images by using an overhead projector or interactive whiteboard or by physically showing the images on laminated cards. Before doing this routine, make sure that students are familiar with the particular model that you will use.

Introducing the routine

Tell students that you will quickly show them several items and that you want them to figure out how many items you are showing them. Make sure that everyone can see the image. The 3×4 array above can illustrate the routine:

1 Show the image for only three seconds—enough time for students to see the image, but not enough for them to use a counting strategy. Then say, "I am going to show you the image again, and I want you to check your answers."

2 Show the image again for only three seconds. After waiting for students to think, call on a student.

3 Ask, "How many did you see and how did you see them?" A student might explain the array by saying, "I saw 12 dots; 4 plus 4 is 8. And another 4 is 12."

4 Record by circling the quantities that the students identified and labeling with the equations. Ask, "How many of you also saw it this way?" Give students time to think and respond. Then ask, "Who saw it a different way?"

5 Call on two to three more students. Use a new blank image to record each different way children see the quantities, so all ways are visually clear and accessible to all students.

6 Below is an example of how you could record such a conversation.

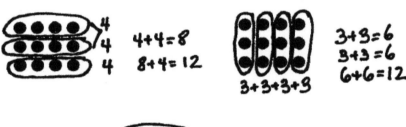

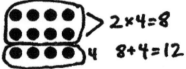

6 Show another related image, such as one that shows the commutative property of multiplication:

7 Repeat the procedure of soliciting students' different ways of seeing how many dots are in the array. You can anticipate that some students will make a connection to the first image: "It's the same as the last one, just turned over on its side." If students do not see the relationship, you can ask, "How does this array compare with the last array?" By having students explore and discuss the relationship between 3 × 4 and 4 × 3, you support them in making an explicit generalization about the commutative property of multiplication.

Continuing the routine

Over time, engage students in exploring quick images that elicit more complex strategies or ideas.

Suggestions for recording

Listen carefully to students' explanations so you can accurately record their strategies. You can give students the option to come to the board to point to or circle the arrangements they see and explain how they figured out the total. Also keep in mind the importance of tapping the brain's power to process visual images and to search for patterns. If you record the images and students' strategies neatly and in an organized manner, they are more likely to see and understand important mathematical patterns, relationships, and structures.

Choral Counting (K–5)

Mathematical goals

- Recognizing numerical patterns and explaining why they occur

- Making generalizations (for example, when you multiply any number by 10, the product always has a zero in the ones place)

Setup

- Prepare a large section of board space for recording the numbers students say as they count.

- Decide what number patterns or relationships you want students to focus on.

- Think about how you can record the numbers students will say in a way that makes that pattern stand out visually. For example, if you want students to notice that the ones digit does not change when you add ten to a number, record it like this:

57
67
77
87
97
107
117
127
137

Introducing the routine

Tell students that they are going to skip-count together as a class and the number they will count by—for example, 5.

1 Begin the count slowly and ask students to count with you. As students say the multiples of 5, record them on the board. Record the numbers in a way that you think will highlight the patterns you want students to see:

5	10	15	20	25	30	35	40	45	50
55	60	65	70	75					

2 Stop and ask students, "What do you notice about the numbers so far?" Students might say, "I see a lot of fives and zeros," or "The numbers go five, zero, five, zero."

3 Follow up with clarifying questions, such as "Where do you see fives and zeros? Can you come show us the fives and zeros that you are talking about?" Call a student to the board to show the class that he or she is referring to the fives and zeros in the ones place of each number. You can underline what the student notices.

4 You can ask, "Why do you think that all the numbers have either a zero or a five in the ones place?" This question both restates (in more precise mathematical language) what students have noticed and asks them to consider why the numbers behave that way. If not many students raise their hands to explain why, ask students to explain to a partner why they think the numbers all have a five or a zero in the ones place. This approach gives all students an opportunity to try out an explanation in a less public way.

Consider exploring the following patterns:

- Why particular numerals appear in the ones place. When you count by 12s, why do the multiples always end in 2, 4, 6, 8, or 0?

- Patterns of odd and even numbers. When you count by an even number, why do you say only even numbers? When you count by odd numbers, why do you say numbers that are both odd and even?

- The tenth multiple always has a zero in the ones place. This is an important pattern to notice. Why does this happen?

- Why the numbers above and below each other are always the same distance apart. For example, in the multiples of 5 above, why are the numbers in the second row 50 more than the number above them?

- Patterns that occur when you count by two different numbers related to one another, such as 4 and 8. See the example below for how to record this.

Continuing the routine

As students' ability to notice relevant patterns and explain why they occur becomes more sophisticated, introduce harder numbers to count by and more complex patterns to explain. For example, have students first count by one number and then by a related number and then record the second set of numbers directly below the first set:

4	8	12	16	20	24	28	32	36	40
8	16	24	32	40	48	56	64	72	80

Recording the two sets of multiples in this fashion makes students more likely to notice that each number in the second row is twice the value of the number above.

Suggestions for recording

To determine the best way to record numbers so students can see the important patterns and relationships, experiment before doing the routine with your class. Recording the first ten multiples of any number across and then next ten multiples directly below might enable students to see this pattern best. However, you can also draw attention to repeating patterns in digits by ending a row with other multiples that end in zero. You might record the multiples of 12 like this:

12	24	36	48	60
72	84	96	108	120

Number Strings (1–5)

Number strings are sets of related problems that engage students in exploring mathematical ideas and strategies.

Mathematical goals

- Developing fluency with number facts

- Visualizing patterns and relationships that occur in number and operations

- Developing accurate, efficient, and flexible strategies for computing with numbers

- Developing clear, efficient ways to record different computation strategies

- Using models such as open number lines and open arrays to solve and represent computation problems
- Making generalizations about strategies and properties of numbers and operations

Setup

- Clear a large amount of board space.
- Collect several different-colored markers for recording. Use a black marker only for numbers in the string.
- Decide on the mathematical ideas or strategies you want students to explore.
- Choose five to seven related problems that showcase the ideas or strategies you want students to explore.

Here are some examples of number strings. Look at the numbers in each set of problems. In each set, problems are sequenced so students can use answers and strategies from previous problems to solve later problems.

Grade 1	Grade 2	Grade 3	Grade 4	Grade 5
$4 + 4 =$	$52 + 10 =$	$200 - 25 =$	$1 \times 48 =$	$4 \times 10 =$
$4 + 5 =$	$52 + 20 =$	$200 - 26 =$	$2 \times 24 =$	$8 \times 5 =$
$6 + 6 =$	$52 + 22 =$	$200 - 40 =$	$4 \times 12 =$	$16 \times 2\frac{1}{2} =$
$7 + 6 =$	$52 + 26 =$	$200 - 41 =$	$8 \times 6 =$	$7 \times 7 =$
$8 + 9 =$	$46 + 33 =$	$300 - 52 =$	$16 \times 3 =$	$14 \times 3\frac{1}{2} =$

Introducing the routine

Explain to your students that you will give them math problems and that they should solve them in whatever way makes sense to them. Tell them they can solve the problems mentally or that they can use their whiteboards or notebooks.

When students are asked to solve problems mentally (without paper and pencil), they often decompose and recompose numbers in flexible ways and invent their own strategies. This is the type of thinking that you want to elicit. However, when the numbers become larger or you want students to experiment with using models such as open number lines or open arrays to keep track of their thinking, using whiteboards or notebooks to record their steps can benefit them.

1 Using a black marker, write the first problem on the board, one that all students can quickly figure out.

2 Say the problem aloud. Wait until most students have their thumbs up before calling on anyone. (If most of your students do not know the answer, your problem is too hard. Start over with an easier problem.)

3 Call on a student and ask for his or her answer. Record the answer on the board.

4 Ask the student, "How did you figure that out?" Students should "just know" the first problem in a number string. (For example, first-grade students might "just know" that $4 + 4 = 8$, or second-grade students might "just know" that $52 + 10 = 62$.) If the student "just knows" the answer, you do not need to record anything but the answer. Some teachers write "IJKI" ("I just know it") next to the problem.

5 Write the second problem in the string in black marker. Usually, the second problem requires some kind of strategy or reasoning. Often, students use what they know from the first problem to help them solve the second. (For example, if the first problem is $4 + 4 = 8$ and the second problem is $4 + 5 = $ _____, a first-grade student might say, "I know that $4 + 4$ is 8 and 5 is one more than 4, so $4 + 5 = 9$.")

6 Say the problem aloud, and give students wait time. Wait until most students have thumbs up before you call on anyone.

7 Call on a student and ask for his or her answer.

8 Ask, "How did you figure that out?" Record the student's thinking next to the problem in a color other than black. Be sure to accurately represent the student's reasoning with the models and strategies used so that everyone has access to the solution.

9 Then ask, "Did anyone solve it a different way?" You can record a second way of solving the problem in a different color of marker; doing so enables students to readily see the differences between the solutions. You can continue by asking whether anyone else solved it that way.

10 You can either ask for another solution or move on to the third problem in the string, repeating the process above.

At any time, you may choose to draw students' attention to the patterns and relationships that occur in problems, strategies, and models. Students may point out observations about patterns and relationships as strategies are shared. In either case, students need to discuss the patterns and relationships they notice. Here is an example of how a teacher supports a class of first-grade students as they begin to generalize the doubles-plus-one strategy. The teacher is using the following string:

$$4 + 4 =$$
$$4 + 5 =$$
$$6 + 6 =$$
$$7 + 6 =$$
$$8 + 9 =$$

Notice how the teacher responds after a student shares a strategy for the second problem in the string:

Enrique: I know that 4 + 4 is 8 and 5 is one more than 4, so 4 + 5 equals 9.

Teacher: [*Records the following on the board*]

$$4+4=8$$
$$4+5=9 \qquad 4+4+1=9$$

$$4+\overset{5}{\underset{\wedge}{}}$$
$$4+4+1 = 9$$

Teacher: Wow, you used what you knew about 4 + 4 to figure out 4 + 5. That's so interesting. [*Turning to the rest of the class*] Raise your hand if you understand what Enrique just said. Who can explain it in his or her own words? [*One or two students do so.*] Do you think this strategy would always work? [*Many students put a thumb up, but others are not sure.*]

Teacher: Let's see whether this strategy works on the next two problems. [*Students notice that the strategy works on the next two problems.*]

Teacher: This strategy that Enrique used has a name. It is called the doubles-plus-one strategy. [*Adds "Doubles + 1" to their class chart of addition strategies, using words and equations to clearly represent it.*]

Suggestions for recording

At first, try to record student thinking as faithfully as you can, using equations and models the students use. If you explore these models in your own problem solving, you will develop a deeper understanding of how they support the development of important mathematical ideas. Once you understand them, you will become more proficient at using them to facilitate and record student thinking.

Here is an example of what a completed class number string looks like when students' strategies are recorded clearly using both equations and an open number line. This number string supports the addition strategy of keeping one number whole and adding on the other number in parts. Problems in the string are written in black marker so they stand out, enabling students to more easily see how problems in the string are related. For example, one student used the answer from the first problem to help him solve the second problem. He saw that 52 + 10 = 62, so for 52 + 20, he just added 10 more to 62. Also (though it can't be shown here because this book is in two-color format), the teacher recorded strategies for each problem in different colors so students can more easily see the differences between them:

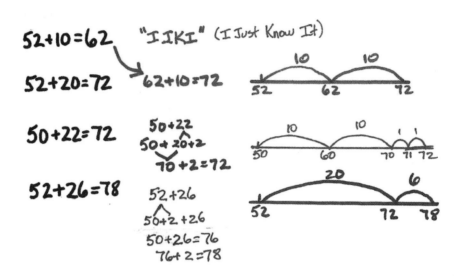

Continuing the routine

As students develop increasingly sophisticated ideas, you can use number strings to help them develop a wider range of strategies. As you deepen your own understanding of the big ideas, models, and strategies that are important for your students to develop, you will get better at choosing strings that support their learning. You can also develop your ability to facilitate explicit class discussions about generalizations important for your students to make and prove.

Designing number strings that develop mathematical ideas and strategies requires expertise. The following books can help choose appropriate number strings for your students:

- Fosnot, Catherine Twomey, and Willem Uittenbogaard. *Minilessons for Early Addition and Subtraction*. Portsmouth, N.H.: Heinemann, 2007.

- ———. *Minilessons for Extending Addition and Subtraction*. Portsmouth, N.H.: Heinemann, 2007.

- ———. *Minilessons for Extending Multiplication and Division*. Portsmouth, N.H.: Heinemann, 2007.

- Imm, Kara Louise, Catherine Twomey Fosnot, and Willem Uittenbogaard. *Minilessons for Operations with Fractions, Decimals, and Percents.* Portsmouth, N.H.: Heinemann. 2007.

- Uittenbogaard, Willem, and Catherine Twomey Fosnot. *Minilessons for Early Multiplication and Division.* Portsmouth, N.H.: Heinemann, 2007.

Start with one routine, and schedule a consistent time for it. Work to foster broad participation in the routine—for example, by giving students wait time after posing questions and by periodically asking students to think, turn, and talk with a partner. You should also work on understanding and recording students' thinking as accurately and clearly as possible. As you and your students become more proficient with each routine, you will become more comfortable facilitating conversations about students' mathematical thinking, and their thinking will become more flexible and sophisticated.

MAKE GENERALIZATIONS EXPLICIT TO DEVELOP COMPUTATIONAL FLUENCY

Elementary students engage in complex thinking about math when they are challenged to explore patterns and relationships, make conjectures, and prove whether the conjectures are true and why. The routines described earlier engage students in building mathematical ideas and offer opportunities to generalize. Through explicit, guided inquiry, you can further develop these routines.

You can use questions to guide students to make and prove generalizations. Consider the generalization that the product of any number and zero is zero (the zero property of multiplication). To begin, you might use the following number string, presenting one problem at a time. Ask students to explain their reasoning for each solution:

$$5 \times 0 =$$
$$4 \times 0 =$$
$$0 \times 10 =$$
$$7 \times 0 =$$
$$25 \times 0 =$$

After students solve all the problems, prompt them to look for patterns and relationships by asking, "What do you notice?" Students might notice that all the products are zero.

Next, challenge students to generalize by asking them to form a conjecture related to their observation. Ask why they think this happens: "Why do you think all the products are zero?" or "What conjecture [or rule] can you make about multiplying a number by zero?" Students might say, "When you multiply a number by zero, you always get zero as an answer."

Then challenge students to prove whether their conjecture is true by asking whether it will always work: "If I multiply any number by zero, will I always get a product of zero?" Ask how they can prove it: "How can you prove that any number multiplied by zero equals zero?" Students might say, "I know that 12×0 means $0 + 0 + 0$ twelve times. It doesn't matter whether I add 12 zeros or 20 zeros—all those zeros together still equal zero."

Finally, after students prove that the conjecture is true, ask them to restate the generalization: "So, what rule can we make about multiplying any number by zero?"

Guiding students to make and prove generalizations is an important aspect of developing computational fluency. As you become more aware of the generalizations your students are ready to make, you will recognize opportunities in your routines, lessons, and class discussions to explicitly engage students in making and proving them.

CONCLUSION

Computationally fluent students have a deep understanding of number and operations as well as facility with procedures. They take time to look at the numbers in problems to determine the most efficient strategy. They think flexibly about changing numbers in problems to make them easier to solve. They solve problems accurately. Students develop computational fluency by inventing strategies and exploring the mathematical structures and properties underlying those strategies.

You can use the instructional routines in this chapter to support your students' development of computational fluency. These routines also give you opportunities to support your students' development of their problem-solving dispositions—curiosity, flexibility, persistence, risk taking, and reflection. Consistent and frequent work with these routines will support your students' problem solving in and out of math class.

III The Lesson Cycle

Students and teachers benefit when teachers plan effective lessons, enact the lessons as planned, and carefully reflect on evidence of student learning. Engaging in this lesson cycle helps teachers develop and refine several essential habits of effective teaching: planning lessons purposefully, observing students at work, assessing student learning, and reflecting on their practice. Through purposeful lesson planning, enactment, and reflection, teachers learn more about—and explore connections among—the mathematics they are teaching, their students' mathematical thinking, and effective instruction: They become better math teachers. Share and discuss these chapters with colleagues, and collaborate to plan and reflect on lessons as often as possible.

Effective lessons revolve around good tasks. Chapter 8 describes tasks most likely to result in significant learning and suggests how to make tasks in your curriculum more mathematically rigorous. Chapter 9 explores planning a lesson. Chapter 10 focuses on the in-the-moment decisions teachers must make while teaching a lesson and how careful planning can make those decisions easier. Chapter 11 examines reflecting on a lesson, emphasizing how to analyze student work, how to plan next instructional steps, and how to improve instruction.

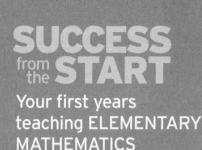

chapter **eight**

Tasks That Promote Learning Math with Understanding

Guiding Principles

LEARNING IS MAXIMIZED WHEN STUDENTS—

>> interact in a safe, supportive learning community;

>> activate and build on prior knowledge;

>> process information both visually and linguistically;

>> solve problems with meaningful contexts;

>> engage in reflection, self-monitoring, and metacognition; and

>> engage in complex thinking.

The math problems and activities that you assign will influence what students think about as they solve and discuss problems; what tools, strategies, and representations they use; and what mathematical connections they make. Tasks will also influence how hard students think and persevere during math class and, ultimately, what they come to believe math is all about.

Essential Practices

TO ENSURE THAT STUDENTS LEARN MATH DEEPLY AND WITH UNDERSTANDING—

>> assign appropriately challenging, mathematically rigorous tasks;

>> give students time to problem solve; and

>> engage students in reasoning, representing and communicating their thinking and making connections.

For students to engage in genuine problem-solving that involves reasoning and proving, creating and using representations, communicating ideas, and making connections, you must give students tasks that promote these processes. Not all math tasks elicit these processes, and students need not engage in all of them every day. Sometimes students need to practice procedures or math facts to consolidate that knowledge. However, students should solve challenging problems and engage in the NCTM Process Standards and the Common Core Standards of Mathematical Practice regularly. Many math programs offer challenging problems that can support students in learning math with understanding. Other programs contain fewer problems or tasks like these, and you need to know how to improve such tasks.

CHARACTERISTICS OF TASKS THAT PROMOTE LEARNING MATH WITH UNDERSTANDING

In general, tasks that promote learning math with understanding have the following characteristics:

- They require students to engage in mathematical thinking that focuses on concepts and relationships rather than just procedures or rules.
- They have multiple entry points and are therefore accessible to a range of students.
- They are engaging to a wide variety of students.
- They offer opportunities for students to communicate ideas.
- They require students to represent, explain, or justify their thinking.

Tasks that promote understanding invite students to use mathematical reasoning and to explore mathematical ideas. Students with different levels of prior knowledge or different ways of thinking can use what they know to begin. Different students may choose different tools and strategies to complete tasks, or they may use the same tools and strategies but in different ways. The contexts pique students' curiosity and motivate students to persist in finding solutions. Because the tasks invite students to use different strategies and representations, they give students genuine reasons to share their thinking, ask questions, and listen to the thinking of others. The tasks require students to reflect on and communicate their strategies and why they think their answers are correct. This supports students' reasoning and metacognition and allows teachers to assess students' levels of mathematical thinking.

Here is an example of an appropriately challenging, mathematically rigorous task that comes from a standards-based math program. It is written for third-grade students.

Book Orders (page 1 of 2)

Title	Price	Title	Price
Monster Jokes	$1.99	Sillyt Kid Jokes	$3.42
10 Projects with Wood	$1.73	10 Projects with Paper	$2.54
Mystery of Owl Island	$2.50	Mystery of the Silver Wolf	$3.35
Going West	$4.28	About America	$4.46
Time Machine	$3.15	Upside-Down Town	$4.25

If you have $10.00, which books can you buy?
Find combinations of at least three different books that cost
close to $10.00 in all. Then find how much money you have left.
Write equations to show your solutions.

Book Order 1 List titles and prices.

_____   _____

_____   _____

How much did you spend? _____   How much is left? _____

Equations:

Book Order 2 List titles and prices.

_____   _____

_____   _____

How much did you spend? _____   How much is left? _____

Equations:

From Investigations Student Activity Book Single Volume Edition Grade 3 by Sussan Jo Russel and Karen Economopoulos, copyright 2008 Pearson Education, Inc. or its affiliates. Used with permission. All rights reserved.

Solutions to the problem

You probably started by making sense of the problem. You figured out that the table was a section of a book order form and that the problem asks you to pretend to order three or four different items, find the total cost, and find the change you would receive from $10. You then consciously or unconsciously planned how to begin.

Once you began solving the problem, what kinds of mathematical thinking did you engage in? You may have begun by estimating. Perhaps you thought about buying the *Monster Jokes* book for $1.99 and *10 Projects with Wood* for $1.73 and thought of each book as close to $2.00. Together they would cost a little less than $4.00. You might have then looked for a third book that would make the total close to $10. For example, adding *Going West* for $4.28 brings the total to approximately $8. You then might have found the exact total by using either a procedure you learned in school or a mental math strategy and then calculated the change from $10.

STOP+REFLECT

>> First, solve this problem for yourself. Reflect on your process. What kinds of mathematical thinking do you engage in?

>> Think about how a third grader might solve this problem. How might his or her thinking compare with yours? (Assume that the third grader can solve the problem.)

>> Consider whether this problem fits the criteria for tasks that promote learning math with understanding and why.

Monster Jokes $1.99 → $2.00 *10 Projects with Wood* $1.73 → $2.00 $2.00 + $2.00 = $4.00	$4.00 + ? = $10.00 *Going West* $4.28 → $4.00 $4.00 + $4.00 = $8.00	$1.99 + $1.73 + $4.28 = $8.00 $10.00 − $8.00 = $2.00

Or you might have begun differently by looking for combinations of prices that are easy to add, such as $2.50 and $2.54. You might have found the sum of $5.04, looked for another convenient price, such as $4.46, and arrived at a total of $9.50. This total makes finding change from $10 easy. People who use this approach focus on finding "friendly numbers" to make the computation easier, instead of using estimation. Both approaches are valid and require mathematical reasoning.

"What prices would be easy to add?" *Mystery of Owl Island* $2.50 *10 Projects with Paper* $2.54 $2.50 + $2.50 = $5.00 $5.00 + $0.04 = $5.04	$5.04 + ? =$10.00 "What price would be easy to add to $5.04?" *About America* $4.46 $5.04 + $4.46 = $9.50	$10.00 − $9.50 = $0.50

A third approach is trial and error. Students might choose books with titles that interest them without considering prices. These students may end up with a total greater than $10 and then have to trade in one or more books for less expensive ones. These students will do less mathematical reasoning initially. However, because of the constraint that they spend no more than $10, they will have to engage in mathematical reasoning to determine which book(s) to trade in and for what.

"What books would I like to buy? I like mysteries and fantasy."	"What book should I trade in and what should I buy instead?"	$10.00 − $9.90 = $0.10

"What books would I like to buy? I like mysteries and fantasy."

Mystery of Owl Island $2.50
Mystery of the Silver Wolf $3.35
Upside-Down Town $4.25

$2.50 + $3.35 = $5.85
$5.85 + $4.25 = $10.10
"Oops. Too much."

⇨

"What book should I trade in and what should I buy instead?"

$3.15 is a little less than $3.35.

"I'll trade in *Mystery of the Silver Wolf* for *Time Machine*. I'll spend 20 cents less."

$2.50 + $3.15 + $4.25 = $9.90

⇨

$10.00 − $9.90 = $0.10

Characteristics of this problem

This problem fits four of the five characteristics of problems that support learning math with understanding:

1 It requires mathematical thinking that focuses on concepts and relationships, not just procedures. The problem requires students to alternate between addition and subtraction and see relationships between these two operations. The problem also invites students to use mathematical reasoning to either estimate or choose combinations of prices that will be easy to add.

2 The problem has multiple entry points and is therefore accessible to many students. The problem has multiple solutions and solution paths.

3 The problem context is likely to be engaging to most students. It presents math as connected to students' lives and useful in everyday situations and offers students the opportunity to wonder about the many combinations of books and prices that could be chosen.

4 It offers genuine opportunities to share and discuss mathematical ideas, such as the usefulness of estimating, different ways to approach the problem, and different strategies to add prices and find change.

5 It does not ask students to show their work and explain their choice of books. However, you could easily modify the directions to ask students to show their work and explain their choice of books.

THE POWER OF MEANINGFUL CONTEXTS

Story problems

Not all tasks that promote learning math with understanding need be as complex as the book-order task. One- and two-step story problems can be excellent tasks.

Current math programs contain many story problems, and for good reason. Meaningful contexts can facilitate student learning. They can support students in reasoning about concepts and relationships and in developing meaning for operations. They can make problems more engaging and accessible, and they can help communicate mathematical ideas. Here are two examples of story problems:

1 Stephan is 12 years old. He is three times as old as his cousin Rosa. How old is Rosa?

2 Nina uses $\frac{3}{4}$ of a cup of sugar to make 1 batch of cookies. How many batches of cookies can she make with 6 cups of sugar?

These contexts make the problems engaging. Students are generally interested in the ages of their relatives and how they compare with their own. Who is older? Who is younger? By how much? Students are also familiar with and generally enjoy cooking. Furthermore, by seeding the idea that there is mathematics to be thought about when playing with cousins or when cooking, these problems encourage students to notice and wonder about mathematics outside math class.

The Problem with Teaching "Key Words"

It is important not to teach your students key words to determine what operation to use when solving story problems. Though it may seem like a simple strategy to help students choose the correct operation, looking for key words short-circuits sense making. This strategy discourages students from making sense of what is happening in the story problem and using the story context to figure out how to solve the problem. If students understand the actions in a story problem and what the numbers in the problem refer to, they should be able to figure out the correct operation to solve the problem.

Furthermore, key words can mislead. For example, the following problem contains the word *altogether*, which is usually considered a key word for addition. However, it is not an addition problem:

Sally and her brother have 64 baseball cards altogether. If Sally has 49 baseball cards, how many does her brother have?

As students move up in the grades, the story problems they encounter will be more complex in their structure and more difficult to analyze with a code of key words. Instead of teaching key words, teach your students how to make sense of and solve problems by using the metacognitive problem-solving routine from chapter 6.

Using the same story context more than once

Giving students the same type of problem with the same context on multiple occasions can be useful. For example, one second-grade teacher helped her students understand and solve comparison subtraction problems by regularly sharing with her students the scores of recent basketball games. For each game, she asked students to figure out how many more points the winning team scored than the losing team. These students developed efficient strategies for solving subtraction problems and were motivated by the context. They even began bringing in scores from basketball games themselves.

Repeated use of the same context can be especially helpful for struggling students and English language learners: Students do not have to take time and energy to understand a new problem situation each time they solve a problem. When the context remains the same, students can focus on developing or refining methods to solve the problem.

At some point, all students should be asked to solve problems in a variety of contexts to transfer what they have learned to new situations. However, if students are allowed to first develop deep understanding of the concepts and relationships embedded in one context, they can use what they know about that context to understand others.

Investigations

An investigation is another type of task that allows students to explore the math in one context over a series of lessons. Investigations engage students with particular concepts and models that the context supports. For example, when students learn about place value, experiences packing items in groups of 10 and 100 are useful. You can ask students to imagine that they work in a candy factory and can "package" quantities such as 37 candies in packs of 10. Students act this out by organizing 37 connecting cubes into three stacks of 10 and seven "singles." Over several days students "pack" many different quantities and keep track in a class table:

Total number of candies	Packs of 10	Singles
21	2	1
37	3	7
54	5	4
58	5	8
62		
75		
102		

During each day of the investigation, students discuss the patterns they notice, why they think they occur, and whether they believe they will always occur; they continue to pack other quantities to see what happens. Through such context-driven investigation, students develop a deeper understanding of place value.

Math games

Although math games do not usually involve real-world contexts, they also can serve as meaningful contexts to learn mathematics. Many math games support developing mathematical thinking by incorporating mathematical models such as number lines, hundred charts, ten-frames, arrays, and decimal grids. Often the game board is a particular model, such as a ten-frame or hundred chart. In these games, the mathematical model is the context that the students engage with. As students play the same game again and again, they become more familiar with the model and begin to use it to think about number relationships and operations.

WHY AND HOW YOU MIGHT MODIFY TASKS

Now you may be wondering about the tasks in your math program and how well they fit the criteria here. When analyzing your tasks, ask yourself:

- Will these problems challenge students to think about mathematical concepts and relationships? Are they likely to engage in mathematical reasoning?

- Are the problems open-ended and accessible for all students?

- Are the problems engaging?

- Do the tasks ask students to show their work and/or explain their thinking?

The following sections describe how you can modify problems to meet these criteria.

Minimize directions for how to solve problems

A surprising number of math problems contain specific directions for how to solve them. Sometimes the directions specify particular materials that students should use. A story problem might be followed by directions to "use counters" or "draw a picture" to solve it. Other times, the directions specify a general problem-solving strategy such as "work backward." Still other times, the directions suggest using a particular computational strategy, such as "partial products," or a particular model, such as an array.

Consider when directions for how to solve problems are likely to enhance students' understanding of concepts and relationships and when they are likely to get in the way, and then adjust accordingly.

When students first encounter a particular type of story problem, asking all students to draw a representation of the problem or to act it out with cubes makes sense. These actions help students fully understand the problem structure and enable you to assess whether students understand it. When introducing a particular model, such as an array, asking students to use the model to solve problems also makes sense.

However, letting students decide what tools and strategies to use when solving problems is usually better. First, this approach supports differentiation by making the same problems both more accessible and more challenging. Students who need to use counters to solve a problem can do so, and those who can use more sophisticated strategies can work at their level of challenge. Second, it supports sense making and persistence. All students may not be able to figure out how to use the strategy of "working backward" to solve a particular problem. When students are allowed to use whatever strategy makes sense to them, all students can engage with the problem. Third, it supports engagement. Students like having choices and they like discussing with others the choices they have made. Finally, it supports making connections. After students solve problems in a variety of ways, you can ask students to look for connections among different strategies and representations.

Add or modify a context or ask students to create a context

Some contexts are harder for students to understand or model than others. For example, students in a first-grade class were having trouble solving comparison problems about the weights of different animals. The teacher changed the context to the heights of different buildings. The students could more easily model the new problems with cubes and were more successful in solving the problems.

Other times, the given contexts do not seem that interesting or engaging. Make contexts more engaging by thinking of situations directly related to students' lives or the topics they are studying in other subjects. Or ask students to create their own story problems. Writing story problems for a particular operation engages students in thinking more deeply about what types of actions and relationships that operation represents.

Ask students to estimate

Estimating is an important part of the metacognitive problem-solving routine. Asking students to make an estimate requires them to reason about the quantities involved in the problem, what the operation really means, and what size answer is reasonable. Your tasks should often ask students to make an estimate before solving problems and to explain the thinking behind their estimates.

Ask students to show their work and explain their thinking

Routinely ask students to show and explain their strategies. Their writing need not be long and laborious. Students can develop efficient ways to record strategies so that they can share their work and thinking with peers and teachers. At first, some students may find it difficult to record or explain how they solved a problem. However, with your consistent support, all students can learn. You can model this process by listening to students' reasoning and showing them how to translate their strategies into appropriate math language and representations. You may need to rewrite worksheets with space for students to record their work and thinking or ask students to record their work in a math notebook.

Ask students to check their answer by solving the problem in a different way

Asking students to prove their answer is correct reminds them to check their work. It is the last step in the metacognitive problem-solving routine. This practice reinforces habits of reflection, self-monitoring, metacognition, and attention to precision. Asking students to solve problems in different ways challenges them to think flexibly and to wonder whether they could solve them a better way. Thinking flexibly enables students to consider alternative strategies when confronted with a problem and to choose the most efficient strategy.

Examples of modifications

Here are some examples of the modifications described above. Some problems are modified in more that one way.

Ten birds were sitting in a tree. Then 4 birds flew away. How many birds are left in the tree? Use counters to solve the problem.	⇨	Ten birds were sitting in a tree. Then 4 birds flew away. How many birds are left in the tree? Solve the problem in a way that makes sense to you, and show your work.
A cat weighs 18 pounds. A dog weighs 35 pounds. How much heavier is the dog than the cat?	⇨	One building is 18 stories high. Another building is 35 stories high. How much taller is the second building? Solve the problem in a way that makes sense to you, and show your work.
Solve this problem by regrouping: 92 – 49	⇨	Rosa is reading a book. Her book has 92 pages. Rosa has just finished reading page 49. How many more pages does Rosa need to read to finish her book? Solve this problem in a way that makes sense to you, and show your work.

Solve this problem: $$17\overline{)238}$$	⇨	Write a word problem for $$238 \div 17 =$$ Solve the problem in a way that makes sense to you, and show your work.
Solve this problem using partial products. $$\begin{array}{r} 51 \\ \times\,27 \\ \hline \end{array}$$	⇨	$$51 \times 27 =$$ Before solving the problem, decide whether the product will be more than 1,000 or less than 1,000, and explain your thinking. Solve the problem in a way that makes sense to you, and show your work.

Open-ended tasks

Most tasks that support students in learning math with understanding still have one correct answer. However, students can arrive at that answer in different ways. Tasks with one correct answer but multiple solution paths are sometimes called open-routed tasks because students can choose different routes to solve them. Other tasks, called open-ended tasks, have multiple solution paths and multiple solutions (the book-order problem and the "Today's Number" routine from chapter 7 are examples).

Open-ended tasks can prompt especially productive mathematical thinking. They encourage flexible thinking, systematic thinking, and reflection. Students often use one solution to find other solutions and, in the process, make important mathematical connections. Furthermore, because open-ended problems allow for so many different correct answers, students at many levels can solve them. As a result, these tasks can engage a range of students in noticing connections among solutions. They can be used to assess student understanding and to engage students in complex thinking.

Examples of modifications

Here are some examples of tasks with only one correct answer that have been modified to make them open-ended tasks with multiple correct answers.

STOP+REFLECT

>> What modifications do you notice in the problems above?

>> Look through the problems for an upcoming lesson. Try modifying one according to one or more of the suggestions above.

>> How might students engage with the problem differently because of the modification?

What is the value of these coins?

Show your work.

⇒

What is the value of these coins?

What other coin combinations would equal the same amount? How many different combinations can you find?

Write down all the combinations you can think of.

Andrew picked 4 apples. Ella picked 5 apples. How many apples did they pick in all?

Solve the problem in a way that makes sense to you, and show your work.

⇒

A bowl has 9 apples. Some are red and some are green.

What combinations of red and green apples might be in the bowl?

Write down all the combinations you can think of.

Jessica puts cupcakes in rows on a tray. She makes 6 rows of cupcakes with 8 cupcakes in each row. How many cupcakes does she put on the tray?

Solve the problem in a way that makes sense to you, and show your work.

⇒

How many different arrays can you make with 48 tiles?

Create as many arrays as you can with 48 tiles. After you build each array, record it on graph paper. How do you know if you found them all?

How many ¼s are equal to ½?

How many ⅛s are equal to ½?

Solve the problems and show your work.

⇒

How many different combinations of fractions can you think of that equal ½?

Record the different combinations.

You can also follow open-ended questions with a prompt to make a generalization based on the multiple solutions the student has generated or to compare responses.

$\frac{1}{2} = \frac{\square}{8}$ $\frac{3}{4} = \frac{\square}{12}$ Solve these problems and show your thinking.	Write ten fractions greater than $\frac{1}{2}$. How do you know that these fractions are all greater than $\frac{1}{2}$?
Write a story problem for this equation: $$12 \times 6 =$$ Solve the problem and show your thinking.	Write one multiplication story problem and one division story problem. How are multiplication and division story problems alike and different?

CONCLUSION

This chapter highlights the most important things to consider as you select tasks and math problems for your students. The problems you assign will influence how well students can access the problems; what tools, strategies, and representations they use; and what mathematical connections they make. If you have trouble finding tasks with the characteristics described in this chapter, modify the ones you have to make them more likely to support students in learning math with understanding. Your students will learn math more deeply.

STOP+REFLECT

>> Solve each open-ended problem on the right side of the page and reflect on the kinds of thinking you do.

>> What might you learn about students' thinking from their work on these tasks?

chapter **nine**

Lesson Planning

Guiding Principles

LEARNING IS MAXIMIZED WHEN STUDENTS—

>> interact in a safe, supportive learning community;

>> activate and build on prior knowledge;

>> process information both visually and linguistically;

>> solve problems with meaningful contexts;

>> engage in reflection, self-monitoring, and metacognition; and

>> engage in complex thinking.

A detailed lesson-planning framework is an important tool. Specific to teaching mathematics and designed to support teaching as described in this book, the framework in this chapter (1) prepares you to observe and support key mathematical ideas that students develop as they solve problems and (2) helps you anticipate and minimize common difficulties that hinder student engagement with mathematics.

This framework is designed primarily to help you plan and facilitate lessons in which students solve challenging tasks. Such a lesson generally has four parts:

1 A challenging task that meets the criteria described in chapter 8

2 A launch in which you introduce the task, activate students' prior knowledge, and communicate expectations for how students will work

3 A work time during which students solve the problem and you circulate and ask questions to assess and build on student thinking

4 A class discussion in which you focus students' attention on two to three student-generated strategies, to help students communicate their ideas, consider the ideas of others, and deepen their mathematical understanding.

PREPARING TO OBSERVE AND SUPPORT MATHEMATICAL THINKING

Planning math lessons requires planning for what your students will learn during a lesson, not just what they will do. Planning for learning requires the following:

- Clarifying the mathematical goals of the lesson. What concepts, strategies, skills, or connections should students develop or deepen during the lesson?

- Anticipating how students will solve the problems you give. What strategies might students use? What tools might they use? How might they represent their thinking? What mistakes might they make or misconceptions might they have?

- Planning for how best to elicit, assess, and respond to students' solutions and ideas. What should you look for as students work? What questions can you ask to get students to describe their thinking? What types of student thinking and student work would show evidence of understanding the main ideas of the lesson? What questions can push students' thinking further?

Because mathematical thinking is complex, making sense of students' thinking and responding to it on the fly can be hard. Anticipating students' strategies ahead of time makes you more likely to observe and understand those strategies when students use them. Similarly, if you think ahead of time of questions to ask students during lessons, you will ask better questions when the time comes. Most important, if you are clear about the goals of a lesson and the student thinking and work that shows evidence of meeting those goals, you can better focus your conversations with students on the math that is important to learn.

MINIMIZING COMMON DIFFICULTIES

In any lesson, unanticipated difficulties can keep students from learning what is intended or keep you from interacting with students in the ways that you planned.

Difficulty launching lessons

Tasks can be challenging for you to introduce and for students to make sense of. Giving students the right amount of support and direction can be hard. With too little, students may not know how to approach or complete the task. Too much reduces the mathematical thinking students must do to solve problems. By carefully thinking through and scripting a launch during lesson planning, you are more likely to give appropriate scaffolding and directions.

Difficulty maintaining focus on the learning of the class

Some students invariably get stuck when solving challenging problems. Other students finish early. Teachers often find themselves responding in the moment to the needs of particular students instead of assessing and responding to the learning of the class as a whole. Although giving extra help and extensions is appropriate, doing so in planned and structured ways is best, so you do not spend most of math class "helping" the same students day after day. Planning modifications and extensions ahead of time supports all students in being independent and frees teachers to assess and focus on the learning of the class.

The following planning framework contains valuable questions for planning each component of a lesson. Time constraints make it difficult to answer all questions for every lesson. However, planning lessons by using the entire framework, perhaps once every week or two, is worthwhile—especially if you plan lessons with colleagues. It will help you see the value of each question and develop your instruction. Teachers who plan lessons by using these questions develop habits of thinking about students and mathematics that make the process easier and more efficient.

Lesson Planning Framework

Do the math and define the learning goals

- Read the lesson. What are the math learning goals? What is the task?

- What related prior knowledge and experiences will students bring to the task?

- Do the task with your students in mind. What tools and strategies might students use? What connections and understandings should they develop? What mistakes or misconceptions might arise?

- Review the task. Should you differentiate it to meet the diverse learning needs of your students? Does the task require students to show their work?

- Review the learning goals. Should you clarify or revise them?

Plan the launch

- How will you activate students' prior knowledge and engage them in the task?

- What visual aids, including models and vocabulary words, will make the task accessible?

- What directions will help students to think and work autonomously?

Plan the work time

- How will you group your students as they work? (Individually? In pairs?)

- What materials do students need, and how can you make them accessible?

- What is important to observe as students work (strategies, tools, representations)?

- What questions will you ask to support student learning?

Plan the class discussion

- What big ideas, strategies, or representations do you want all students to explore more deeply in the class discussion?

- What connections are important for students to make? What questions can you ask to help students make those connections?

- What visual aids, including models and vocabulary charts, will make the discussion visual and accessible?

PLANNING A DIVISION LESSON

To understand how to use this framework, read how two fourth-grade teachers use these questions to plan a division lesson. Notice how Ms. Ellis and Ms. Kramer work together and how their collaboration helps both to hone their instruction. They each teach fourth grade in the same school. Ms. Kramer has taught for more than fifteen years and at many grade levels. Ms. Ellis has been teaching for three years. They meet twice per month to plan math lessons together that they will teach in their own classrooms. Ms. Ellis will teach the lesson first. Ms. Kramer will teach the lesson one or two days later. Because Ms. Ellis will teach the lesson first, the teachers focus on her students when planning the lesson, and she takes the lead in making decisions. Ms. Kramer will adapt the lesson for her own students on the basis of how things go in Ms. Ellis's classroom. They plan for an hour the day before the lesson.

For the past several weeks, their students have been studying multiplication. They have found factors and multiples of different numbers, solved and written multiplication story problems, and developed increasingly efficient strategies for solving multiplication problems with two-digit numbers. The teachers are now planning the year's first formal lesson on division. Although the students had done some work with division in third grade, these teachers are unsure of what the students learned or remember.

Reading the lesson: What are the learning goals? What is the task?

The teachers begin by reading the lesson as it is described in their teacher guides. The lesson begins with the following story problem:

> Ms. Santos owns a neighborhood grocery store. She has 56 apples to arrange in rows for her window display. She has room for 4 rows in her window. How many apples will there be in each row if she puts the same number in each row?

The guide suggests that the teacher present the problem to the class, ask students to solve the problem in any way they can think of, and then discuss the different ways that students solved the problem. After the discussion, the teacher is supposed to send students off to solve more division problems. The stated goals of the lesson are (1) solving division story problems and (2) using and interpreting division notation.

After the teachers read through the lesson, Ms. Kramer starts the conversation.

Ms. Kramer:	So what are the goals of this lesson?
Ms. Ellis:	The first one is "solve a division story problem." [*Now talking about the task rather than the goal*] The lesson seems almost like a preassessment—to show what strategies students are using so that we can build on them. It seems that the teacher is supposed to present the problem and then observe what students do.
Ms. Kramer:	I'd be curious to see how the students would approach this without a lot of explanation. Will they recognize it as a division situation?
Ms. Ellis:	You want students to come away from the problem knowing that it is division, but let them figure it out. I think they will use what they know about multiplication to solve the problem. And it might even feel like a multiplication situation as they deal out tiles—if that is what they do.

These teachers plan to observe and support student mathematical thinking. The conversation begins with one teacher asking what the goals of the lesson are and another teacher reading the first goal from the teacher's guide. Then, instead of hurriedly copying down that goal word for word on a recording sheet, the teachers begin wondering aloud about the lesson and about their students. Ms. Ellis wonders about the underlying purpose of the lesson and the teacher's role ("The lesson seems almost like a preassessment." "It seems that the teacher is supposed to present the problem and then observe what students do."). Ms. Kramer wonders about the students' experience. ("Will they recognize it as a division situation?")

STOP+REFLECT

>> What do you notice about how these teachers begin planning the lesson?

>> Why do they begin talking about the underlying purpose of the lesson, the teacher's role, and what students might think about as they solve the problem?

Defining lesson goals means more than reading a set of bullet points from a teacher's guide and writing them down. It involves making sense of the guide's stated goals, the recommended sequence of instruction, and how students at this point in the curriculum are likely to experience the task. Read through the lessons in your math program with the care, thoughtfulness, and curiosity that these teachers are demonstrating. Also, because different teachers are likely to attend to different aspects of a lesson as they read and analyze it, collaborate in lesson planning as much as possible.

What prior knowledge and experiences will students bring to the task?

Ms. Kramer: Let's talk about what the students know and understand and what they have done before. Let's remind ourselves of their prior knowledge.

Ms. Ellis: We've done a lot of work in multiplication in terms of groups of things—we've done that through pictures and arrays. We're working on the strategy of breaking a problem into friendlier problems to solve it and building on what you know to figure out what you don't know. If you gave the students a story problem about 6×14, most students would break it into 10×6 and 4×6.

Ms. Kramer: What do your students know about division?

Ms. Ellis: Many are nervous. I asked this morning what they knew about division because I know they did some in third grade. Only four students shared ideas. Those who shared said some nice things. Kathryn [all names are pseudonyms] said, "It is multiplication but backwards." Dana said, "It's the action of splitting something into parts." Daniel said, "How many groups of something are in something else." Sydney shared that she knew what the division symbol was. But the others stayed quiet. I know most are anxious about it.

Ms. Kramer writes down a few statements about the students' prior knowledge of multiplication and the fact that many of them are anxious about division.

STOP+REFLECT

›› What does Ms. Ellis mean when she says, "working on the strategy of breaking a problem into friendlier problems to solve it"?

›› What do Ms. Ellis's comments about her students' knowledge of division tell you about the range of understanding within her class?

To help you better understand Ms. Ellis's comments about her students' prior knowledge of multiplication, here is some additional information. In the past few weeks, students in both classes have used arrays to explore breaking multiplication problems into smaller problems to make them easier to solve. An array is a mathematical model that can represent multiplication situations. The problem 6×18 can be represented with an array. The array shows 6 rows of 18 squares and 18 columns of 6 squares (6 groups of 18 and 18 groups of 6):

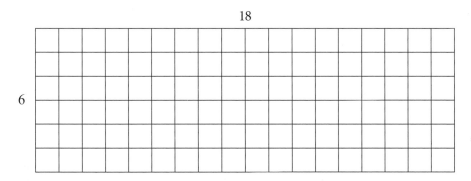

To find the total number of squares in the array, we can break down the array into smaller arrays and determine the number of squares in each smaller array. The 6 × 18 array could be broken up like this:

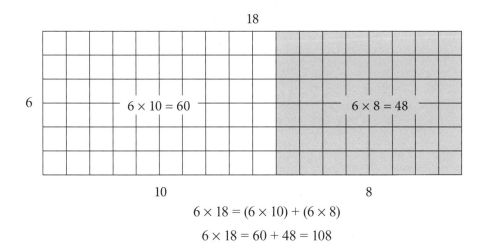

$$6 \times 18 = (6 \times 10) + (6 \times 8)$$
$$6 \times 18 = 60 + 48 = 108$$

The same array could be broken up like this:

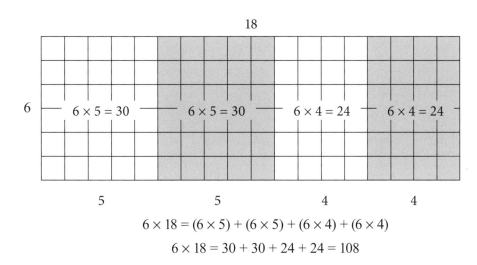

$$6 \times 18 = (6 \times 5) + (6 \times 5) + (6 \times 4) + (6 \times 4)$$
$$6 \times 18 = 30 + 30 + 24 + 24 = 108$$

The same array could be partitioned in other ways. The total squares in the larger array will always equal the sum of the squares in the smaller arrays within it. The students in this school spent many lessons experimenting with different ways to break apart arrays to find the total number of squares and discussing which ways were most efficient and why.

The students' prior knowledge of division is less extensive and more varied. A few students articulated some important aspects of division ("It is multiplication, but backwards." "It's the action of splitting something into parts." "How many groups of something are in something else."). Together these statements indicate a rather sophisticated understanding of division. However, most students did not share any knowledge of division.

Continuing to define learning goals

Ms. Kramer:	So going back to the lesson goals . . .
Ms. Ellis:	The second goal is "Interpret division notation." Hmm . . . I guess what they are saying is, "What does it mean to divide?" [*Pause*] That will be a huge goal. What does it mean to divide? What are you doing when you are dividing?
Ms. Kramer:	Can we agree that "solving division story problems" is a goal? Should we also write, "What does it mean to divide?"
Ms. Ellis:	Yes. And how about "understand what it means to divide and how to interpret division notation"?
Ms. Kramer:	OK.

Ms. Ellis and Ms. Kramer use a Circle Map (one of eight Thinking Maps, http://thinkingmaps.com) to facilitate and document their thinking through this part of their planning. Ms. Kramer writes "lesson goals" in the center circle and identifies lesson goals in the outer circle. The frame surrounding this map identifies students' prior knowledge and experience. It also includes a prediction about how some students may react to the problem. This visual (fig. 9.1) keeps the focus on the students as the teachers discuss and refine the lesson goals.

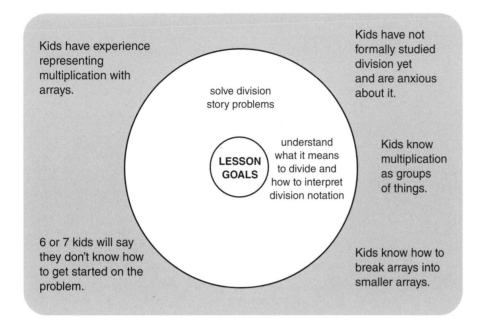

Kids have experience representing multiplication with arrays.

Kids have not formally studied division yet and are anxious about it.

solve division story problems

LESSON GOALS

understand what it means to divide and how to interpret division notation

Kids know multiplication as groups of things.

6 or 7 kids will say they don't know how to get started on the problem.

Kids know how to break arrays into smaller arrays.

Fig. 9.1. *Circle Map showing lesson goals framed by students' knowledge*

STOP+REFLECT

>> Why does Ms. Ellis rephrase the goal "Interpret division notation" as "What does it mean to divide?"

The teachers continue to make sense of a lesson goal. At first Ms. Ellis seems puzzled by the goal as written. What does it mean to interpret division notation? And how does that fit into this lesson? Then she realizes that interpreting division notation means more than just being able to say, "Here's the division sign." It means understanding the operation of division. A student who can interpret division notation is a student who, when faced with a division sign, knows how to begin solving a problem because he or she knows what it means to divide. After Ms. Ellis thinks through the meaning of the lesson goal, Ms. Kramer thinks of a way to phrase the goal that includes both the meaning of the operation and the interpreting of the notation.

So far the teachers have written down both the lesson goals and the prior knowledge that students will bring to the task. This helps them keep these important pieces of information in mind while they plan the rest of the lesson. As you plan, you should do the same.

Doing the task with students in mind

Ms. Kramer suggests that they think about the problem and imagine what approaches students might use. They decide that students will solve the problems individually but then share their strategies with a partner.

Ms. Ellis begins naming strategies that students might use.

Ms. Ellis: Some students may deal out by ones.

She gets a bin of color tiles and begins dealing out the tiles one by one into four rows:

1	5
2	6
3	7
4	8

Ms. Ellis: Here are four shelves. Now each shelf has two apples. The only thing to keep track of is "Here are my four rows. Have I dealt out all the apples yet?" So, I think some students might deal out one by one all the way up to 56.

Ms. Kramer: So that is one strategy.

Ms. Ellis: Some other students might start like this. [*She begins placing five tiles in each row.*] And think about . . . OK . . . if each row has 5 . . . how many apples have I used? And I think they'll say, "OK, I've used 5, 10, 15, 20. I've used 20 apples. How many apples are there? There are 56." And then I would guess that they might add another 5 apples to each row so they have 40, and then count on from there.

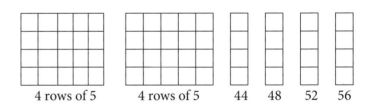

4 rows of 5   4 rows of 5   44   48   52   56

Ms. Kramer: Could you see some students seeing the first 20 and then saying, "I don't need to keep using tiles; I can use what I know"?

Ms. Ellis: Yeah, I do. They might think, "OK, if I have 4 rows and I put 5 in each row, I have used 20 apples and I have 36 left." If I have 36 left and 4 rows, I can add 9 more to each row.

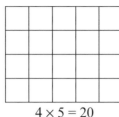

56 − 20 = 36

36 ÷ 4 = 9

I can add 9 more apples to each row.

Each row has 14 apples.

$4 \times 5 = 20$

Ms. Kramer: Will you have any students who use pictures rather than tiles?

Ms. Ellis: Yes. Definitely. But they'll use the same strategies, just with pictures. [*Pauses to think*] So one strategy is dealing by ones. Another one might be dealing by ones and then chunking them in into arrays of friendly numbers. Another is starting out with arrays of friendly numbers and then reasoning without having to build the rest. So we've got those three.

Ms. Kramer: [*Records the three strategies*] Will some students just use pencil and paper and write equations? For example, will anyone use a ten-times strategy and say, "If there were 10 in a row, that would be 40, and 4×10 is 40. What do I have left?"

$$4 \times 10 = 40 \rightarrow 56 - 40 = ? \rightarrow 56 - 40 = 16$$
$$4 \times ? = 16$$

Ms. Ellis: I have one or two students who might do that. They might multiply by 10.

Ms. Kramer: [*Adds the "multiplies by ten" strategy to the chart*] I'll leave blanks because we will see others. You never know what will come up.

Figure 9.2 is a visual of their notes.

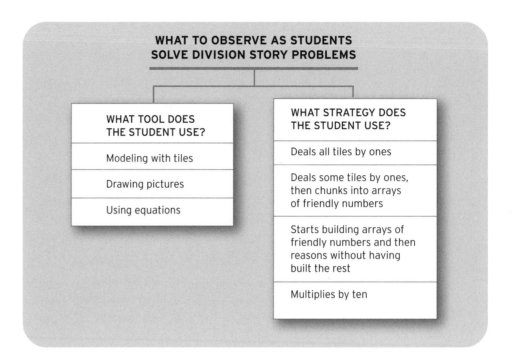

WHAT TO OBSERVE AS STUDENTS SOLVE DIVISION STORY PROBLEMS

WHAT TOOL DOES THE STUDENT USE?	WHAT STRATEGY DOES THE STUDENT USE?
Modeling with tiles	Deals all tiles by ones
Drawing pictures	Deals some tiles by ones, then chunks into arrays of friendly numbers
Using equations	Starts building arrays of friendly numbers and then reasons without having built the rest
	Multiplies by ten

Fig. 9.2. *Planning notes for a division word problem*

STOP+REFLECT

>> Do you understand all these strategies? If not, take the time to make sense of them.

>> In what other ways might students solve this problem?

The teachers anticipate four different strategies, each of increasing sophistication. The first strategy is a direct-modeling strategy. Students who use this strategy simply act out the problem. They do not need to think about multiplication or division to solve it. The other three strategies all entail some thinking about multiplication or division, but with different levels of efficiency and sophistication.

As these teachers anticipate how students will solve the problem, they distinguish between the tools students will use and the strategies students will use. Strategies describe the physical and mental actions students take as they solve a problem. Tools are the materials students use. "Using tiles" is not a strategy. Students can use tiles in different ways. Similarly, students can use the same strategy, such as "dealing out by ones," with different tools. For example, some students might use tiles and other students might draw circles.

The teachers record the tools and strategies so that they can remember to make these tools available and to look for these strategies as they observe students at work. The teachers will also use this chart later in the planning meeting to generate questions to ask students as they work.

Do learning goals need to be clarified or revised?

Ms. Ellis now raises a potential difficulty for some students.

Ms. Ellis:	At first, there are going to be six or seven students who immediately think, "I don't get it. I don't know what I am supposed to do." It's the same students that I struggle with across the curriculum. I'm trying to get them to think about how to help themselves, instead of just saying, "I don't get it."
Ms. Kramer:	So the challenge is, how do we help students understand the problem?
Ms. Ellis:	The first thing they need to do is wrap their heads around the language of the problem and ask, "What is this question asking me?"
Ms. Kramer:	Right.
Ms. Ellis:	Often my students will see a lot of text and just say, "I don't get it."
Ms. Kramer:	That relates to the work we've started in teaching our students how to think through solving a problem. We want them to ask themselves, "What are the things that I need to do and think about as I solve problems?" "What do I know that is going to help me solve this?"
Ms. Ellis:	So that might be a secondary goal, developing independence in problem solving.
Ms. Kramer:	Let's call that "developing metacognitive problem-solving skills." It's about developing thinking and self-monitoring skills throughout the process of problem solving. [*Pauses to think*] We could also change the context of the problem to make it more meaningful to the students.

The teachers briefly talk about changing the context of the problem but keeping the numbers the same. They decide to create a story problem about the Mayan civilization because that is what they are studying in social studies. The story problem will involve balls used in the Mayan game pok-a-tok.

Figure 9.3 shows their revised goals.

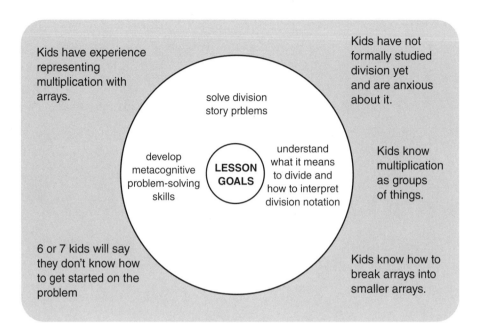

Fig. 9.3. *Revised goals for students learning division*

The figure shows a central circle labeled "LESSON GOALS" surrounded by three goals: "solve division story prblems," "develop metacognitive problem-solving skills," and "understand what it means to divide and how to interpret division notation." Surrounding notes read: "Kids have experience representing multiplication with arrays." "Kids have not formally studied division yet and are anxious about it." "Kids know multiplication as groups of things." "6 or 7 kids will say they don't know how to get started on the problem" "Kids know how to break arrays into smaller arrays."

STOP+REFLECT

>> Why do the teachers decide to add a third goal of "developing metacognitive problem-solving skills"?

Ms. Ellis raises a common difficulty: how to support students who quickly say "I don't get it" when faced with a challenging problem. In response, the teachers think proactively about how to help all students make sense of the problem and begin solving it. They have recently introduced their students to the problem-solving routine in chapter 6. They recognize that the questions in the routine will help their students become more confident and competent in their ability to independently solve problems. The teachers decide that developing this skill is important enough to make it an additional goal for their lesson.

This section of dialogue illustrates the value of anticipating students' difficulties as well as their strategies. Difficulties can take many forms: misconceptions about mathematical ideas, lack of prior knowledge, unfamiliar vocabulary, and various logistical issues. Whatever the potential problems, if teachers can anticipate them and plan in ways that minimize those difficulties, lessons will run more smoothly. Students will spend more time on task, and teachers can better attend to the learning of the class as a whole.

Planning the launch

How will you activate prior knowledge? What visual aids will make the task accessible? What directions will enable students to think and work autonomously?

Ms. Kramer: What will happen in the launch? What will you say? How will you direct students, and so on? Let's use words that get to the point, to get across what students need to hear and understand as clearly and succinctly as possible.

Ms. Ellis:	I'll say that I have a problem that I want us to think about [*Ms. Kramer scribes*], and I'll have the problem on a piece of chart paper. I will read them the problem.
Ms. Kramer:	How will you activate their prior knowledge about problem solving?
Ms. Ellis:	[*Talking slowly so that Ms. Kramer can record*] I might say, "We've been thinking about how good problem solvers approach a problem. What's the first thing a good problem solver does?"
Ms. Kramer:	And at least some students will say something about needing to understand the problem.
Ms. Ellis:	Right. And then I think I'd say, "Let's read the problem together."
Ms. Kramer:	OK.
Ms. Ellis:	And then I think I will say, "So a good problem solver understands the problem first. Who thinks you understand the problem and can explain what the problem is about and what it's asking you to find out?"
Ms. Kramer:	OK. You have choices. How can you increase students' engagement and give them more think time?
Ms. Ellis:	Oh, turn and talk! [*Ms. Ellis pauses to choose her words.*] I think I will say, "Think, turn, and talk. Listen to what your partner says. If you agree, restate what your partner said. If you do not agree, restate your understanding of the problem."
Ms. Kramer:	[*Writing*] Without giving a solution or an answer, right? Just explain what the problem is about and what the problem is asking them to find out.
Ms. Ellis:	Right.
Ms. Kramer:	So now they understand the problem. What is the next thing that you want them to do? What is the next thing that good problem solvers need to ask themselves?
Ms. Ellis:	What's my plan? How will I solve this problem?
Ms. Kramer:	When they think of that next step in problem solving, making a plan, they need to activate their prior knowledge. You want them to think, "What do I know that can help me solve this? What does this problem remind me of? What math do I know that will help me solve it?" We want them to go through that repertoire of questions.

Ms. Ellis:	I should say that. "Before you solve the problem, think, 'What do I know that can help me solve this? What other problems does this remind me of?' Then use what you know to solve the problem."
Ms. Kramer:	Do you need to tell them that they will be working individually but sharing their work with a partner?
Ms. Ellis:	Yeah—so in the launch let's say, "You will be solving the problems individually, but you will be sharing your solutions with your partner." I'll also ask them to ask their partner if they need help.
Ms. Kramer:	So that is your launch. We've got that scripted out.

Figure 9.4 shows the script of their launch.

STOP+ REFLECT

>> Why do the teachers decide to focus on activating students' prior knowledge of problem solving rather than other types of prior knowledge?

>> What do you notice about the collaboration between the teachers?

The teachers are planning the launch. They think of questions they want to ask students and carefully choose what language to use. A launch makes the task accessible and clarifies expectations. The teachers want to do this as succinctly as possible so that students will have more class time to spend solving problems. The teachers even create a script to keep themselves focused during the lesson.

Most launches involve activating some kind of prior knowledge. Here, the teachers activate prior knowledge of problem solving, because problem solving is central to the lesson goals. When planning a launch, consider what prior knowledge will best help your students for the lesson you are planning.

Finally, notice how these teachers are talking with each other. They do not always or immediately agree. They push one another to think about how best to frame questions so that students will learn the most.

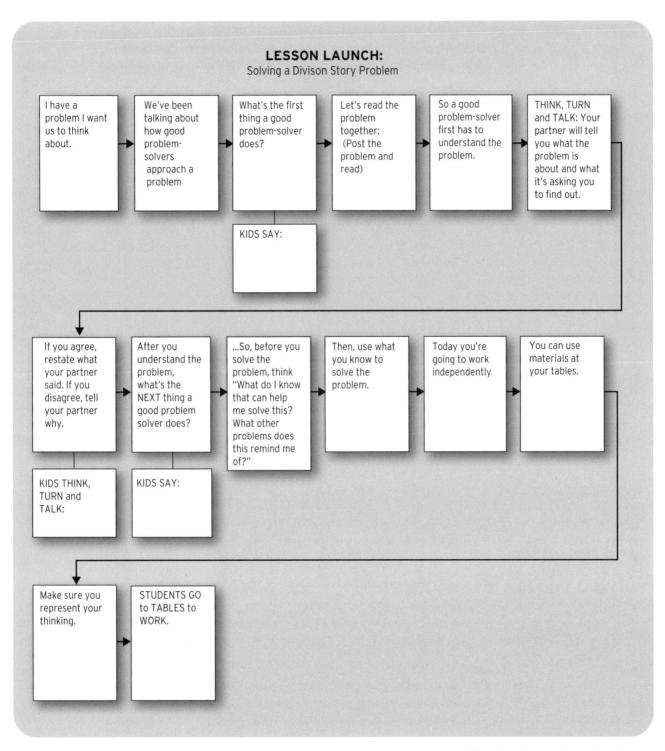

LESSON LAUNCH:
Solving a Divison Story Problem

Fig. 9.4. *Lesson launch script*

Planning work time: What to observe, what questions to ask

For these teachers, planning work time means reminding themselves of strategies they anticipated students would use and thinking of questions they can ask to assess and build on students' thinking. To begin, the teachers look back at their chart entitled What to Observe.

Ms. Kramer:	What questions do we want to ask students as they work?
Ms. Ellis:	If someone is dealing by ones, I think I might ask them, "Could you deal out more than one ball at a time?"

Ms. Kramer records that question on the chart of student strategies.

Ms. Ellis:	What if they make an array using friendly numbers? If they make four rows of five, we could say . . . "Do you think there you could make another four rows of five?" [*Pauses to think*]
Ms. Kramer:	Or we could say, "Why are you putting out rows of five? How did you decide on five?" Then if they say, "Well, five's a friendly number," or "I know 5×4 is 20," we could ask, "Do you know any other friendly numbers, or is there another fact you know?"
Ms. Ellis:	[*Pauses to consider*] Yeah, I think asking, "Why did you use fives?" and "Why did you chunk by a friendly number?" are better questions because they get students to explain their thinking more.

Ms. Kramer adds these questions to the chart, under the respective strategies (fig. 9.5).

STOP+REFLECT

>> During planning, why do teachers spend time thinking of questions to ask students as they work?

>> Why do the teachers craft different questions for different strategies?

While planning the work time, the teachers focus on assessment and questioning to support students' development of key mathematical ideas. The questions relate to anticipated student strategies and are designed to prompt students to share their thinking and to push students to think of more sophisticated and efficient ways to solve the problem.

Planning the class discussion

Ms. Ellis:	After solving the first problem, students will go on to solve the other problems in their student books. I'll stop them after a certain point, have them turn and talk with their partner, and then pull them back together for a whole-class discussion.

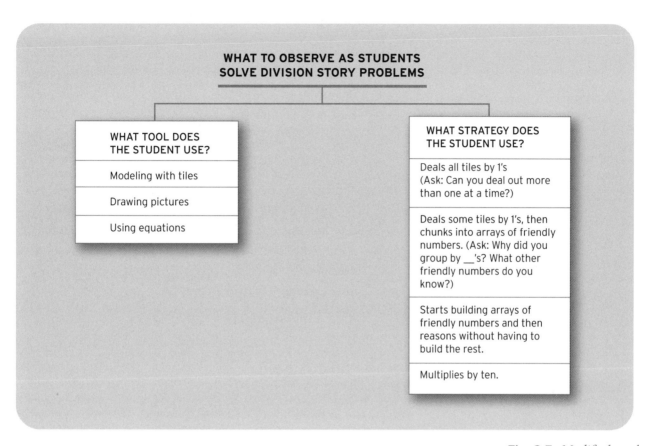

Fig. 9.5. *Modified teachers' planning notes for a division word problem*

Ms. Kramer: So what do we want to focus on in the class discussion? What strategies do we want to share, and what connections do we want students to make?

Ms. Ellis: Well, we'll want to have two to three students share their strategies, probably in order from less complex to more complex. We probably need to wait to see what strategies students use before we can decide which ones to share. If not many students deal out by ones, we might not need to start there, but if many students use that strategy, that will definitely be one we choose.

Ms. Kramer: Do you want to ask, "What information did you use to help you solve the problem?" or "How did you get started?" "How did you help yourself?" That would reinforce the metacognitive problem solving. We could ask students those questions when they share their solutions.

Ms. Ellis: That sounds good. We definitely need to do some talking about how this is a division problem.

Ms. Kramer: Could you talk about division after students share their strategies? Remember, we said some students might solve the problem without knowing it was division. [*Pauses to think*] Oh, after the sharing we could say, "Is this problem division or multiplication?" and do another think, turn, and talk.

Ms. Ellis: Then I could ask them why they think it's division or multiplication. I like that idea—but what about the notation? How do we fit that in?

Ms. Kramer: What if you asked students for an equation that would match the problem?

Ms. Ellis: When?

Ms. Kramer: You could do that after they discussed why the problem was division. And if some students still think the problem is multiplication, they can give a multiplication equation. I assume that some students will know it's division, so we might get more than one equation.

Figure 9.6 shows the script for their class discussion.

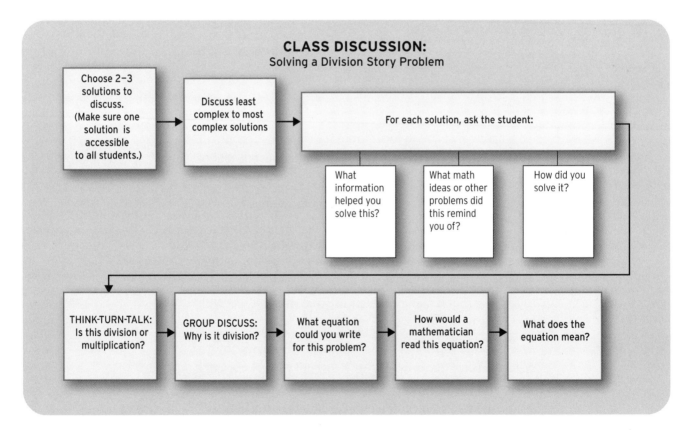

Fig. 9.6. *Script for class discussion of division word problems*

STOP+REFLECT

>> Why does the chart consist mostly of questions?

>> Why do the teachers plan the order of questions to ask in the class discussion?

The planned discussion is connected to the lesson goals. The script addresses each lesson goal. Students will share strategies, showing different ways to solve division story problems. Then the teacher will ask what information students used to help solve the problems, which will help them reflect on their problem-solving process. Finally, the teacher will ask students to consider what makes the problem a division problem and how to read a division equation.

The script is written almost entirely in questions because these teachers know that their students will be more actively involved and learn more if asked to think for themselves. The teachers have also carefully thought through the order of questions. The discussion will move from the concrete sharing of solutions, to considering whether this problem represents division and why, to the more general question of what division means.

CONCLUSION

Throughout planning, Ms. Ellis and Ms. Kramer modeled the dispositions and actions of thoughtful teachers. They took a stance of curiosity toward both the lesson goals (what did they mean?) and their students (how might they solve the problem?). They anticipated everything they could: strategies and tools students might use, student difficulties, how the launch should sound, questions to ask, and how to focus class discussion on the goals. Finally, they used visual tools to facilitate and document their thinking. These documents are readily accessible to support the lesson enactment and reflection.

This framework can help you plan lessons in ways that will prepare you to observe and support students' mathematical thinking and minimize difficulties. The more consistently you use these questions to plan your lessons, the more familiar they will become. Over time, you can incorporate more questions from the framework as you develop the habits of a skillful mathematics teacher.

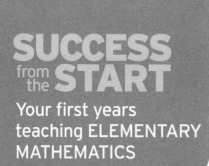

SUCCESS
from
the START

Your first years
teaching ELEMENTARY
MATHEMATICS

chapter **ten**

Lesson Enactment

Guiding Principles

LEARNING IS MAXIMIZED WHEN STUDENTS—

>> interact in a safe, supportive learning community;

>>activate and build on prior knowledge;

>> process information both visually and linguistically;

>> solve problems with meaningful contexts;

>> engage in reflection, self-monitoring, and metacognition; and

>> engage in complex thinking.

W hat happens when lessons are enacted? Does the teacher remember and follow the plan? Do the students solve problems in the predicted ways? Can the teacher understand what students are doing and thinking and ask questions to deepen their thinking?

Experienced teachers know that real lessons are inevitably messier than our most well-thought-out plans. During lessons, teachers must decide which students to talk with, for how long, what questions to ask, and whose work to share with the whole class and why. Teachers must quickly respond to nonacademic issues that arise and adjust when students' responses reveal more or less knowledge or understanding than anticipated. Furthermore, even when events unfold as predicted, teachers must shift between focusing on individual student thinking and the needs of the group. They must also shift between assessing student thinking and choosing ways to respond to that thinking. Skillful teachers coordinate many things at once.

A well-thought-out lesson plan can greatly reduce how much complicated thinking teachers must do on the fly. This chapter documents how the division lesson that Ms. Ellis and Ms. Kramer planned unfolds.

Both teachers bring their scripts of the launch and class discussion. Ms. Ellis uses them to guide her launch and class discussion. Ms. Kramer writes observation notes on them as Ms. Ellis teaches. They decide that during the work time, Ms. Kramer will observe and interact with students at two tables and Ms. Ellis will observe and interact with the rest of the class.

Pay attention to the decisions that Ms. Ellis makes and how she interacts with her students. Notice the choices she makes and how they are aligned with or different from her plan. Also, look for evidence of how Ms. Ellis's actions, comments, and questions affect her students' learning.

LAUNCH: ACTIVATING PRIOR KNOWLEDGE ABOUT PROBLEM SOLVING

Ms. Ellis gathers students on the rug in her meeting area.

Ms. Ellis:	I want us to think about a problem. We talked earlier in the year about things that good problem solvers do. What is the first thing that a problem solver needs to do when given a problem? [*Pauses for wait time*] Stefan?
Stefan:	Read the question.
Ms. Ellis:	Yes. You have to read the question, but what else? [*Pauses*] Jordan?
Jordan:	You have to explain it so that a stranger would understand it.
Ms. Ellis:	Well, you want to explain your work so that a stranger would understand it, but when Stefan said you have to read the problem, you have to do something else. What else do you have to do? Melissa?
Melissa:	You have to understand the problem.
Ms. Ellis:	[*Nodding*] You have to understand the problem. Why is understanding the problem important? [*Pauses*] Max?
Max:	Because if you don't understand it, you won't get it and you will need a lot of help.
Ms. Ellis:	Yes. If you just read the problem and you don't understand it, you are not going to know what to do. Right? [*Pause*] So first you want to understand the problem. To understand the problem you have to ask yourself: "What is the problem about?" and "What do I have to find out?"

Ms. Ellis:	I have a problem for you. [*She has written the following problem on chart paper and hangs it on the board where all the students can see it.*]
	Two Mayan kingdoms disagree over who owns some land. Instead of going to war, the kings decide to settle things on the ball court with a game of pok-a-tok. The referee must arrange 56 rubber balls on the court in rows before the game, and he has room for four rows. How many balls will each row have?
Ms. Ellis:	So now I want you to think and then turn and talk to someone on the rug—first explain to your partner how you understand the problem. "What is the problem about, and what do I have to find out?" And if you are the person listening, decide whether you agree or disagree. If you agree, restate what your partner said. If you disagree, share your own understanding of the problem. OK. Think, and then turn and talk about how you understand the problem.

All the students turn to a person sitting next to them and begin to talk about the problem. Ms. Ellis listens to the conversations of a few different pairs. She hears Selena say to her partner, "It's about the referee has 56 rubber balls and they are trying to see how many rubber balls can go in four rows." After two to three minutes of partner talk, Ms. Ellis asks the students to stop talking and face forward again.

Ms. Ellis:	Who can tell me—not any solutions—but just what is this problem about? Selena?
Selena:	This problem's about two Mayan kingdoms, and they are trying to play a ball game . . . and the referee has to set up the ball court . . . and there are 56 rubber balls and they can fit in only four rows. We are trying to figure out how many rubber balls can go in those rows—like, the number.
Ms. Ellis:	OK, you said a lot. I heard you say what the problem is about. I also heard you say what the problem is asking you to find out. Raise your hand if you heard what Selena said and agree with her understanding of the problem. [*Most students raise their hands. Ms. Ellis decides to move on.*]
	What is the next thing problem solvers do after they have understood the problem? [*Pauses*] Andre?
Andre:	Um, guesses and checks.
Ms. Ellis:	OK. Guessing and checking is a problem-solving strategy. Wylie?
Wylie:	They break it up.

Ms. Ellis:	If you were choosing a strategy like chunking you might break the number up—but take a step back. In general, what do problem solvers have to do once they have understood a problem? Max?
Max:	Write the equation?
Ms. Ellis:	[*Sees that no hands are raised*] The next thing that a problem solver does is make a plan to solve the problem. And when you are making a plan, what question do you need to think about? [*Only a few hands are up.*] Melissa?
Melissa:	What do I know that will help me solve the problem?
Ms. Ellis:	What do I know that will help me solve it! We've talked a lot about building on what you know that can help you figure out what you don't know. Right? So, today, before you start trying to solve the problem, ask yourself, "What do I know that will help me solve this problem?" So today you'll work independently. I'll put materials on your tables in case you need them. Showing all your work is important. Work independently, record all your work, and then share your work with your partner.

STOP+REFLECT

>> What is the first thing that Ms. Ellis wants students to do when solving a math problem?

>> What question does Ms. Ellis want students to ask themselves as they make a plan to solve the problem? Why is this question important?

>> Review the script that the teachers wrote when they planned the launch. How does this compare to what actually happened?

>> A launch introduces the task, activates prior knowledge, and communicates expectations for how students will work. Does Ms. Ellis accomplish these goals? What is your evidence?

Ms. Ellis uses this launch to activate prior knowledge about problem solving. She wants her students to become metacognitive, to become aware of and monitor their thinking as they solve problems. She wants her students to make sure they understand the problems they read. She also wants her students to stop to ask themselves what they know that could help them solve a problem before they rush to solve it.

The launch mostly follows the script that the teachers wrote. Ms. Ellis asks the questions that she planned. She has the students think and then turn and talk to practice making sense of a problem, and she monitors whether the students interpret the problem correctly. They have difficulty answering her question about what students do next after they understand a problem, so after fielding several answers, she explicitly names the next step in the process. She also asked students what question they should ask themselves when making a plan. A student answered, "What do I know that will help me solve this problem?" Eventually, with more conversations like these, students will internalize the problem-solving steps and questions to ask themselves.

Ms. Ellis spends most of the launch time introducing the task and activating prior knowledge about problem solving. Although she explains her expectations for how students will work, she does not spend much time on it. Her students have had enough practice working with math materials such as tiles, recording their work clearly, and sharing their work with a math partner. Earlier in the year, Ms. Ellis devoted more launch time to explaining her expectations and making sure her students understood them.

STUDENT APPROACHES TO THE PROBLEM

After the launch, students return to their tables and begin solving the problem in various ways. Ms. Ellis moves around the room, observing students as they work. She and her colleagues anticipated some, but not all, of these strategies.

Dealing by ones (using tiles or drawings)

Some students begin by placing 56 tiles or 56 circles in four rows of four equal groups. Ms. Ellis sees something like this:

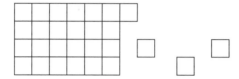

Starting with 4 × 10 = 40

Some students begin by thinking about four groups of 10 balls. They write $4 \times 10 = 40$ on their papers and then think about how many more balls can fit in each row.

Guessing and checking

Four students begin by guessing and checking, a strategy the teachers did not anticipate. All four students begin with 15 balls in each row and check whether that works. Two students use tiles to create rows of 15. The other two students use equations. They write $15 + 15 = 30$, $30 + 30 = 60$.

Using a division algorithm

Some students begin solving the problem using the long division algorithm. They write

$$\begin{array}{r} 14 \\ 4\overline{)56} \\ \underline{4} \\ 16 \\ \underline{16} \end{array}$$

STOP+ REFLECT

>> Why might students who were guessing and checking have started with 15 balls in each row? What question(s) could you ask to elicit and assess their thinking?

>> When you see students using an algorithm, you need to assess whether they understand what they are doing. What questions(s) could you ask the students using the division algorithm to elicit and assess their thinking?

QUESTIONING SELENA: ELICITING A STUDENT'S REASONING

As Ms. Ellis observes the students at work, she stops to talk with particular students to assess what they know. She first checks in with Selena. When Ms. Ellis approaches, Selena has a pile of tiles next to her and 30 tiles in front of her, arranged in two rows of 15.

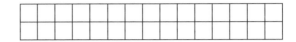

Ms. Ellis asks Selena to explain what she is doing.

Selena:	I have to find out how many times 56 can go into four groups. I am splitting the cubes into 15 to see whether that works.
Ms. Ellis:	How many tiles do you have here right now? [*She waves her hand over both the tiles in the rows and the pile of tiles next to the rows.*]
Selena:	Fifty-six.
Ms. Ellis:	OK, and how many rows were there again in the problem?
Selena:	Four.
Ms. Ellis:	OK, so tell me why you are starting with two.
Selena:	Well, because like I said, we are splitting them in four rows, so we're trying with a big number. So this is 15, so there's two rows of 15. So we are going to see whether there's two more rows of 15.
Ms. Ellis:	OK, let's see.

Selena creates a third row of 15. Ms. Ellis watches.

Then Selena adds the remaining tiles. The tiles now look like this:

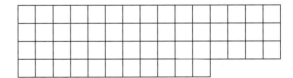

Selena:	So we see that there's not enough cubes. There's four cubes leftover. So now, because these are groups of 15, we'll try to make the groups smaller. [*Looks thoughtfully at the arrangement of tiles*] So we can probably do [*stops to think*] let's see if 13 works.

Ms. Ellis first assesses Selena's understanding by asking how many tiles she has and how many rows exist in the problem. She then tries to understand Selena's strategy by asking her why she has created only two rows. Selena explains that she is guessing and checking, although she does not use those terms.

Once Ms. Ellis understands Selena's strategy, she decides to simply observe Selena as she places the rest of the 56 tiles in rows of 15. Without prompting, Selena realizes that 15 balls is not the answer and reasons that because she does not have enough tiles to make a complete fourth row of 15, she needs to put fewer tiles in each row. Selena's choice of 13 as the next row length to try indicates that she realizes that she needs only to make each row a little shorter.

QUESTIONING SHAWN: WHAT DO THE NUMBERS MEAN?

When Ms. Ellis approaches Shawn, he has already finished solving the problem. On his paper he has written the answer 14. Underneath, he has written the following equations:

$$10 \times 4 = 40$$
$$4 \times 4 = 16$$
$$16 + 40 = 56$$

Ms. Ellis begins by asking Shawn to explain how he found his answer.

Shawn:	I did 10 times 4 equals 40 and then 4 times 4 equals 16. And then 16 plus 40 equals 56. So 10 and 4 equals 14, so that's the answer.
Ms. Ellis:	If we are thinking about this situation . . .
Shawn:	Each row had 14.
Ms. Ellis:	Each row had 14 what?
Shawn:	Balls.
Ms. Ellis:	Fourteen balls in each row. [*She points to the equation 10 × 4 = 40 on his paper.*] Here, the 10 represents what and the 4 represents what?
Shawn:	The 10 represents some of the rubber balls in one row, and the 4 equals the rows.
Ms. Ellis:	So, what's the 40?
Shawn:	[*Pointing to the 10 and the 4 in the equation 10 × 4 = 40*] The 40 is how much this times that equals: 40.
Ms. Ellis:	In the problem, what does the 40 mean?
Shawn:	It's part of how many balls there are in total.

Ms. Ellis:	OK.
Shawn:	And once I do this [*points to the equation 4 × 4 = 16*], I get 16 and add that up and get 56; I know it's the answer.
Ms. Ellis:	OK. [*Pointing to 4 × 4 = 16*] So this is four more balls in each row.
Shawn:	[*Nodding*] Yup.

STOP+REFLECT

➤➤ What do you notice about Ms. Ellis's questions? What is she trying to find out?

➤➤ What does Shawn mean when he says that the 10 in

4 × 10 means some of the balls in each row?

Shawn used an efficient strategy to solve the problem. He used what he knows about multiplication and the distributive property to find the answer, and he clearly recorded his thinking with equations. Ms. Ellis decides to assess whether Shawn can relate the numbers he used back to the context of the problem. She asks him questions about what the numbers 14, 10, 4, and 40 mean in the context of the problem. Shawn answers each question correctly. He even realizes that the 40 refers to some of the 56 balls that the referee has to place in 4 rows.

QUESTIONING MAX: DOES THIS MAKE SENSE?

Ms. Kramer has been observing students at two tables. As she approaches Max, he shows her his paper. He has written 56 × 4 = 156. Underneath that he has written the following:

$$50 \times 2 = 100$$
$$50 \times 1 = 50$$
$$6 \times 1 = \underline{6}$$
$$156$$

Ms. Kramer:	Does this answer make sense?
Max:	[*Looks puzzled and doesn't respond*]
Ms. Kramer:	What does this answer mean?
Max:	There are 156 balls.
Ms. Kramer:	Let's read the problem again.

Max reads the problem aloud. When he gets to the part about having 56 balls for 4 rows, Ms. Kramer asks, "Does this answer [*pointing to 156*] make sense?"

Max:	No, it's too much!
Ms. Kramer:	What do you know that can help you solve this problem?
Max:	Can I use an array?
Ms. Kramer:	Of course—if you think that will help you figure it out.

Max reaches for the tiles. He counts out 56 tiles and then places them in an array, one at a time, building columns of 4.

Ms. Kramer leaves and returns later to find that Max has constructed a 4 × 14 array:

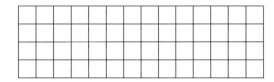

Ms. Kramer:	What did you find out?
Max:	Each row has 14 balls.
Ms. Kramer:	How can you check to see whether your array has 56 balls?
Max:	I can count by fours [*pointing to each column*].
Ms. Kramer:	Could you check in an easier way?
Max:	[*Looks excitedly at Ms. Kramer*] Can I use friendly numbers?
Ms. Kramer:	What friendly number can you use?
Max:	Five.
Ms. Kramer:	How can you use 5 to help you?

Max separates a 4 × 5 array of tiles from the larger array like this:

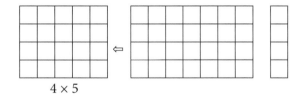

4 × 5

Ms. Kramer:	So what do you have here [*pointing to the 4 × 5 array*]?
Max:	Well, 4 times 5 is 20. Here's 20 [*covering the 20 tiles with his hand*].
Ms. Kramer:	How can you break up the rest of the tiles into friendly arrays?
Max:	I can do 4 × 7—that's 28. [*He counts 7 tiles by ones and separates the 4 × 7 array from the remaining tiles)*]

The tiles now look like this:

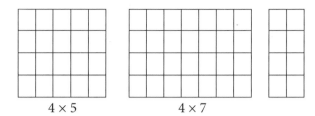

4×5	4×7

Ms. Kramer: So how many do you have now?

Max: [*Pointing to the 4 × 5 array*] This is 20 and this [*pointing to the 4 × 7 array*] is 28. So 20 and 28 is . . . 48.

Ms. Kramer: So what do you do next?

Max: I have 8 left; that's a 4 by 2. And 48 plus 8 is . . . 56.

Ms. Kramer: So, you just proved that you have 56 balls. What did you have to find out?

Max: [*Thinks for a moment*] I had to find out how many balls the referee put in each row.

Ms. Kramer: So . . . what's your answer?

Max: Each row has 14 balls.

Ms. Kramer: Max, you did a great job thinking through this problem. Can you draw these arrays on your paper so you can show the good thinking you did?

Ms. Kramer leaves as Max represents his work.

STOP+REFLECT

>> How does Ms. Kramer help Max rethink his answer of 156?

>> What question does she ask to prompt Max to solve the problem again in a different way?

>> What questions does Ms. Kramer ask Max after he creates the 4 × 14 array of tiles? Why does she ask these questions?

When Ms. Kramer approaches Max, she sees that he has an incorrect answer on his paper. She also sees that he arrived at this answer by trying to multiply 4 × 56 in a way that does not make sense. Max made two significant errors: He misinterpreted the story problem and multiplied incorrectly. However, instead of correcting the errors, Ms. Kramer asks Max to consider the reasonableness of his answer. She asks, "Does this answer make sense?" When Max has trouble answering, she prompts him to reread the problem and then asks the question again. By asking Max to assess the reasonableness of his answer, Ms. Kramer teaches him to reflect on and monitor his thinking, a habit that will allow him to find and correct his own errors in the future.

Once Max understands the problem, Ms. Kramer asks him the question that she wants all her students to ask themselves before they begin solving a problem: "What do you know that can help you solve this problem?" This question prompts Max to think of using an array. Once Ms. Kramer determines that Max has a viable way to solve the problem, she walks away to observe other students, but she returns later to check on his progress.

After Max solves the problem by placing 56 tiles in a 4 × 14 array, Ms. Kramer continues to ask him questions. She asks him how he could check whether he has

56 tiles. When Max responds by saying he could count by fours, she asks whether he can think of an easier way and prompts him to think about "friendly numbers." These questions prompt Max to think about the array as multiplication rather than simply as a model of the situation. Her questioning not only reinforces good problem-solving habits (checking one's work for accuracy, efficiency, and reasonableness of answers) but also extends Max's mathematical thinking.

CHOOSING WORK TO SHARE

After solving the problem about the rubber balls, the students solve four more division story problems. With about twenty minutes left in class, Ms. Ellis stops to decide whose work to present in the whole-class discussion and why. In the lesson planning, the teachers had decided to focus the class discussion on solutions to the initial story problem.

Ms. Ellis wants to choose work that all students will understand. Because many students solved the first problem by dealing by ones, she decides to share work from a student who used that strategy. However, she also wants to push those students to think of more efficient ways to solve division problems. She decides to have Max present his work first. She wants him to explain to the class how he solved the problem by placing tiles one by one in an array but then used multiplication equations to check his answer.

Ms. Ellis also notices that several students used 4×10 to solve the problem. Because this strategy is so powerful and efficient, she decides to ask one of these students to share. She notices that Sofia started with $4 \times 10 = 40$. However, instead of continuing with equations, Sofia skip-counted by fours from 40 to 56. Ms. Ellis decides that Sofia's solution will be accessible to most students and asks her to share.

CLASS DISCUSSION: TWO STUDENTS SHARE THEIR STRATEGIES

Ms. Ellis asks students to finish working and gather on the rug. She asks them to bring their papers and place them on the rug in front of them. She explains that she has asked two students to share their work and that she wants everyone to give these students their full attention and respect.

Max shares

Max sits in front of the class with a 4×14 array in front of him. Ms. Ellis asks him to tell the class how he solved the problem.

> *Max:* I broke the array up into friendlier problems. It really helped me because I didn't have to count all the squares one by one.
>
> *Ms. Ellis:* Before we go there, what did you use to help you solve this?

STOP+REFLECT

>> What factors does Ms. Ellis consider when deciding whose work to share?

>> What other considerations might you take into account when choosing student work to share with the class?

Max:	I used—I used an array because it would help me a lot.
Ms. Ellis:	How did you know how to start your array? What in the problem helped you figure out how to use an array to help you solve this?
Max:	Well, the four rows helped me. I could just make the four rows.
Ms. Ellis:	[*To the rest of the class*] So what helped Max? What information in the problem really helped Max? Omar?
Omar:	The four rows.
Ms. Ellis:	The four rows was really helpful. OK. And Max, tell everyone how you first built that array. Do you remember what you did?
Max:	Yeah.
Ms. Ellis:	Tell everybody what you did. [*To the class*] I should see eyes on Max.
Max:	I had the tiles and I was dealing them out . . . and I was counting by ones . . . and keeping track of how many I put out.
Ms. Ellis:	So you put them one by one in each row?
Isaiah:	Until he got to 56.
Max:	Yeah, I dealt them out and then I just broke them up into friendly problems.
Ms. Ellis:	Can we take a look at these friendly problems?

Ms. Ellis places Max's paper on the document camera:

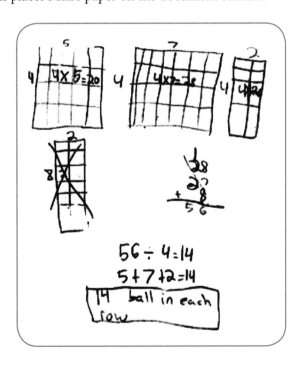

Max:	I split the arrays into a 5 by 4, 7 by 4, and a 2 by 4.
Ms. Ellis:	So you took a chunk of four groups of 5 and then you put out four groups of 7. And then you had four groups of 2?
Max:	[Nods]
Ms. Ellis:	And where is your answer?

Max points to 14 in the equation 56 ÷ 4 = 14 at the bottom of his paper.

Ms. Ellis:	And if we look at your arrays, where is your answer?

Max runs his hand across the top row of each of the arrays.

Ms. Ellis:	Does anyone have a question or comment for Max?
Sofia:	I like that you put it in arrays. I wouldn't have thought to do that.
Melissa:	I like how you split up the arrays. Stefan and I did arrays too, but only after we had solved the problem.
Ms. Ellis:	Raise your hand if you also used arrays or tiles to solve the problem. [About one-third of the students raise hands.]
Ms. Ellis:	Thank you so much Max. OK, we'll also hear from Sofia.

Sofia shares

Ms. Ellis puts Sofia's work on the document camera. Sofia stands at the front of the room, near the screen where her work is projected.

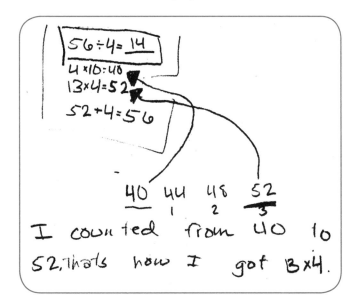

Sofia:	[Pointing to equation at top of page] I thought of the problem as 56 divided by 4, because there were 56 balls and you had to split them up into four groups. So I wanted to use 4 because it was 56 divided by 4. The easiest one I thought of

was 4 times 10. So I got to 40, and then I counted on from 40 to 44, 48, 52. So that's three . . .

Ms. Ellis: Three what?

Sofia: Three more 4s. So from 10, 10 plus 3 is 13. So I got 13 times 4 and that's 52, and one more 4 is 56. So I got 14: 56 divided by 4 equals 14.

Ms. Ellis: So what helped you, Sofia? What helped you get started?

Sofia: Um, the 4 times 10.

Ms. Ellis: So those 10 balls were a nice, easy chunk for you to start with.

Ms. Ellis: [*To the whole class*] So what helped Max get started was thinking about using that array with the four rows. What helped Sofia get started was that friendly chunk of ten groups of four. [*Pauses to give students a chance to think*] How many people solved it in a similar way to Sofia? [*Four students raise their hands.*]

Ms. Ellis: Does anybody have a question or comment for Sofia? Amelia?

Amelia: Was this a quick and easy way for you?

Sofia: Um, I would say it was kind of in the middle. It took me a little while to think about how I should plan it out and think about it—but I would say it was pretty easy.

Ms. Ellis: Anyone else? [*No other hands go up.*]

Ms. Ellis: Thank you, Sofia.

STOP+REFLECT

>> What do you notice about the questions that Ms. Ellis asks Max as he presents his solution? Why does she ask these questions?

>> After each student shares his or her strategy, Ms. Ellis asks, "Does anyone have a question or comment for _____?" Why might she ask this question? What do you notice about the questions and comments that students offer?

>> Why does Ms. Ellis ask each student what helped him or her solve the problem, and why does she summarize this information for the rest of the class?

Ms. Ellis asks several clarifying questions of Max as he presents his work ("Before we go there, what did you use to help you solve this?"). She also revoices some of his statements ("So you put them one by one in each row?"). Her purpose is not to take over his presentation but rather to help him present his work and thinking in a sequence and in language that other students can easily understand.

Ms. Ellis's request for questions and comments serves several purposes. It allows students who do not fully understand a classmate's thinking to ask for clarification. It invites students to share what they notice about the solutions. Finally, it communicates Ms. Ellis's expectation that students pay attention to and work to understand each other's thinking.

Ms. Ellis asks each student what helped him or her solve the problem, and she summarizes this information because she wants students to internalize this question. It addresses the lesson goal of developing metacognitive problem-solving skills.

MORE DISCUSSION: MULTIPLICATION OR DIVISION?

Ms. Ellis: [*To the whole class*] Now think about this: Is this problem division, or is it multiplication? No hands, just think. [*Pauses for wait time*] Now turn to someone next to you and talk about whether this is division or multiplication.

Students turn and talk. Ms. Ellis listens to a few pairs. One student says, "I think it could be both." After about two minutes she asks students to stop talking and look at her.

Ms. Ellis: So what do you think? Is this division, or is it multiplication? [*Most students raise their hands.*]

Ms. Ellis: Isaiah?

Isaiah: I think it's both, actually.

Ms. Ellis: What do you mean, "both"?

Isaiah: It can be stated as multiplication or division.

Ms. Ellis: How did Sofia state it? [*She points to the equation 56 ÷ 4 = 14 on Sofia's paper, still projected on screen.*]

Isaiah: As division.

Ms. Ellis: How could you state it as multiplication? [*Several students raise their hands.*]

Isaiah: Fourteen times 4 equals 56 or—if you didn't know the answer, it would be 4 times what equals 56?

Ms. Ellis: Melissa?

Melissa: I think she thought of it as, um, a division problem but used multiplication to solve it.

Ms. Ellis: [*Matter-of-factly*] Sofia thought of it as a division problem but used multiplication to solve it. [*Several students indicate that they agree.*] Stefan?

Stefan: I agree with Melissa because . . . you can state it as both. You can solve it both ways because multiplication and division are similar like that. Like, 56 divided by 4 is 14, and 14 divided by 56—no, 14 times 4 equals 56.

Ms. Ellis: OK, so Sofia wrote it like this. [*She writes 56 ÷ 4 = 14 on the board.*] Isaiah said we could write it like this [*she writes 4 × 14 = 56*] or Isaiah said if we didn't know what the answer was, we could write it like this. [*She writes 4 × _____ = 56.*]

The board now looks like this:

$$56 \div 4 = 14$$
$$4 \times 14 = 56$$
$$4 \times \underline{} = 56$$

Ms. Ellis:	How would a mathematician read this equation [*points to 56 ÷ 4 = 14*] the way that Sofia wrote it? And we all are mathematicians, so as mathematicians, how do you read it? What does it mean? [*Gives wait time*] I need to see new hands, not the same hands. Hiroshi?
Hiroshi:	I'd read it, "56 divided by 4 equals 14."
Ms. Ellis:	You'd read it as 56 divided by 4, but what does that mean? [*Many hands go up.*]
Ms. Ellis:	Omar?
Omar:	How many times 4 goes into 56.
Ms. Ellis:	Sofia?
Sofia:	Um, 56, if you divide it up in four groups, how many things are in the groups?
Ms. Ellis:	So how many things will be in the groups? So you might see how many balls will be in those four rows? Andre?
Andre:	Also, like, how many groups of 14 go into 56?
Ms. Ellis:	How many groups of 14 go into 56? How many groups of something can be found in something else?
Max:	How many—how many groups of 4 can be found in 56.
Ms. Ellis:	I just heard two really interesting things. I heard "How many groups of 4 fit into 56?" [*Writing that statement on the board*] Right? And I heard something else, something different. Sofia, what did you say?
Sofia:	I said, if you divide 56 into 4 groups, how many things are in the group?

Ms. Ellis writes, "If 56 is divided into 4 groups, how many are in each group?"

The board now looks like this:

$$56 \div 4 = 14$$
$$4 \times 14 = 56$$
$$4 \times \underline{} = 56$$

How many groups of 4 fit into 56?

If 56 is divided into 4 groups, how many are in each group?

Ms. Ellis: [*To the class*] So the equation 56 ÷ 4 = _____ can mean either "How many groups of 4 fit into 56?" or "If I divide 56 into 4 groups, how many will be in each group?" We'll work on division for the next few weeks. We'll have lots of time to come back to these ideas. Now it's time to put away your math papers and get ready for art.

Ms. Ellis ultimately wants her students to understand that they have solved a division problem. However, she knows that students must understand how multiplication and division are related. She also knows that students often use multiplication to solve division problems. Therefore, she does not shy away from Isaiah's statement that the problem is both multiplication and division. In fact, she asks him to explain his thinking further ("What do you mean, 'both'?") and follows up by pointing out that Sofia wrote a division equation for the problem and asking for a multiplication equation. These equations help show that division and multiplication are inverse operations.

Twice, Ms. Ellis pauses to record important student ideas. She poses a question, allows students to talk long enough to generate and consider ideas, and then stops to succinctly restate and record the related multiplication and division equations and the two interpretations of 56 ÷ 4. Her students give two interpretations because division problem are either partitive (How many in each group?) or quotative (How many groups?). The students will revisit this idea in future lessons.

CONCLUSION

Ms. Ellis and Ms. Kramer supported students to engage in problem solving, reasoning and proving, representing their thinking, communicating their ideas, and making mathematical connections. Ms. Ellis launched the lesson in a way that communicated the task and reminded students of questions to ask themselves as they solve problems. During work time, both teachers observed students and asked questions—to assess student thinking, to help students reflect on strategies and whether answers made sense, and to support students in problem solving. Ms. Ellis scaffolded the sharing of work during class discussion by beginning with a piece of work that all students would understand. She also facilitated a discussion in which she helped students make connections between multiplication and division and recorded important equations and ideas to make the mathematics visual.

With experience, your work to plan lessons, develop routines, and foster a supportive community will pay off in well-executed lessons that support students in learning math with understanding.

STOP+REFLECT

>> How does Ms. Ellis respond to Isaiah's statement that the problem they solved could be both multiplication and division? What connections between multiplication and division are Isaiah, Melissa, and Stefan trying to communicate?

>> Reread the two interpretations of 56 × 4. How do they compare?

>> How does Ms. Ellis make students' thinking visible during this class discussion? What does she choose to record on the board and why?

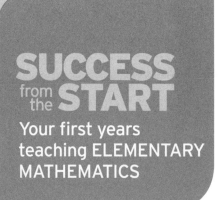

chapter **eleven**

Lesson Reflection

Guiding Principles

LEARNING IS MAXIMIZED WHEN STUDENTS—

>> interact in a safe, supportive learning community;

>>activate and build on prior knowledge;

>> process information both visually and linguistically;

>> solve problems with meaningful contexts;

>> engage in reflection, self-monitoring, and metacognition; and

>> engage in complex thinking.

Teaching is complex and challenging work. Teachers make many instructional decisions every day in response to student thinking and learning needs. Some decisions are planned, and others are made in the moment in response to unpredictable events. Skillful mathematics teachers continually assess how their instructional decisions affect student learning. They reflect on their teaching with curiosity, risk taking, openness to change, and a commitment to students. These dispositions and values enable them to more effectively question, assess, and improve their instruction. Sometimes reflection causes them to examine and perhaps change their beliefs about mathematics teaching and learning.

Reflective teachers observe, analyze, and improve their practice to better facilitate students' development of mathematical ideas and proficiency. This chapter describes a framework for reflecting on mathematics lessons. If you consistently use the framework's questions to guide your thinking as you reflect on your lessons, you will develop the habits of a skillful reflective practitioner.

Time constraints make it difficult to answer all these questions for every lesson. The end of the chapter suggests questions to focus on when you do not have time to answer them all. Reflecting on lessons by using the entire framework, perhaps once every week or two, is worthwhile. At first, using this framework to reflect on lessons will take significant time. However, it will be time well spent, especially if you reflect on lessons with colleagues. Over time, teachers who reflect on lessons with this framework develop habits of thinking about students, mathematics, and teaching that make the process easier and more efficient.

At the end of a lesson, how can you tell whether students learned what you intended them to learn? How do you know what new lessons will advance and support your students' understanding of the mathematics? Systematically reflecting on your lessons can answer these and other questions essential to success in teaching mathematics.

Lesson Reflection Framework

A framework for reflection consists of the following parts:

- Evidence review. What did you observe about students' learning experiences and written work?

- Lesson analysis. What affected students' learning experience?

- Action planning. What actions can you take to improve your instruction and advance student learning?

EVIDENCE REVIEW

Reflective teachers identify events in lessons that stood out for them and determine what students learned. You will first need to gather evidence from your lesson: your observations of students at work during the lesson, their written work, and lesson artifacts (such as class charts and visual representations from interactive whiteboards). Use figure 11.1 to help you think about and organize your reflections for the three parts of the lesson: the launch, work time, and class discussion.

This part of the reflection asks you to reflect on your observations of students during all parts of the lesson and to assess student written work. Assessing student work is the most important aspect of evidence review. It enables you to determine to what extent students learned what you intended them to learn and informs you about next instructional steps. However, you must also reflect on what happened in the launch, work time, and class discussion because you will most likely observe unexpected events or interactions. When you stop and analyze what caused these events, you engage in the next part of lesson reflection: exploring what influenced student learning.

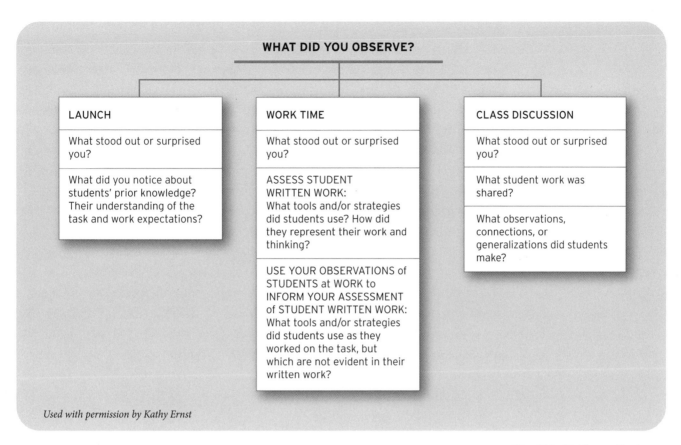

WHAT DID YOU OBSERVE?

LAUNCH	WORK TIME	CLASS DISCUSSION
What stood out or surprised you?	What stood out or surprised you?	What stood out or surprised you?
What did you notice about students' prior knowledge? Their understanding of the task and work expectations?	ASSESS STUDENT WRITTEN WORK: What tools and/or strategies did students use? How did they represent their work and thinking?	What student work was shared?
	USE YOUR OBSERVATIONS of STUDENTS at WORK to INFORM YOUR ASSESSMENT of STUDENT WRITTEN WORK: What tools and/or strategies did students use as they worked on the task, but which are not evident in their written work?	What observations, connections, or generalizations did students make?

Used with permission by Kathy Ernst

Fig. 11.1. *Evidence Review*

LESSON ANALYSIS

Reflective teachers are eager to find out how their instruction affects student learning. To understand this dynamic, they analyze their observation data and explore cause-and-effect relationships between their teaching and student learning. They ask such questions as these:

- Did the lesson go as planned? If not, why not?

- Did students use the strategies I predicted they would use? If not, why not?

- What misconceptions or difficulties arose for students, and what caused them? What were the effects?

- What did I wish had happened but that did not? What could I do to cause that to happen?

You can analyze events to better understand how your instruction affects students at any point in lesson reflection.

After you have identified what happened in the lesson and assessed student work, and after you have analyzed events or interactions in the lesson that stood out for you, focus on the last part of lesson reflection: identifying actions you can take to improve your instruction and advance student learning.

ACTION PLANNING

Reflective teachers look back at their observation data, their assessment of student work, and their analysis of their instruction. They ask, "Now what? How can I use this information to improve my practice and advance my students' learning?" They develop an action plan, using questions such as the following to guide their thinking:

- How can you improve the lesson (for next time)?

- What are the next instructional steps for students?

- What teaching practices/moves supported student learning?

- How can you improve your teaching?

- What actions will you take to improve?

Figure 11.2 will help you organize your action planning and contains further questions to prompt your thinking.

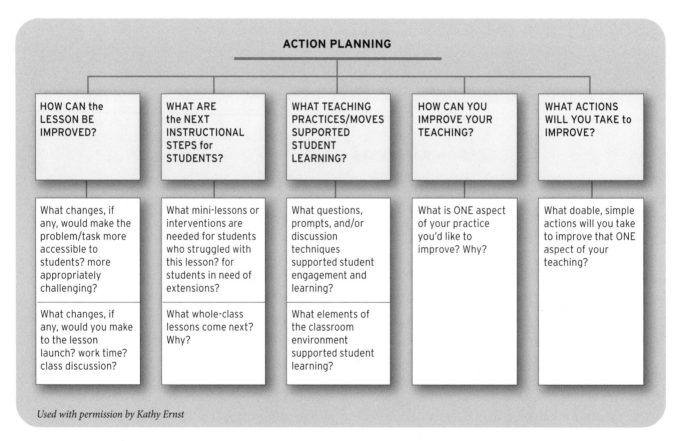

Used with permission by Kathy Ernst

Fig. 11.2. *Action Planning*

Some key points about action planning: First, jotting down a few notes about how to improve the lesson will not take long if you have already reflected on what happened in the lesson, assessed student work, and analyzed surprises that you observed. Second, your assessment of student work and your observations and analysis of students at work will help you decide what instruction they need next. Third, identifying teaching practices or moves that advanced student learning makes you think about how your teaching affects students' learning. Identifying your successes not only builds your confidence but also reminds you to continue these successful practices. Next, skilled teachers reflect on their lessons and generalize how they can improve their instruction. Because improvement for all teachers—novice to expert—occurs when it is incremental, identify only one aspect for improvement. When you focus on one improvement at a time, you increase the likelihood of success and long-term change. Also, small increments in teacher effectiveness advance student learning. For example, giving more wait time can engage more students in mathematical thinking and broaden participation. Finally, to simply identify what you need to improve is not enough. Skillful teachers brainstorm actions they will take to improve their instruction, and they commit to implementing those actions. As you implement your actions, observe how they influence student learning. If your actions are not effective and you have no other strategies in mind, ask colleagues or other math educators for ideas. Try focusing on one improvement at a time, implementing actions often and consistently.

Teachers who collaboratively plan and reflect on lessons learn from each other's expertise, observations, questions, feedback, and thinking. Though such collaboration offers greater potential for professional learning than when teachers work alone, support structures for this approach are not always available. Try to problem solve creatively with your colleagues to find time to plan lessons, observe each other, and reflect on lessons together. Seek support from your principal to make it happen.

You can use the reflection framework for collaborative or individual reflection. This chapter's conclusion suggests ways to get feedback on your teaching if you work alone.

REFLECTING ON A DIVISION LESSON

To understand how to use this framework, we will continue to follow Ms. Ellis and Ms. Kramer as they reflect on the division lesson Ms. Ellis just taught. Their principal has allotted time for them to meet shortly after the lesson so that they can readily recall the "lesson story." They meet for fifty minutes, break to get lunch, and then continue their lesson reflection for another thirty minutes while eating.

Evidence review: What did you observe?

During their lesson planning (chapter 9), Ms. Ellis and Ms. Kramer recorded their thinking and work in the following visual documents:

- Lesson goals framed by students' prior knowledge and experience (Circle Map)
- Script of lesson launch (flowchart)
- What to observe as students work (tree chart)

STOP + REFLECT

>> What dispositions and qualities of a reflective practitioner do you demonstrate?

>> What dispositions and qualities would you like to develop?

>> Chapter 2 discussed how students who engage in reflection, self-monitoring, and metacognition perform best. How is a reflective teacher like a reflective student?

- Script of class discussion (flowchart)

As she taught the lesson, Ms. Ellis used the scripts of the lesson launch and class discussion as guides while Ms. Kramer wrote observations on her own copy. During the work time, both teachers referred to their chart of what to observe as students work while students solved the problem. They bring all their planning documents, student work, and observation notes to their lesson reflection meeting. They begin to share observations about the first part of the lesson, the launch.

What did you observe in the launch?

Ms. Ellis and Ms. Kramer sit at a large table, where they place the stack of student work and documents from their lesson planning. They look at their flowcharts of the lesson launch to recall what happened: In the beginning of the launch, Ms. Ellis focused on the first goal of the lesson: learn how to think through solving a problem. When she asked the students what good problem solvers do, they needed considerable prompting before identifying the first step: understand the problem. The teachers begin their reflection by talking about this first part of the launch. Ms. Kramer records their observations throughout the lesson reflection.

Ms. Ellis:	When I asked the students what good problem solvers do, they could finally name the first step after lots of prompting, but I knew they didn't know what questions to think about that could help them understand the problem.
Ms. Kramer:	What questions did you want them to think about?
Ms. Ellis:	I wanted them to ask, "What's the problem about?" "What do I have to find out?" They didn't know the second step, make a plan. But some seemed to know what to ask themselves as they make a plan—"What do I know that will help me solve it?" I haven't gone over the problem-solving chart with them. [Fig. 6.4 has the problem-solving chart that Ms. Ellis introduced her students to.]
Ms. Kramer:	[*Looking at the flowchart of the launch*] So what happened when you introduced the problem?
Ms. Ellis:	I was worried about changing the context because I thought it would make them too excited. Sometimes excitement can be hard for us to handle, but they did a great job with it today! And when I heard students close to me talking about what the problem was about in the think, turn, and talk, I heard them clearly explain that there were 56 balls, you need to put them into 4 rows, and their partners responded, "I agree."

Ms. Kramer: And why do you think they knew what to do?

Ms. Ellis: I think reading the problem together helped them focus. Giving them wait time and think time gave them a chance to process it.

Ms. Kramer: [*Pointing to the directions in the launch script*] You gave clear, explicit directions. Those are complicated, multistep directions. You asked students not only to process steps in the think, turn, and talk, but also to understand the problem. Making the directions explicit really helped.

Figure 11.3 shows the notes they recorded from their reflection on the launch.

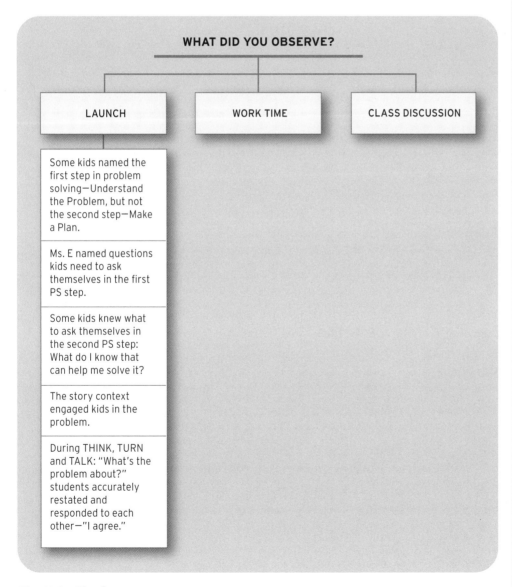

WHAT DID YOU OBSERVE?

| LAUNCH | WORK TIME | CLASS DISCUSSION |

LAUNCH

Some kids named the first step in problem solving—Understand the Problem, but not the second step—Make a Plan.

Ms. E named questions kids need to ask themselves in the first PS step.

Some kids knew what to ask themselves in the second PS step: What do I know that can help me solve it?

The story context engaged kids in the problem.

During THINK, TURN and TALK: "What's the problem about?" students accurately restated and responded to each other—"I agree."

Fig. 11.3. *Teacher observations of the lesson launch*

STOP+REFLECT

>> Why is making descriptive, nonjudgmental observations important? Why is it important that Ms. Kramer recorded their observations?

>> Ms. Ellis observes that her students were unfamiliar with the metacognitive problem-solving routine. How does she respond to this information?

>> In her planning, Ms. Ellis decided to change the problem context by relating it to the class study of the Mayans. At the time, she wondered whether it would distract her students from the mathematics of the problem. Upon reflection, she is surprised that the problem context was not distracting. Why might this be important to observe?

>> Why did the teachers explore what caused students to understand the directions during the think, turn, and talk?

Beginning the reflection with descriptive evidence of what happened in the lesson—what they saw and heard—gives Ms. Ellis accurate feedback. It also allows for productive inquiry and analysis of the teaching and learning rather than judgment of Ms. Ellis and her students. Focusing on descriptive observations supports Ms. Ellis in taking a stance of curiosity, risk taking, honesty, and openness to change. Recording their observations enables Ms. Ellis and Ms. Kramer to see patterns in the teaching and learning and to decide what merits more exploration.

After she shares her observation that the students did not know what questions to ask themselves during problem solving, Ms. Ellis reflects on what affected the learning experience of the students. She shifts her thinking to teaching moves that would cause her students to develop this knowledge about problem solving. She does not get defensive or look to blame her students for not remembering. Instead, Ms. Ellis identifies what was missing in her instruction: "I haven't gone over the problem-solving chart with them."

Ms. Ellis is pleasantly surprised that the modified problem context did not distract students from the mathematics but instead served to interest and engage them in the problem. Every day, teachers make important decisions about instruction, the outcomes of which are never certain. Reflective teachers, like Ms. Ellis, are mindful of those decisions and observe how they influence student learning. Changing the problem context was a decision with potentially significant consequences. Ms. Ellis keeps this in mind and makes a point to observe its effect on student learning.

When teachers analyze and document instructional moves that cause successful student thinking and work, they are more likely to remember and practice them. Through reflection, Ms. Ellis and Ms. Kramer determine that engaging the students meaningfully in the think, turn, and talk was crucial to a successful lesson launch. As they analyze what caused students to be productively engaged, they identify the think time and Ms. Ellis's delivery of clear, concise instructions. Upon further discussion, they note that Ms. Ellis's directions came from the launch script. The teachers agree that rehearsing important directions before the launch maximizes student learning.

What did you observe in the work time?

Ms. Ellis and Ms. Kramer agree that they have no concerns regarding class management during the work time, so they focus on assessing student work.

Deciding how to assess student work. Ms. Ellis and Ms. Kramer assess student work and share their observations of students at work during the lesson. This analysis is essential to assessing what students learned and informing next instructional moves. However, they are mindful of their limited time.

Ms. Ellis:	We have to decide how to assess student work. [*She looks over her Circle Map of lesson goals.*] We had three goals: solve division story problems, understand what it means to divide and how to interpret division notation, and develop metacognitive problem-solving skills.
Ms. Kramer:	Let's look back at what we said was important for us to observe as students worked. [See fig. 9.2.] Which of these would be most important for us to assess?
Ms. Ellis:	Let's look for strategies.
Ms. Kramer:	[*Nods in agreement*]

The teachers begin to sort through student work, focusing on strategies students used.

In their lesson planning, Ms. Ellis and Ms. Kramer intentionally aligned their learning goals with the division problem and what was important to observe as students solved the problem. They graphically recorded their goals and what was important to observe, making this information readily accessible. Doing so enables Ms. Ellis and Ms. Kramer to quickly scan the most important learning goal and the category of student work most closely connected to it. Here, they decide to assess the strategies students used, because the stategies will inform them of the reasoning students used to solve division story problems, the lesson's key learning goal.

Using observations of students at work to inform assessment of students' written work. Looking over student work, the teachers notice that some papers show clear evidence of how students solved the problem, but others do not. Here are two samples of student work from Ms. Ellis's class.

Caleb's work:

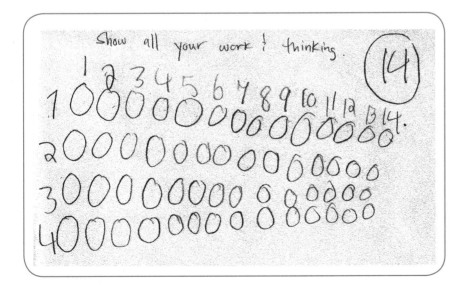

STOP + REFLECT

>> How did the teachers' lesson planning help them to efficiently decide which aspect of the student work was essential to assess?

Ava's work:

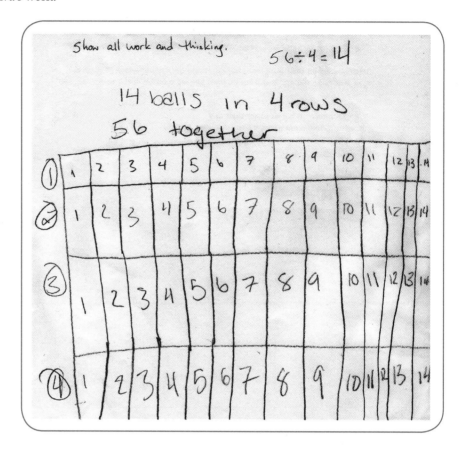

Ms. Ellis and Ms. Kramer cannot tell from the written work what tools or strategies students used, so they rely on their observations of students at work to assess students' approaches and strategies.

Ms. Ellis: So Max, Caleb, Ava, and Selena all used tiles, but in a slightly different way. [*She spreads their papers on the table.*] Ava counted out 56 tiles, started with two rows of 15, then made a third row of 15, and then a fourth row with only 11. So she had to adjust.

Ms. Kramer: So she dealt in chunks, like that strategy we talked about yesterday? Is that how you would describe it?

Ms. Ellis: I think she guessed—like, "Let me try 15 and see whether that works." Selena used the same strategy. Were you watching Caleb and Max?

Ms. Kramer: Yes. Caleb counted out 56 tiles and dealt them out by ones, four in each column. As he dealt, he kept track of his count—like 1, 2, 3, **4,** 5, 6, 7, **8** . . . Max also used the same "dealing by ones" strategy.

Ms. Ellis: Hiroshi and Sebastian were also probably dealing by ones. [*She gathers these papers and spreads them on the table.*] I know they didn't use tiles, so it looks like they used drawings to keep track of their dealing.

Sebastian's work:

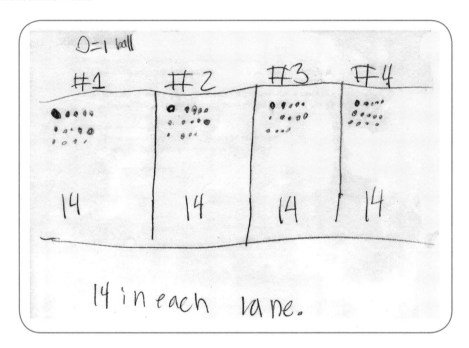

The teachers agree that Sebastian and Hiroshi also used a "dealing by ones" strategy, and the approach of using a drawing is more sophisticated than using tiles. They put these in a pile and sort through other papers to see whether other students used this strategy.

Ms. Ellis and Ms. Kramer are eager to know how students solved the problem. They approach this task with a genuine curiosity about how students think and what they know and understand. As they analyze student work, they look for similarities and differences and begin to sort student work according to the strategies students used.

Just by looking at the written work of these students, Ms. Ellis cannot tell with certainty whether the six students solved the problem by using tiles or by using a drawing. She also cannot assess what strategies they used, because their work lacks explicit representation of their reasoning. Her observations of students at work yield a more complete assessment of what they know and how they are thinking.

Caleb, Max, and Ava used the same tool (tiles) but different strategies. Caleb and Max dealt by ones, and Ava guessed and checked. Some students used the same strategy but with different tools. Caleb and Max dealt by ones using tiles, but Sebastian and Hiroshi dealt by ones and used a drawing.

STOP+ REFLECT

» What do you notice about the way the teachers discuss and analyze student work?

» How did Ms. Ellis's observations of students at work inform her assessment of their written work?

» What did these teachers learn about tools and strategies students used in their problem solving?

The teachers continue to reflect on what they observed during the work time. Ms. Ellis is surprised to hear that Max used a "dealing by ones" strategy. She remembers how confidently and skillfully Max shared his strategy at the class discussion of chunking 56 into smaller arrays by using tiles (see Max's work, chapter 10). She wonders how Max shifted his thinking to this more sophisticated idea.

Learning more about Max. Ms. Ellis asks Ms. Kramer to share what she observed as Max solved the division problem. They look at Max's paper. Ms. Kramer retells the story of her interaction with Max (see chapter 10). She explains how Max initially thought the problem was a multiplication problem, 56 × 4. She talks about the question she posed to facilitate his understanding of the problem and the problem context: "What does this answer mean?" She tells of how she prompted Max to check the reasonableness of his answer: "Does your answer make sense?" She continues to explain how she guided him to make a plan by activating his prior knowledge: "What do you know that can help you solve it?" She explains how he connected the story context to arrays and how he independently solved the problem with tiles. As she tells the story, she recalls not only her prompts but also Max's responses. Ms. Ellis wants to know more about Ms. Kramer's prompts.

Ms. Ellis:	What language did you use with Max to move him from counting the tiles by ones to chunking?
Ms. Kramer:	First I asked how he could check to see whether his answer was right. He started to count by ones. So I said, "Could you check in an easier way?" He asked, "Can I use friendly numbers?" So then he started to chunk the tiles. His face lit up and he said it was like the multiplication array game the students have been playing.
Ms. Ellis:	Oh, that's nice [*she takes notes on Ms. Kramer's prompts*].
Ms. Kramer:	[*Points to Max's paper to show how he chunked the tiles into 4 × 5, 4 × 7, and 4 × 2 arrays*] So I asked him to draw his arrays to show his work and thinking. When he drew the first array, 8 × 2, he checked it on his own and saw that it wasn't right. He crossed it out and drew the 4 × 5 array above it [*points to Max's paper*]:

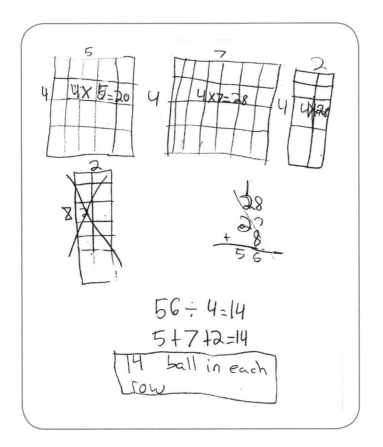

Ms. Ellis: I've got to tell you what a huge leap this is for Max. To work independently and to build on experiences he's had in math is huge for him. In our planning, when I said that some students would say, "I don't know what to do," I had Max in mind. He doesn't approach problems this independently.

Ms. Kramer: I also wonder whether reading comprehension is an issue for him. When I asked him to read the problem aloud, he read it very slowly. When he realized it was about putting the 56 balls into 4 rows, he made the connection to arrays.

Ms. Ellis: He is an English language learner. So are three other kids.

Ms. Kramer: Oh, that could explain why he didn't understand the problem!

Ms. Ellis: I should have previewed the problem with him before the lesson. So looking back at our planning, we didn't address the needs of the English language learners.

STOP+REFLECT

>> Max is an English language learner. What support enabled him to independently solve the problem?

>> What might have prompted Ms. Ellis to ask, "What language did you use with Max to move him from counting the tiles by ones to chunking?"

>> When Ms. Ellis learns that Max did not understand the problem, how does she respond? What does she discover about their lesson planning?

When English language learners struggle to learn a new language, others often underestimate their ability to think. Ms. Kramer did not know that Max was an English language learner, but she interacted with him as she would with any other student: She supported him to think through his problem-solving process. When Ms. Kramer asked Max, "What does this answer mean?" and "Does your answer make sense?" she prompted him to think about monitoring his work and checking the reasonableness of his answer.

When she realized that Max did not understand the problem, Ms. Kramer gave him time to reread it, focusing his attention on the sequence of actions. The story-problem context was accessible to Max because it was about the Mayan culture, a topic in which the whole class was interested and engaged. The problem also had an accessible mathematical context—putting 56 balls into 4 rows relates to arrays, a model Max had explored. Ms. Kramer activated his prior knowledge to help him make that connection: "What do you know that can help you solve it?" Supplying manipulatives enabled Max to solve the problem by modeling the situation. Other questions such as "How can you check your work?" and "Could you check in an easier way?" prompted Max to connect what he knows about decomposing arrays into friendly chunks and this new idea that division is related to multiplication.

Although using concise, accurate mathematical language is fundamental to all students' developing understanding of mathematics, Ms. Ellis knows that such language is essential for English language learners and struggling learners. She recognizes that Ms. Kramer's questions were not only concise but also effective in scaffolding Max's learning. She wants to add these questions to her notes so she will remember to use them in future interactions with students. Ms. Ellis's desire to learn from a colleague shows her curiosity, openness to change, and commitment to students.

When Ms. Ellis learns that Max did not understand the problem, she thinks about what affected this learning experience. Why did he not understand? She shifts her thinking to what would cause him to understand: "I should have previewed the problem with him before the lesson." She also looks back to their lesson plan and discovers what's missing: "We didn't address the needs of the English language learners." This brief analysis, based on a colleague's observation of Max at work, will inform Ms. Ellis's action planning later in the reflection.

So far, Ms. Ellis and Ms. Kramer have assessed the work of students who used tiles to solve the problem. They sort these papers into three piles: dealing by ones, dealing by ones and then chunking with support, and guessing and checking. They look at other work and notice that several students have started by using a multiplying-by-tens strategy, demonstrating an understanding of the distributive property. These students have recorded their thinking with equations, like Jordan:

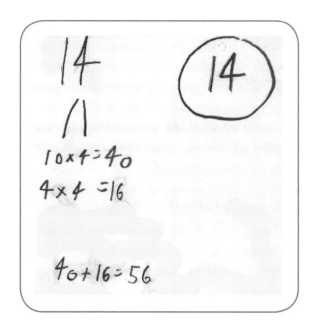

Ms. Ellis and Ms. Kramer put these multiplying-by-tens strategies in a pile and wonder what strategies they predicted students would use. Reviewing their chart of what to observe as students work, they see that they predicted students would use deal by ones; deal by ones, then chunk into friendly numbers; build arrays of friendly numbers, then reason; and multiply by 10. They discover students are using other strategies the teachers did not predict. Scanning other work, they notice that two students used the division algorithm. Ms. Ellis comments that they know the procedure but do not understand it. She places them in a separate pile.

As Ms. Ellis and Ms. Kramer continue to assess student work, they notice that two students have used a similar strategy of guessing and checking with equations.

Assessing student work: Using equations to guess and check. The teachers now analyze how students used equations to guess and check.

Ms. Ellis:	It looks like Isaiah first tried 15. He added 15 and 15 and got 30, and then he added 30 and 30 and got 60. That didn't work, so he crossed out 15. Then he tried 14. He added 14 and 14 and got 28, and then doubled 28 and got 56.
Ms. Kramer:	Would we put them in a category of guessing and checking? It's similar to Selena's strategy, but she used tiles.
Ms. Ellis:	It is the same strategy. But using equations to guess and check is a more advanced approach.

Ms. Kramer agrees. For now, they add Isaiah's and Selena's work to the guessing-and-checking pile.

Isaiah's work:

Ms. Kramer and Ms. Ellis scan the papers, looking for evidence of students' strategies and reasoning. When they identify one student's strategy, such as dealing by ones, they scan all student work, looking for that same strategy. They discuss and analyze each work sample, adding any observations of students at work to inform their assessment. They continue this process of sorting student work by strategy.

When they finish assessing student work, the teachers look at their sorted piles. They record the strategies on their chart and the number of students who used that strategy. If you decide to record your students' strategies in a chart, writing students' names next to the strategy they used could help you keep track of assessment data. Visually accessible data are easier to use and refer to when deciding what instruction your students need next.

So far, Ms. Ellis and Ms. Kramer have spent most of their reflection time assessing student work—as it should be. Assessing student work is the most important part of lesson reflection. If your time for lesson reflection is limited, focus on assessing student work.

Ms. Ellis and Ms. Kramer reflect on the sequence of events in the class discussion. They discuss how both students, Max and Sofia, shared their strategies with clarity and accuracy. They recall that the think, turn, and talk ("Is this problem multiplication or division?") gave all students time to think and verbalize their reasoning. Recalling the class discussion, Ms. Kramer and Ms. Ellis conclude that the students understand the relationship between multiplication and division.

Continuing to reflect on the class discussion, Ms. Ellis and Ms. Kramer revisit the students' responses to Ms. Ellis's question: "What does $56 \div 4 = 14$ mean?" Students have a variety of interpretations, including "How many groups of 4 are in 56?" (quotative division) and "How many are in each group if you divide 56 into 4 groups?" (partitive division).

Ms. Ellis and Ms. Kramer record their observations of the class discussion on their chart and end this part of the reflection (fig. 11.4):

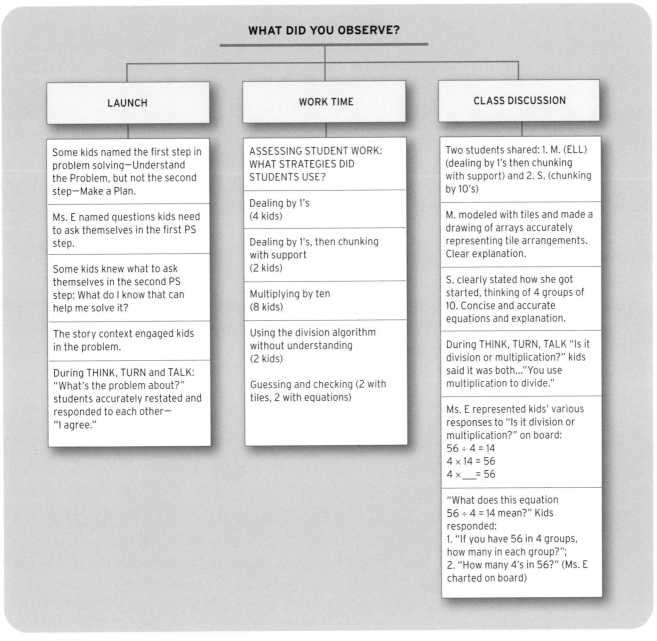

WHAT DID YOU OBSERVE?

LAUNCH

Some kids named the first step in problem solving—Understand the Problem, but not the second step—Make a Plan.

Ms. E named questions kids need to ask themselves in the first PS step.

Some kids knew what to ask themselves in the second PS step: What do I know that can help me solve it?

The story context engaged kids in the problem.

During THINK, TURN and TALK: "What's the problem about?" students accurately restated and responded to each other— "I agree."

WORK TIME

ASSESSING STUDENT WORK: WHAT STRATEGIES DID STUDENTS USE?

Dealing by 1's
(4 kids)

Dealing by 1's, then chunking with support
(2 kids)

Multiplying by ten
(8 kids)

Using the division algorithm without understanding
(2 kids)

Guessing and checking (2 with tiles, 2 with equations)

CLASS DISCUSSION

Two students shared: 1. M. (ELL) (dealing by 1's then chunking with support) and 2. S. (chunking by 10's)

M. modeled with tiles and made a drawing of arrays accurately representing tile arrangements. Clear explanation.

S. clearly stated how she got started, thinking of 4 groups of 10. Concise and accurate equations and explanation.

During THINK, TURN, TALK "Is it division or multiplication?" kids said it was both..."You use multiplication to divide."

Ms. E represented kids' various responses to "Is it division or multiplication?" on board:
$56 \div 4 = 14$
$4 \times 14 = 56$
$4 \times \underline{\quad} = 56$

"What does this equation $56 \div 4 = 14$ mean?" Kids responded:
1. "If you have 56 in 4 groups, how many in each group?";
2. "How many 4's in 56?" (Ms. E charted on board)

Fig. 11.4. *Completed chart of observations*

STOP+REFLECT

>> Why do Ms. Ellis and Ms. Kramer record their observations of what happened in the class discussion?

Documenting observations of the class discussion creates data about student work and thinking that can inform Ms. Ellis's future lesson planning. Ms. Ellis can use it to keep track of students whose work has been shared at class discussions. Doing so enables her to make sure that she does not always call on the same students. She can also keep track of students' big ideas, connections, and misconceptions. This information reminds her of what important ideas students need to develop further. This documentation is also a record of her teaching. She can reflect on it later to assess her growth.

So far, Ms. Ellis and Ms. Kramer have completed the first part of lesson reflection: evidence review, framed by the question "What did you observe about students' learning experiences and written work?" Ms. Ellis and Ms. Kramer noted their observations of students at work, identified any surprises or interactions that stood out for them, and assessed student written work.

Lesson Analysis: What affected the learning experience of the students?

In the evidence review, Ms. Ellis and Ms. Kramer also analyzed surprises and interactions that stood out for them. They explored causes and effects of those events in the division lesson. For example, they analyzed what caused Max to understand the problem and how this understanding affected his ability to solve the problem independently. This part of the lesson reflection is called lesson analysis, guided by the question "What affected the learning experience of the students?"

Skillful teachers continually reflect on how their instruction affects student interactions and learning. They also assess whether their instruction advances student learning. This analysis, as well as their analysis of student work, informs both their instructional decisions and decisions about how to improve their teaching. Thinking about causes and effects of moments in teaching and learning occurs throughout lesson reflection.

STOP+REFLECT

>> Think of a moment in your teaching that surprised you or stood out. What caused that event? How did it affect student learning?

Action planning

In this last part of lesson reflection, action planning, see whether you can identify other moments when the teachers analyze the impact of their instruction on student learning. What changes do they plan to make in their instruction as a result of their analysis?

Ms. Ellis and Ms. Kramer are guided by the key question "What actions can you take to improve your instruction and advance student learning?" (fig. 11.2).

Ms. Ellis has been thinking about Max ever since hearing how he misunderstood the problem at the beginning of the work time. Max and her other English language learners are on her mind.

How can the lesson be improved?

Ms. Ellis:	In thinking about Max, Mia, Diego, and Caleb (all English language learners), I think it's important for me to check in with them in the beginning of the work time to make sure they understand the problem. I'd have them restate to me what the problem is about, what they have to find out, and what they know that can help them solve it.
Ms. Kramer:	What about previewing the problems with them before the launch?
Ms. Ellis:	That's a good idea. I'm not sure that it's necessary for all problems, but I'll keep that in mind.
Ms. Ellis:	[*Continues to reflect on different aspects of the lesson*] I thought the problems were appropriate for all the kids. They were engaged and had materials that made the task accessible. I could have done more work with the problem-solving steps and what questions problem solvers ask themselves.

Ms. Ellis and Ms. Kramer talk about how teaching students to transfer these metacognitive problem-solving skills requires scaffolded instruction over weeks of lessons (see chapter 6). They agree that reinforcing these skills should happen in every lesson, not just this lesson on division. They decide to address problem solving in their discussion about planning next instructional steps for students.

Ms. Ellis and Ms. Kramer note that the students did productive work related to the learning goals. They do not recommend any changes in the lesson because the launch, work time, and class discussion went smoothly.

What are the next instructional steps for students?

As they consider next instructional steps for students, Ms. Ellis talks about how she plans to teach and reinforce the metacognitive problem-solving routine. Recently, she introduced the problem-solving routine to her students with a chart of the steps and questions students should ask themselves as they problem solve. However, she realizes that she has not used this tool frequently because it hangs in an obscure place. Ms. Ellis realizes that if she wants her students to learn and transfer this thinking to their problem solving, she has to first make it visually explicit. She decides to display the chart in front of the meeting area. She also decides to make individual charts for students to keep in their notebooks.

Ms. Ellis knows that students will develop metacognitive and self-monitoring problem-solving skills only if she teaches the routine with fidelity and frequency. She states that she will be more deliberate about helping students learn and apply these questions to their problem solving in every math class.

STOP+REFLECT

» Why is reflecting on how you can improve the lesson important?

» How could you keep track of changes you want to make in your lessons so that you remember them the next time you teach the lesson?

Ms. Ellis and Ms. Kramer now focus on their piles of student work. They also look at their chart of student strategies. As they consider next instructional steps, they wonder how to give more support to the students who dealt by ones. Ms. Ellis and Ms. Kramer want to move them from dealing by ones to building arrays by using a chunking-by-tens strategy. Do they explore this idea further in a minilesson with all students? Just the group who dealt by ones? They look at their "What Did You Observe?" chart and notice that only eight students used a chunking-by-tens (a "times ten") strategy. Most students need tasks that would develop their understanding of how to use this strategy to solve division problems. However, Ms. Ellis and Ms. Kramer also note that this is a big idea that students develop over time in their division unit. They decide to continue to explore this idea of using the times-ten strategy and partial products with all students as they continue with the unit.

STOP+REFLECT

>> How did the teachers' technique of assessing student work help them plan next instructional steps for students?

What teaching practices/moves supported student learning?

As Ms. Ellis and Ms. Kramer consider what teaching moves supported student learning, they think about moves that caused constructive shifts in students' learning. Ms. Ellis thinks about the questions and prompts they posed to students as they worked.

Ms. Ellis:	When you asked the students to check their work, it reminded them of the problem-solving process and what they should do when they're finished with a problem. I also liked your question "Could you check in an easier way?" because it pushed students to be more efficient and moved them from counting on to multiplying.
Ms. Kramer:	I heard you asking, "What do these numbers mean?" You rooted students in the context of the problem (putting 56 balls into 4 rows). That question really helped them make sense of the problem.
Ms. Ellis:	I also think that giving explicit directions in the launch gave them smooth entry into the task. That's why their work was so productive.

STOP+REFLECT

>> Why is it important to identify practices and moves that supported student learning ?

>> What practices and moves of yours support student learning? What evidence do you see of their effects?

Ms. Ellis and Ms. Kramer move to the next question in action planning. Only Ms. Ellis reflects on this question because she taught the lesson. However, she shares her thinking with Ms. Kramer.

How can you improve your teaching?

Ms. Ellis reflects for a moment to generalize from the lesson only one aspect of her teaching she would like to improve. She says, without hesitation, "I have to support my English language learners. I need to be more cognizant of their needs."

What actions will you take to improve your teaching?

Ms. Ellis brainstorms actions she will take to be more cognizant of her English language learners. Ms. Ellis has learned about meeting the needs of English language learners, so she readily identifies actions that will support her particular group of students.

Ms. Kramer:	What are some actions you can take to be more cognizant of your English language learners?
Ms. Ellis:	I can preview problems before the launch.
Ms. Kramer:	That will help them learn any unfamiliar vocabulary in the problems. Previewing will make the problems more accessible.
Ms. Ellis:	They also need accessible problem contexts. And I can give the students opportunities to explain their thinking and ideas.

Many teachers know what practices advance student learning, but they assume that because they know it, they practice it. This is not always so. For example, most teachers know that giving wait time is essential to student learning, yet in practice, they often do not. The only way you can know whether you are "walking the talk" with your practice is to get feedback on your teaching. Ms. Ellis gets feedback from a colleague who observed her lesson and joins her in reflecting. The end of this chapter lists more ways for you to get feedback on your teaching.

Ms. Ellis and Ms. Kramer are now finished with the last part of their lesson reflection, action planning. They documented their decisions about how to advance student learning and improve instruction as they reflected on each question. Figure 11.5 shows what they recorded.

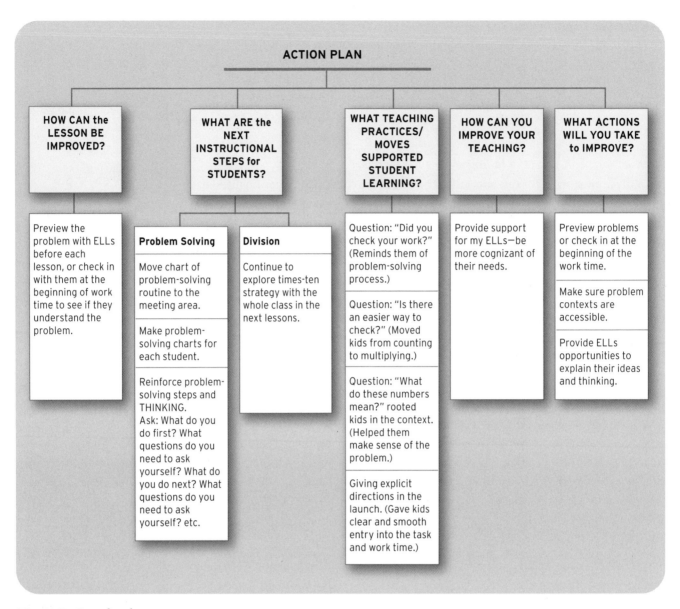

Fig. 11.5. *Completed action planning chart*

OTHER WAYS TO GET FEEDBACK ON YOUR TEACHING

This chapter presented a model of collaborative lesson reflection, in which Ms. Ellis had the benefit of getting feedback on her teaching from her colleague. However, Ms. Ellis, like most teachers, does not have the structures in her school to allow for such collaborative work on a regular basis. Ms. Ellis must rely on getting feedback on her teaching in other ways. If you are in a similar situation, think creatively about getting feedback on your teaching. The following are some suggestions.

Videotape or audiotape your lesson

Recording your lesson (video or audio) enables you to get feedback on your launch, student work time, and class discussion. You may decide to replay parts of the lesson that are important to you. For example, if you are trying to improve your launches by making student expectations clear and concise, you may want to listen to only that part of the lesson. Or you may want to more closely listen to students' explanations of how they solved a problem so you can better understand what they know, what strategies they are using, or what misconceptions they have.

Invite a colleague to observe parts of your lesson

If scheduling constraints prohibit colleagues from observing your whole lesson, choose a part of the lesson on which feedback is most important to you. Tell your colleague what you would like him or her to observe so that the feedback will be focused, purposeful, and more likely to guide your instruction in constructive ways. Feedback in the form of descriptive observations is essential. As you reflect on observations of moments that surprise or stand out, inquire, discuss, and analyze. What caused this to happen? What are the effects on student learning? What do I wish had happened, and how could I cause that to happen?

Assess student work with colleagues

When you and your colleagues collect common work samples and analyze them together, you can learn much about your students' math proficiency and your own instruction. Your students' work reflects your teaching. For example, if your students do not represent their reasoning and strategies in writing, you probably have not taught them to do so. You may not realize the extent to which students can show their work and thinking until you see work samples from other classes. Conversely, you may discover that your students' work does show evidence of their strategies and thinking.

Assessing student work with colleagues offers opportunities to get feedback on your teaching in other ways. When teachers assess student work together, they usually discuss other related aspects of their instruction: how they introduced the task, how they grouped students, what materials they used, and what questions and prompts supported students as they worked. Hearing from colleagues about effective practices gives you an opportunity to ask yourself, "Is this a practice I use in my work? If not, what changes in my teaching can I make to implement it?"

CONCLUSION

Throughout lesson reflection, Ms. Ellis demonstrated and modeled dispositions of a successful mathematics teacher. She approached her work with curiosity, risk taking, openness to change, and commitment to her students. Most important, she assumed the stance of a learner. She was eager to learn how her students reasoned mathematically. She welcomed feedback and fearlessly analyzed how her instruction influenced her students' learning. She was open to making changes in her teaching to better advance her students' development of math ideas.

This chapter focused on all parts of lesson reflection. When you start to reflect on lessons, focus on the most important aspects:

Evidence review

Assess student work and review your observations of students at work. This is the most important aspect of lesson reflection: It informs you about whether students learned what you intended them to learn and about what next instructional steps will advance their learning.

Lesson analysis

Identify one or two moments in the lesson that surprised you or stood out. Analyze the causes and effects of those moments.

Action planning

Plan next instructional steps. If unsure how to proceed, consult with colleagues, a math coach, or a curriculum specialist. Implement a change in your instruction that you may have identified when you analyzed causes and effects of the moment that surprised or stood out.

* * *

As you gain experience teaching, you can use the questions in the reflection framework to guide your thinking. The more consistently you use them to reflect on your practice, the more familiar they will become. This approach will become more intentional as you develop the habits of a skillful and reflective mathematics teacher.

IV

Essential Elements of Effective Mathematics Teaching

Section IV gives more detailed information about essential elements of teaching: classroom discourse, assessment, differentiation, homework, technology, and building family-school partnerships.

Chapter 12 describes engaging students in productive mathematical discourse. Chapter 13 explains how to assess students' understanding of mathematical ideas and give students feedback that enhances their learning. Chapter 14 offers strategies to differentiate math instruction, emphasizing how to meet the needs of English language learners and struggling learners. Finally, chapter 15 explains how to plan purposeful homework that supports student learning.

Available online at this book's More4U site, two chapters offer more resources. These bonus chapters explore how technology can support students' math learning and offer strategies to create family-school math partnerships.

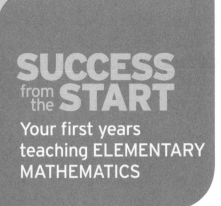

chapter twelve

Mathematical Discourse

Guiding Principles

LEARNING IS MAXIMIZED WHEN STUDENTS—

>> interact in a safe, supportive learning community;

>> activate and build on prior knowledge;

>> process information both visually and linguistically;

>> solve problems with meaningful contexts;

>> engage in reflection, self-monitoring, and metacognition; and

>> engage in complex thinking.

All students need opportunities to discuss their mathematical thinking with others. When students regularly share their mathematical ideas and representations with peers and make sense of the ideas and representations of others, they make more mathematical connections and deepen their understanding. Chapters 1 and 9 gave examples of elementary students engaged in rich mathematical discourse. In this chapter you will learn more about how to foster and facilitate mathematical discourse in your own classroom.

Mathematical discourse supports students' learning in four ways:

1 Communicating and representing mathematical ideas help students both process new ideas and clarify their thinking. As students talk, represent, and write about mathematical ideas, they process the ideas more deeply. As students explain their strategies and reasoning, they can listen to themselves and reflect on whether their ideas make sense. When students have repeated opportunities to use mathematical vocabulary, they become more precise in their communication and in their thinking.

2 Hearing and seeing other students' explanations and representations deepens students' understanding. When students are exposed to the strategies and representations of their peers, they gain access to new ways of thinking about problems. When they see different strategies and representations presented side by side, they are more likely to notice connections between them. When students hear and see concepts expressed in several ways, they develop deeper understandings.

3 Listening to students' understandings and misconceptions helps teachers assess student learning. When teachers ask students to explain and represent their thinking, teachers develop more awareness of what students truly understand and where students have misconceptions or confusions.

4 Discourse shapes thinking. How students communicate about mathematics influences how they think about mathematics. When students regularly participate in mathematical discussions within a community of learners, they develop important habits of mathematical thinking, such as the following:

- Recalling and explaining the thinking behind an answer or idea
- Using models and representations to solve problems and explain ideas
- Looking for patterns and relationships
- Using reasoning to determine whether answers and ideas make sense
- Making generalizations and justifying them

At its heart, fostering and facilitating mathematical discourse is about communicating with students to understand and support their thinking, rather than hoping to merely transmit your thinking to them.

Mathematical discourse refers to both the talk and the visual representations used to communicate thinking. Chapter 2 emphasized the importance of making mathematics and mathematical thinking visual to help students make sense of it. Students develop more complex networks of connected knowledge when ideas and information are communicated both linguistically and nonlinguistically. That chapter also highlighted three ways to make mathematics and mathematical thinking visual:

1 By making models and other math materials available for students to use when solving problems and explaining their thinking

2 By hanging vocabulary charts and strategy charts where students can see and refer to them

3 By recording students' strategies and ideas during discussions

As you read this chapter, keep in mind the need to also support thinking visually.

Engaging students in productive math discourse is complex work. It requires asking open-ended questions to prompt students to reveal their strategies, their reasoning, and their misconceptions. It requires understanding and recording students' strategies and ideas. It requires engaging students in understanding and responding to each other's thinking. Fortunately, these are skills that you can learn.

Essential Practices

>> Develop productive discourse patterns for your classroom.

>> Ask questions that elicit student thinking.

>> Make mathematical thinking visual.

>> Foster broad participation and rich discussion.

>> Teach students explicit behaviors and language for math discussions

DEVELOP PRODUCTIVE DISCOURSE PATTERNS FOR YOUR CLASSROOM

Much discourse in math classrooms follows two familiar patterns: IRE (initiate–respond–evaluate) and funneling.

In IRE, a teacher asks a question, a student answers, and the teacher evaluates whether the answer is correct. It can sound like this:

Teacher:	What is the answer to 5×18?
Student:	90.
Teacher:	Good.

Or this:

Teacher:	What is the answer to 5×18?
Student 1:	80.
Teacher:	[*Pause*] Not quite. Does anyone have a different answer?
Student 2:	90.
Teacher:	Yes.

Teachers engaging in IRE focus only on the correctness of an answer and do not draw out the thinking behind either correct or incorrect answers. These conversations generally do not invite broad or active participation. They often occur without giving students much wait time and reward students who give correct answers quickly. Students who need more time or who make mistakes may become discouraged and stop trying.

When funneling (Herbal-Eisenmann and Breyfogle, 2005), a teacher asks follow-up questions in response to a student's idea or answer. However, instead of genuinely probing the student's thinking, the questions funnel student responses in the way that the teacher is thinking:

Teacher:	What is the answer to 5×18?
Student:	80.
Teacher:	Hmm, let's think about that. What is 5×10?
Student:	50.
Teacher:	What is 5×8?
Student:	Um, 40?
Teacher:	So, what would 5×18 be?
Student:	Um . . .
Teacher:	Well, what is 50 plus 40?
Student:	90?

Teachers who funnel do most of the talking and thinking. Although the teacher may appear to be offering helpful scaffolding, this is often not the case. The student may guess rather than genuinely follow the logic of the teacher's thinking. The teacher may ask less demanding questions as she works to help the student give the correct answer. For example, the question the student answers is "What is 50 plus 40?" This is a much easier question than "What is 5×18?" Used often, funneling encourages passive learning and makes assessment difficult. Teachers do not find out what misconceptions or mistakes are causing students' errors.

Teachers need productive patterns of discourse around mathematics to engage all students in mathematical discussions and to gain accurate assessment information. Teachers need questions and responses that draw out students' mathematical thinking rather than evaluate or funnel it. Students need opportunities to understand and explore mistakes without feeling criticized. Both teachers and students need ways to think and talk about math as a subject that involves more than finding the correct answers to problems.

ASK QUESTIONS THAT ELICIT STUDENT THINKING

Most math conversations, whether with individual students or groups, begin with a question. As chapter 8 described, questions you ask should be related to your lesson goals and the mathematics that you want students to learn. However, you need not craft new questions for every lesson. Some questions are useful for many different math conversations, to elicit and support important types of mathematical thinking.

Although the following are not the only questions that facilitate productive math conversations, they are good ones to start with. Asking these questions regularly will engage students in habits of mathematical thinking. You will gather information about what students understand and do not understand. And you will develop a culture in which students expect to share their thinking and learn from the thinking of others.

"What do you notice about _____?"

Examine the following dialogue between a fourth-grade teacher and her students.

> *Teacher:* This is a picture of some colored tiles in a bag. Take a look at the picture and think about what you notice. [*Gives about one minute of wait time*] Now tell your partner what you see.

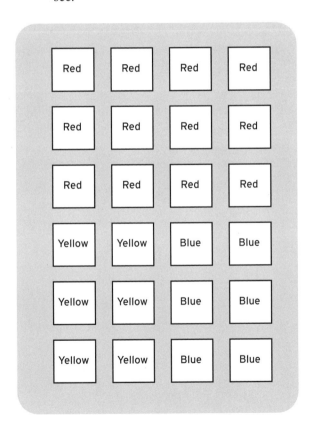

Students turn to their partners, share what they noticed, and then when asked, turn back toward the teacher.

> *Teacher:* [*To the class*] What did you notice?
>
> *Amber:* Yellow is one-fourth of the shape.
>
> *Janaya:* Four groups with six in each group.

> Darnell: If this was probability, the chances of landing on red would be more likely.

> Chris: Yellow and blue are less likely to be picked if they were in a bag because red has more.

> Addie: If you put them in a bag, the chance of picking a yellow or a blue are equally likely.

This teacher is beginning a lesson on probability, a topic his students have been studying. During the lesson students are going to pull tiles out of a bag like the one he shows on the board. Before they begin, he wants students to notice and think about the proportion of tiles of each color. By asking students, "What do you notice?" instead of telling them what he wants them to notice, the teacher quickly and more effectively engages his students in thinking about the math of the lesson. He also gathers information about what his students remember and understand that he can build on.

The question "What do you notice?" prompts students to attend to and consider a problem, strategy, or representation more carefully. It is a low-risk question that invites students to share their observations and thoughts without fear of being wrong. It is also a good conversation starter.

Teachers often ask, "What do you notice?" and variations of this question when launching a lesson or when working with a student who is stuck. When asking these questions, give students time to generate multiple ideas. You can follow up by asking, "What else do you notice?" or "What else do you know?"

"How did you figure that out?" or "Why do you think that?"

> Teacher: What is 5×18?

> Student 1: 90.

> Teacher: How did you figure that out?

> Student 1: Well, I split the 18 into a 10 and an 8. I know that 5×10 is 50, and I know that 5×8 is 40. Then I added 50 plus 40 and I got 90.

* * *

> Teacher: What is 5×18?

> Student 2: 80.

> Teacher: How did you figure that out?

> Student 2: I know that 10×18 is 180. Because 5 is half of 10, I did half of 180. Half of 180 is, um, wait . . . is 90. Oh, I was wrong—the answer is 90, not 80.

Above, the teacher asks, "How did you figure it out?" after students give both correct and incorrect answers. She asks the question in the same matter-of-fact tone and with the same sense of curiosity regardless of whether students' answers are correct. By responding in the same way to both correct and incorrect answers, she makes it safe for students to reveal their thinking and gives students the opportunity to determine whether their answers make sense.

"How did you figure that out?" is one of the most important math questions that you can ask. It draws out student thinking instead of funneling it. When students explain their solutions to problems, they reveal the reasoning, mathematical relationships, and tools they use to solve problems. They make their thinking available to others, and they become more aware of their own thinking, often catching mistakes in the process.

You can ask "How did you figure that out?" and a similar question, "Why do you think that?" whenever students share their answers to problems or state a mathematical idea. At first, students may have difficulty explaining their solutions. They may not be aware of their own thought processes or unsure of how to communicate them to others. You can help your students with questions and prompts such as the following:

- "How did you get started?"
- "Did you use any tools or materials to help you?"
- "Did you break apart any of the numbers?"
- "Show me how you used the one hundred chart."
- "Tell me how you counted."

"How are these similar? How are they different?"

Ms. Davis:	How is Tiffany's strategy similar to Michael's strategy? Crystal?
Crystal:	They both did tens and ones.
Ms. Davis:	Can you say more about how they both used tens and ones?
Crystal:	They both split numbers into tens and ones. Tiffany wrote 40 and 6 and 30 and 7. Timmy drew 4 ten sticks and 6 ones and 3 ten sticks and 7 ones.
Ms. Davis:	How else are the strategies similar? Thomas?
Thomas:	They both used addition.
Ms. Davis:	Are they similar in any other ways? Andre?
Andre:	I know a way they are different.
Ms. Davis:	How are they different?

Andre:	Michael used the hundred chart and Tiffany didn't.
Ms. Davis:	That's true, but let's keep talking about how these are the same. Hannah? How do you think these strategies are the same?
Hannah:	Most of it is the same. They mostly have the same numbers. But Michael drew tens and ones and Tiffany just did numbers.

The teacher in this vignette wants her students to notice connections between two strategies that have been shared. By asking for similarities and by calling on multiple students to answer the question, Ms. Davis prompts her students to notice many significant connections.

"How are they similar?" and "How are they different?" are powerful questions. They engage students in complex thinking. They help students develop the habit of looking for connections and relationships. If you purposely choose two or three pieces of student work to share in your whole-class discussions and then ask the class to compare the strategies, students will pay more attention to the strategies of their peers and will notice more connections.

You can use questions like these to help students notice connections among representations and among problem types:

- How is _____ (what Alicia just did with the cubes) similar to _____ (what Tajik did with his fingers)?
- How is _____ (Sam's drawing of groups of 8) similar to _____ (Cassie's array)? How is it different?
- How is _____ (this problem about balloons) similar to _____ (yesterday's problem about snakes)?

"Why do you think that works? Do you think it will always work?"

Teacher:	What is 5 × 18?
Student:	80.
Teacher:	How did you figure that out?
Student:	I know that 10 × 18 is 180. Because 5 is half of 10, I did half of 180. Half of 180 is, um, wait . . . is 90. Oh, I was wrong—the answer is 90, not 80.
Teacher:	So you used 10 × 18 to help you figure out 5 × 18?
Student:	Yeah.

Teacher:	Why do you think that works? Why is 5 × 18 the same as half of 10 × 18?
Student:	Well, it's like . . . 5 times 18 is . . . 18 . . . 36 . . . 54 . . . um . . . 72 . . . 90. On your way to ten times a number, you get five times the number . . . and if you do two of those, you get ten times the number.
Teacher:	That's an interesting idea. So two sets of five times a number is the same as ten times that number? Hmm. Do you think your strategy will always work? Could you use 10 × 25 to figure out 5 × 25?
Student:	I think so: [*Pauses to think*] . . . 10 × 25 is 250 . . . half of 200 is 100 . . . half of 50 is 25 . . . that's 125. I'll check: 5 × 25 is 25, 50, 75, 100, 125. Yeah, it works.
Teacher:	Do you think your strategy will work for other numbers too? Will five times a number always be half of ten times that number?

Above, a student explains how she figured out the answer to 5 × 18. Her method surprises the teacher. This approach is not something the teacher has taught anyone in the class. The teacher probes the student's thinking by asking why she thinks the method works. The student responds by skip-counting by 18s five times. She then makes a generalization: "On your way to ten times a number, you get five times the number . . . and if you do two of those, you get ten times the number." The teacher follows up by asking the student whether she thinks the strategy will always work and asks her to try her strategy with a different number. The student solves 5 × 25 by finding half of 250 and then checks her answer by skip-counting by 25s.

Asking students to explain why computation methods work and whether they will always work or why patterns occur and whether they will always occur engages students in reasoning and proof, a form of complex thinking. The questions "Why do you think that works?" and "Do you think that will always work?" push students to make generalizations and justify them. As students do, they explore the structures of mathematics and deepen their understanding.

Your students will notice patterns and develop shortcuts. Ask them why they think the patterns occur or why they think their strategies work, and whether they think they will always occur or always work:

- When you add 10 to a number, why does the ones digit stay the same? Will that always happen?

- Why is 742 the biggest number you can make with the digits 7, 4, and 2? Will putting the digits in order from largest to smallest always give you the biggest number? Why?

- Why is $\frac{3}{8}$ greater than $\frac{3}{10}$? If two fractions have the same numerator, will the fraction with the smaller denominator always be greater? Why?

Do not answer these questions for your students. These questions engage students in the habits of looking for patterns and relationships and developing generalizations and justifying them. If you supply your reasoning, you are likely to short-circuit theirs. Instead, model curiosity. Say, "I wonder why that works. There must be a reason. We'll have to keep thinking about this. Let me know if you figure anything out or if this works with other numbers." Then walk away and let your students continue to think. Minutes, hours, or even days later, students will come back to you with their thoughts.

MAKE MATHEMATICAL THINKING VISUAL

Previous chapters emphasized the need to make student thinking visual. Doing so is especially important during whole-class discussions. Without visual representations, students will have difficulty making their own thinking clear and following the ideas of others. Before class discussions, make sure that any references that might be helpful for students, such as vocabulary charts, strategy charts, number lines, or lists of student ideas from recent lessons, are hanging where all students can see them. Also, make sure that you have enough board space to clearly record the new ideas, strategies, vocabulary, and representations that will be shared in the upcoming lesson. If you think students might benefit from using physical materials or virtual manipulatives to show their thinking, make sure these are accessible.

During class discussions, try to record as clearly as possible the important information shared. Doing so is harder than it would appear. Many teachers who are working hard to understand and record their students' ideas end up recording information in messy and haphazard ways. By the end of the lesson, the board is a jumble of mathematical terms, diagrams, equations, and half-erased statements. Instead, plan what type of information you will need to record and where on the board you can record it.

Accurately recording students' strategies with equations and representations may be hard at first. Some strategies that your students use will be new to you. Be patient with yourself. During discussions, try to record what students say as faithfully as you can. Later, when you have time to reflect, think about whether your recording was clear and concise. If not, ask your colleagues or look in your curriculum materials for ideas about how to record strategies more clearly.

To support all students in understanding the thinking of their classmates, try to develop consistent names for strategies and consistent ways of recording them. Whenever possible, rewrite the most important ideas and strategies that emerge from a discussion on a piece of chart paper to help students recall and refer to that information in future lessons. Here is an example of how a teacher makes his students' thinking visual during a class discussion.

Today's Number

Mr. Becker is conducting the Today's Number routine with his class. He has asked his students to think of equations that equal 28. He now calls on students to share their equations.

Mr. Becker: Brandon?

Brandon: 10 + 10 + 8 equals 28.

Mr. Becker: [*Writes 10 + 10 + 8 = 28 on the board*] Brandon, how did you figure out that 10 plus 10 plus 8 equals 28?

Brandon: I know that 10 plus 10 is 20, and 20 plus 8 equals 28.

Mr. Becker draws two lines connecting the 10s and writes 20 underneath. He writes 20 + 8 next to the original equation:

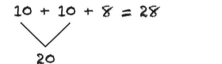

Mr. Becker: Brianna?

Brianna: 20 + 4 + 4.

Mr. Becker: [*Writes 20 + 4 + 4 = 28*] Brianna, how did you know that 20 plus 4 plus 4 equals 28?

Brianna: I know that 4 plus 4 is 8, and 20 and 8 equals 28.

Mr. Becker adds two lines connecting the 4s and writes 8 below them. He writes 20 + 8 = 28 next to the original equation:

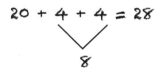

Mr. Becker: Eddie?

Eddie: 32 − 5.

Mr. Becker: 32 minus 5. [*Writes 32 − 5 = 28 on the board; several students raise their hands.*] Eddie, how did you figure that out?

Eddie: I counted back on my fingers [*holds out the fingers on one hand and touches each one as he says the following numbers*]: 32, 31, 30, 29, 28.

Mr. Becker draws a hand on the board. Above the fingers and thumb he writes the numbers 32, 31, 30, 29, and 28.

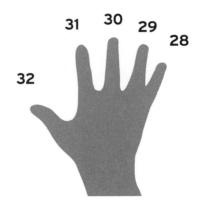

Mr. Becker:	Anthony, you have a question?
Anthony:	I disagree. I don't think he counted right. It should be 32 take away 4, not 5.

Other students nod and make audible sounds of agreement.

| Mr. Becker: | Hmm, so some of you think this equation is not correct. Anthony thinks that maybe Eddie made a mistake counting back. |

Several students nod.

| Mr. Becker: | Let's try to figure this out. I want everyone to think about this. If we start at 32 and subtract 1, what number do we get? |
| Students: | 31! |

Mr. Becker writes 32 and then draws a jump backward of 1; then he writes 31. The board looks like this:

| Mr. Becker: | If we subtract another one, what do we get? |
| Students: | 30! |

Mr. Becker draws another jump backward of 1 and then writes 30.

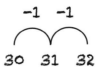

| Mr. Becker: | If we subtract another one, what do we get? |
| Students: | 29! |

Mr. Becker draws another jump backward of 1 and then writes 29.

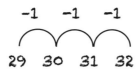

Mr. Becker:	How much have we subtracted so far?
Students:	3!
Mr. Becker:	How much more do we need to subtract to get to 28?
Students:	1!

Mr. Becker draws another jump backward of 1 and then writes 28.

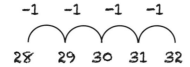

Mr. Becker:	So we started at 32 and we made four jumps backward, and we landed at 28. But we have five numbers up there. Why is that? [*Gives wait time*] Ashleigh?
Ashleigh:	You say only the numbers you land on. Can I show on the hundred board?
Mr. Becker:	Sure.

Ashleigh walks to the front of the room where the hundred chart is.

Ashleigh:	[*Touching the numbers 31, 30, 29, and 28 on the chart*] One, two, three, four. I started at 32 and I landed on 28. That's four.
Mr. Becker:	Eddie, what do you think?
Eddie:	I disagree with myself. I think the answer should be 4.

Mr. Becker erases the 5 in the equation $32 - 5 = 28$ and replaces it with a 4.

At the end of the lesson Mr. Becker's board looks like this:

Today's Number is 28

$10 + 10 + 8 = 28$ $20 + 8 = 28$

20

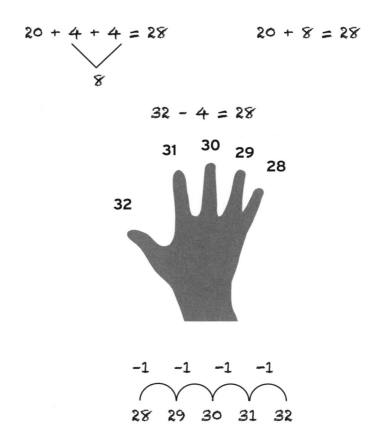

STOP+REFLECT

>> How does Mr. Becker make each student's thinking visually clear to the rest of the class?

Mr. Becker is an experienced teacher familiar with the strategies that his students use to add and subtract numbers. He works to record his students' strategies as accurately and clearly as possible. He draws lines to show which numbers Brandon and Brianna added first. He draws a hand with numbers above it to show how Eddie counted back on his fingers.

Mr. Becker also knows that it is common for first-grade students to mistakenly count the first number they say when they either "count on" or "count back" to solve problems. Mr. Becker has had time to think about this misconception and about how to address it. He realizes that students need to understand that they need to count the jumps backward, not the numbers that they say when they count. He makes this idea visual by drawing the jumps above the numbers. In this way students can see that although five numbers are present, only four jumps occur between 32 and 28.

FOSTER BROAD PARTICIPATION AND RICH DISCUSSION

Two hallmarks of productive classroom discourse are broad participation by a range of students and thoughtful consideration of one another's ideas. For all students to learn from math discourse, discussions need to involve all students in thinking about mathematics, sharing ideas, considering the ideas of others, and responding to the thinking of their classmates. Such inclusive conversations may seem difficult to achieve at first. However, you can take actions and ask questions to engage all your students in sharing their thinking and responding to the thinking of others.

This book has described several techniques for involving many students in class discussions:

- Gathering students on a rug or other meeting area where they can see the board and can easily see and hear one another

- Using wait time to give all students enough time to think through the answer to a question

- Using think, turn, and talk to give all students the chance to put their ideas into words for a classmate

- Calling on more than one student to answer the same question

Consistent use of these techniques will foster broad participation in discussions. Make sure that students are gathered so that they can see and hear one another and see the board. Always give enough wait time for most students to answer each question. If only a few hands go up, calmly tell your students that you expect every-one to think of an answer, and then give a little more wait time. Say, "I'm waiting for more students to raise their hands before I call on anybody." If you think your students have ideas but are reluctant to share them with the whole group, ask them to turn and talk to their partner. After students share their answers with a partner, try again to have a group discussion. Once many students do raise their hands, call on a range of students to share their answers and explanations. To acknowledge the thinking your students have done, call on more than one student to share the an-swer or to share his or her thinking behind the answer.

Once you have fostered broad participation in discussions, you can then deep-en your discussions by having students consider and respond to each other's ideas. *Classroom Discussions: Using Math Talk to Help Students Learn* (Chapin, O'Connor, and Anderson, 2009) highlights five talk moves to help students understand and re-spond to the thinking of their classmates:

- Giving wait time— both after posing questions and after calling on a stu-dent to answer.

- Revoicing—restating what a student has said in clearer or more math-ematically precise language. Sometimes teachers tentatively restate what a student has said because they are not sure what the student means. Here a teacher asks, "Are you saying that _____?" By working to clarify what a student has said, the teacher makes the student's thinking easier to under-stand for the group. Other times, teachers understand a student's thinking but restate the idea to introduce mathematical terms or to use more pre-cise language.

- Prompting students for further participation—inviting other students to add to what has already been said about a topic. Teachers can ask questions like "Who else has something to say about equivalent fractions?" or "Who else can explain why 16 is an even number?" This talk move invites more students into the discussion, focuses the discussion by asking for a particular type of contribution, and enriches the discussion by eliciting more information, ideas, and examples. For this move to be effective, you will need to give wait time after asking students for further participation.

- Asking students to restate someone else's reasoning—asking students to repeat what someone else has just said, but in their own words. This move can highlight something important that a student has just contributed and help the rest of the class make sense of it. After a student makes an insightful comment, check in with the rest of the class by asking, "Who heard what Jamila just said?" Then ask, "Who can say it in your own words?" After someone restates what the first student said, check back with the first student: "Jamila, is that what you said?" These questions may need to be asked and answered a few times before most of the class understands the original idea. However, this is time well spent. Having students restate one another's reasoning helps them to process each other's ideas. It also gives you valuable assessment information about how well students are understanding ideas.

- Asking students to apply their own reasoning to someone else's—asking students to decide whether they agree or disagree with an idea and to explain why. Learning to evaluate an idea and decide whether it makes sense is an important skill. However, the focus should be on evaluating the idea, not the person who expressed the idea. After a student introduces an important idea, the idea has been recorded on the board, and you think most students understand, ask other students to apply their own reasoning. You can do this in a few ways. You can simply ask, "Do you agree with this idea? If so, why?" Or you can poll the class. Say, "I want you to think about _____ (state the idea) and decide whether you agree, disagree, or are not sure." Give wait time and then ask for a show of hands. "Who agrees?" Then, "Who disagrees?" Then, "Who is not sure?" Acknowledge that being unsure is OK. Then ask different students to explain why they agree, disagree, or are not sure.

In the following class discussion, Ms. Chen uses some of these talk moves to support students in understanding each other's thinking and making a generalization. She begins a conversation by asking for fractions that are equal to $\frac{1}{2}$. She gives students time to think of a fraction and then calls on several students to share their answers. She records their fractions on the board without asking them to justify their thinking. At this point in the discussion four students have contributed and the board looks like this:

$$\frac{1}{2} = \frac{2}{4} = \frac{5}{10} = \frac{6}{12} = \frac{10}{20}$$

Ms. Chen:	Isabelle?
Isabelle:	One hundred two hundredths.

Ms. Chen writes $^{100}/_{200}$ on the board.

Ms. Chen:	How do you know that one hundred two hundredths is equal to one half?
Isabelle:	Well—it's like . . . 100 and 100 . . . is 200.
Ms. Chen:	Who heard what Isabelle just said?

Four or five hands go up.

Ms. Chen:	Isabelle, can you say that again so that everyone can hear you? How do you know that one hundred two hundredths is equal to one half?
Isabelle:	Um . . . it's like . . . I know that 100 plus 100 is 200 . . . so one hundred two hundredths equals one-half.
Ms. Chen:	Now who heard what Isabelle said?

Many hands go up.

Ms. Chen:	Who can say what Isabelle just said in your own words?

A few students put their hands down. About ten hands remain raised.

Ms. Chen:	Victor?
Victor:	She said that 100 and 100 is 200, so that's how she knows that one hundred two hundredths is one-half.

Ms. Chen writes on the board:

$$100 + 100 = 200$$
$$So \; \frac{100}{200} = \frac{1}{2}$$

Ms. Chen:	[*To the whole class*] Do you agree with this idea? Do you think that one hundred two hundredths is equal to one half because 100 plus 100 equals 200? [*Wait time. Many students raise their hands.*] Annie?
Annie:	I think so . . . if the fraction is equal to a half . . . you can add the top number two times and you get the bottom number. It works for the fractions we have so far.

Ms. Chen: Who heard what Annie just said? [*Wait time. Most students raise their hands.*] So Annie thinks that if you double the numerator and get the denominator then the fraction is equal to one-half.

Ms. Chen writes on the board under the list of fractions:

> If you double the numerator and get the denominator, the fraction is equal to $\frac{1}{2}$.

Ms. Chen: Phillipe, you have something to add?

Phillipe: You could also say it another way. You could say, "If the numerator is half of the denominator, then the fraction is equal to one-half."

Ms Chen writes:

> If the numerator is half of the denominator, the fraction is equal to $\frac{1}{2}$.

STOP+REFLECT

>> Which talk moves described earlier does Ms. Chen use?

>> How does each talk move broaden participation or deepen the discussion?

Ms. Chen wants her students to make a generalization about fractions that are equal to $\frac{1}{2}$. After Isabelle explains why she thinks that 100/200 is equal to $\frac{1}{2}$, Ms. Chen uses three talk moves to get the whole class to consider and respond to Isabelle's idea: She first asks someone else to restate Isabelle's reasoning. After Victor does this, Ms. Chen asks the rest of the students to apply their reasoning to Isabelle's reasoning by asking them whether they agree or disagree and why. After Annie explains why she agrees with Isabelle's reasoning, Ms. Chen revoices Annie's generalization, using the terms *numerator* and *denominator*. By using these talk moves, Ms. Chen focuses the conversation on Isabelle's idea, brings more students into the conversation, and facilitates a discussion in which Isabelle's explanation of why one fraction is equal to $\frac{1}{2}$ is developed into two generalizations that apply to all fractions equal to $\frac{1}{2}$.

TEACH STUDENTS EXPLICIT BEHAVIORS AND LANGUAGE FOR MATH DISCUSSIONS

This chapter has explained many things that you can do and say to foster deeper, more inclusive math conversations. Students also need to learn how to do their part. If you teach your students explicit behaviors and language for participating in math discussions, even young students can learn to listen to and question one another with respect and curiosity.

Chapter 5 explained how to develop class norms so that "We can help each other do our best thinking, work, and problem solving." As needed, revisit the chart of what it looks and sounds like when students work and talk supportively with one another. Add more norms as students demonstrate them or as you see a need. You may want to add phrases to your list of what students say to support each other, such as the following:

- I didn't understand. Can you please explain that again?

- I agree with _____ because . . .

- I disagree with _____ because . . .

- I noticed . . .

When first leading whole-class math discussions, explicitly teach students the behaviors you expect, such as turning their bodies and faces toward the speaker and speaking both loudly enough for others to hear and slowly enough for others to follow. Also, discuss the importance of listening with an ear for understanding what the speaker is saying. Once students have learned these behaviors, begin your discussions by asking, "What should you say and do in a class discussion?" You can also encourage genuine listening by asking students whether they have comments or questions after a speaker shares a strategy or an idea.

MORE IDEAS TO REINFORCE MATH TALK

Use academic routines and the problem-solving routine from chapter 7

The academic routines in chapter 7 have discourse patterns built into them. Each routine includes questions to elicit particular responses. The routines also include making the math visual. As you and your students gain more comfort and skill with these routines, your math discourse outside the routines will also improve.

Encourage productive conversations when students work together

During work time, encourage productive discourse among partners. When you check in with students working in pairs, direct your comments and questions to both students. Ask questions such as, "Did you understand what your partner just said? Can you say what she said in your own words? How did your partner figure out the answer to the problem?"

Build talk into games

Chapter 6 showed how to introduce the game of "Double Peace." In that example, the teacher built talk into the directions of the game. The directions specify that each student explain to his partner how he figured out the sum of the cards, and the partner says whether he agrees. You can add similar directions to most games. When directions for explaining one's thinking are built into a game, students explain their thinking more frequently, and there is more parity in the amount of talk that each partner contributes.

CONCLUSION

Each productive discussion among a group or pair of students is a sign that you have given interesting problems to talk about, have asked good questions to prompt thinking, and have taught students how to explain their thinking and respond to the thinking of others. As you work to incorporate more math discourse into your classroom, continue to—

- ask questions that elicit student thinking;
- make the mathematical thinking visual;
- foster broad participation and rich discussion; and
- teach students explicit behaviors and language for math discussions.

Also, periodically stop and reflect on the amount and quality of discourse in your classroom. Think about the following:

- Who is doing most of the talking in your classroom—you or your students? Are all students sharing their strategies and ideas, or do a few students do most of the talking and sharing? Do students ask their peers questions about their strategies and reasoning?
- How are you making the mathematics and the mathematical thinking visual?
- Does the math talk further your lesson goals? Are your math discussions helping students understand new strategies and make connections? Are students incorporating new strategies, concepts, and vocabulary into their work because of the discussions?

Although few teachers experienced rich mathematical discourse as students, many teachers are finding ways to cultivate it in their classrooms. With time, consistency, planning, and reflection, you too can foster genuine math discourse among your students.

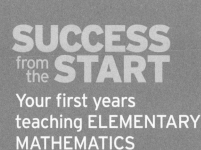

chapter thirteen

Assessment and Feedback

Guiding Principles

LEARNING IS MAXIMIZED WHEN STUDENTS—

>> interact in a safe, supportive learning community;

>>activate and build on prior knowledge;

>> process information both visually and linguistically;

>> solve problems with meaningful contexts;

>> engage in reflection, self-monitoring, and metacognition; and

>> engage in complex thinking.

Assessment and feedback are powerful tools to improve both learning and teaching. You can use assessment information to decide which ideas to focus on when discussing problems with students, to give feedback to students about their work, and to reflect on what aspects of your teaching either advance student learning or need improvement. Students can use self-assessment to adjust their work and learning. However, assessment and feedback are often not used in these ways. When assessment and feedback are limited to putting checks, smiley faces, and grades on papers or tests, they do not have much effect on either learning or instruction.

Chapter 2 explained that you should continually assess students to give instruction that builds on their understandings. Chapters 2, 5, and 6 explained the importance of helping students become metacognitive about their thinking and problem solving. The lesson cycle chapters showed how you can use a combination of clear learning goals, observations of students at work, and analysis of students' written work to discern what students know and can do, reflect on your teaching, and plan future instruction. The discourse chapter highlighted questions and talk moves that elicit student thinking, allowing teachers to better understand and assess students' reasoning.

Essential Practices

>> Set and communicate clear goals and expectations.

>> Use assessment to elicit what students know and can do, as well as reveal difficulties.

>> Teach students to assess their own work and thinking.

>> Give descriptive feedback.

SET AND COMMUNICATE CLEAR GOALS AND EXPECTATIONS

Setting clear learning goals and expectations keeps you and your students focused on what you want them to learn. You cannot assess mathematical thinking and performance effectively if you do not know what to look for. Students cannot learn math effectively if they do not know what they are supposed to learn or how they are supposed to learn it. Developing clear learning goals and communicating and sustaining clear expectations is challenging. However, it is worth your time and energy. It will improve your teaching and make your classroom easier to manage.

Management problems often arise when students are not clear about what they are supposed to learn or how they are supposed to learn it. Explicitly telling students what you expect them to learn enables them to focus their efforts. Setting clear expectations for how you want students to learn (such as what showing work means or how to talk with a partner) teaches students important work habits necessary for deep learning.

Identify learning goals and communicate them to students

As the lesson planning chapter indicated, you must identify the mathematical goals of your lessons and keep those goals in mind throughout your lessons. Communicate these goals to your students in language that they can understand. For example, if first-grade students are playing a game to practice combinations that make 10, you can tell them that they are playing the game to learn the combinations that make 10. If third-grade students are exploring strategies to compare fractions, you can tell them that many different ways to compare fractions exist and that their job is to figure out ways to compare fractions that make sense to them. The reason for sharing learning goals with students is not to funnel students to one particular method of solving problems but rather to more deeply engage them in their own learning.

Rephrasing lesson goals as questions invites inquiry. For example, you might write on the board at the beginning of the lesson, "What are some different ways that you can make 10 by adding two numbers?" Or "How can you figure out which of two fractions is greater?" Communicating related expectations is also helpful. For example, "Be prepared to share one combination you found that equals 10," or "Be prepared to share in the class discussion how you figured out which fraction was greater."

Use goals and anticipated solutions to focus assessment and questioning

As the lesson enactment chapter showed, identifying learning goals and anticipating students' strategies and tools enabled Ms. Ellis to focus her observations of students at work and ask questions tailored to particular strategies. When the lesson was over, those same goals and observation criteria guided her analysis of students' written work, which in turn helped her plan for the next day. Without clear learning goals and clear ideas about what to look for in students' work, Ms. Ellis could not have observed and questioned her students as intentionally or analyzed their work as carefully.

Develop clear expectations for what it means to communicate one's thinking

In-depth assessment of student thinking requires evidence. That evidence usually comes from what students say about their thinking and how they record or explain their thinking in writing. Therefore, you will need to teach your students to attend to their thinking, to explain it to others, and to record it clearly and succinctly. The discourse chapter discussed ways to question students about their thinking, how to orchestrate discourse that presses students to examine and explain their thinking more clearly, and how to model clear recording of strategies and representations.

USE ASSESSMENT TO ELICIT WHAT STUDENTS KNOW AND CAN DO, AS WELL AS REVEAL DIFFICULTIES

You should always be engaged in assessment: before you teach a unit, as you teach the unit, and at the end of the unit. You should also focus your attention on evidence of what students seem to understand and can do, as well as gather evidence of difficulties and misconceptions. By identifying what students know and can do, you position all your students as knowledgeable and capable of making sense of math. You practice seeing them through a positive lens, which is essential for partnering with students around their learning. Identifying what students know and can do informs your instruction. It can give you ideas for where to start with students and what knowledge and ideas to build on. Your job is not to get all students to the same place at the same time but rather to move students along in their understanding of mathematical ideas and in their level of computational fluency.

Diagnosing and Responding to Errors

When students make repeated errors in answering particular types of problems, they are probably misunderstanding something either about the structure of the problem or about the concepts or number relationships necessary to solve the problem. To better understand what a student making errors does understand, back up and pose easier problems, ones with a simpler structure or smaller numbers.

Keep posing easier problems until the student can solve them. Then analyze the successful responses to see what concepts the student does understand and what number relationships the student can use to solve problems. This information allows you to design interventions that build on what the student already knows and understands.

The following sections describe types of assessment that can elicit students' thinking and inform instruction.

Preassessment for each unit

Preassessment yields useful information. It identifies students who lack prior knowledge that curriculum materials assume students to have. It gives you a sense of the range of understanding that students already have about a topic. It also identifies students who already understand many of the concepts, strategies, and representations that the unit develops. If you think that several students in your class lack necessary prior knowledge or vocabulary, give your preassessment a few weeks before you plan to teach the new unit. Doing so will give you or a support teacher time for additional instruction that develops the prerequisite knowledge or vocabulary.

Written preassessments are most appropriate for students in grades 2–5. Such assessments need not be long or elaborate. Pose two to four open-ended questions that elicit what students already know about the topic. Share the purpose of the preassessment with your students to reduce their anxiety and encourage them to put forth their best effort. Explain that the class will be studying a particular topic and that you are giving a preassessment to understand what they already know about that topic so that you can teach them better. Explain that not knowing much about the topic is OK because they will be learning about the topic over the coming weeks. The following are types of preassessment questions that you might use.

Pose a bare number problem and ask students to write a story problem

Pose a bare number problem. Then ask students to write a story problem that represents the problem and then to solve the problem and show their work. Example: "Write a story problem for 43 − 18 = _____. Solve the problem and show your work." If you will be teaching a unit on two related operations (such as addition and subtraction), ask students to solve one of each type of problem.

Ask students to tell you what they know about the topic

Ask students to tell you what they already know about the topic they will be studying. Examples: "What do you know about subtraction?" "What do you know about odd and even numbers?"

Ask students to use particular models or representations

Ask students to use particular models or representations that feature in the upcoming unit. Examples: "Draw an array for 15×7. Use the array to find the product and show your work." "Place $3/8$ and $4/6$ on the number line below [give a number line between 0 and 1 with $1/2$ as the midpoint] and explain how you decided where to put each fraction."

Observe and question students to assess and build on what they know

As your students work on problems, your primary role is to circulate around the room, observing and questioning students to assess and build on what they know. As you notice how your students solve problems and probe and extend their thinking, you may stop to help students with difficulties. You may also spend particular math periods facilitating small-group lessons while the rest of the class works independently or in pairs. However, beware of helping the same students again and again as your primary activity during math time. Instead, observe a range of students to find out the following:

- How are they solving problems? What strategies, tools, and models do they use?

- What concepts do they seem to understand (or not) and what number relationships do they use (or not)? What do their solutions and mistakes reveal about their level of understanding and their computational fluency?

- How do they represent and record their solutions and thinking? Do their representations and explanations match their tools and strategies?

- Are the problems appropriately challenging? Are the problems accessible enough that all students can find an entry point? Are the problems challenging enough for all students to make new connections while solving and discussing them?

Observing your students at work lets you assess the learning of both individual students and the whole class. Your observations will help you decide what questions to pose to individual or pairs of students to extend their thinking. Your observations will also help you decide whose work to share and what questions to ask in the whole-class discussion to extend the learning of your class as a group.

Making Sense of What Students Do and Say

Making sense of what students do and say while they work is an acquired skill. Amidst a busy classroom, understanding students' strategies and representations and recognizing and diagnosing errors may be hard at first. Effective lesson planning will prepare you to observe and respond to your students' thinking. As Ms. Ellis showed in the lesson-planning chapter, anticipate strategies, tools, or representations that students might use, and think of questions that will help you assess and build on what your students know and understand. Then write this information down and carry it with you during the lesson to help you stay focused.

With experience you will learn to tailor your questions to the strategies, tools, and representations that students are using. Meanwhile you can ask more general questions, such as "How did you figure that out?" "Does your answer make sense?" "Can you think of an easier way to solve the problem?" "Can you prove that your answer is correct by solving it a different way?"

Other actions you can take to make observing students easier include the following:

- Create a system to record and track your daily observations. Your math program may suggest ways to do this and supply templates.

- Because carefully observing all your students at work during one lesson is impossible, create a system that ensures that you focus on each student over a week or two. You might choose a set of students to observe each day and write the names of these students on your observation sheet.

- If the problems are too hard for some students, modify them so that these students can work productively.

- If you do not understand something a student says or does, write it down and wait until after class to make sense of it.

Analyzing written work

Analyzing students' written work is another important way to gain insight into their thinking. The lesson reflection chapter showed that analyzing student work gives you a sense of the range of thinking within your classroom and tells you about students you did not observe. Analyzing the work after students have left the room also gives you time and space to make sense of strategies and explanations in a less hectic setting.

Analyze students' written work on a daily basis. Doing so will give you valuable information about how well your students understand the math you teach. If you do not have time to analyze each student's entire paper, chose one question that will give you the most information and analyze each student's response to it. When analyzing student work, keep the following recommendations in mind:

- Take time to make sense of your students' solutions. Student work is not always clear, especially when students are first learning to record their thinking. Do your best to decipher what your students have written. Count the tally marks. Try to read what students have erased. Assume that all students were engaged in sense making even if their answers are incorrect or their work looks messy and unclear.

- Assess whether students met expectations for clear and complete work. Student explanations need not be long or elaborate. However, you should be able to tell from looking carefully at their papers how they solved each problem.

- Sort work by particular criteria, as the teachers did in chapter 11. You can sort work according to the strategies, tools, or representations students used to solve the problems. This approach will give you more useful information than if you sort work solely on the basis of correct answers. It requires you to first figure out how each student solved a problem, which develops habits of noticing and making sense of student thinking. Then, by putting papers in piles according to strategies, you can more easily see which students are using which strategies. You can then think about what prior knowledge of concepts, number relationships, or models students in each category seem to be drawing on. This diagnostic information can help you plan whole-class discussions or small-group lessons to move students along the landscape of learning.

Strategies, Tools, and Representations

When analyzing student work, pay attention to the strategies, tools, and representations that students use. You need to understand the distinctions among these three features of students' solutions.

Strategies are physical and mental actions students take as they solve problems. For example, a student who solves a problem about adding 3 fish and 4 more fish by putting up 3 fingers on one hand and putting up 4 fingers on another hand, and then counting all 7 fingers, is using the strategy of "counting all." The student is counting all 7 fingers (representing the fish) to solve the problem. A student who solves the same problem by saying "3" and then holding up 4 more fingers and counting, "4, 5, 6, 7" is using the strategy of "counting on." The student is counting on from the first group of 3 fish.

A student who adds 3 and 4 by thinking, "3 plus 3 equals 6, so 3 plus 4 would equal one more than 6, which is 7," is using the strategy of "doubles plus one." The student is using a doubles fact that he knows and adding 1 to the sum. Students' strategies vary in sophistication and efficiency. Paying attention to students' strategies can give you important information about what concepts your students understand, what number relationships they have constructed, and how flexible they are in their thinking.

Tools are the materials, models, and representations that students use to organize and keep track of their thinking as they solve problems. Manipulatives, drawings, equations, and models such as ten-frames, number lines, and arrays are all examples of tools. The first two students in the example above use their fingers as tools. They use the same tool but different strategies. The first student uses fingers to "count all." The second uses fingers to "count on." The third student uses equations to organize and keep track of his thinking. Students can also use different tools but the same strategy to solve a problem. For example, a fourth student might add 3 fish and 4 fish by counting out 3 cubes, then counting out 4 cubes, and then counting all 7 cubes to find the total. That student would be using the strategy of "counting all" but using cubes instead of fingers as his tool.

Representations are the ways that students show their thinking to others. For example, the first student might draw 3 fingers and then 4 fingers to show that he first counted 3 fingers and then 4 fingers to solve the problem. The second student might write the number 3 and then draw 4 fingers and write the numbers "4, 5, 6, 7" above the fingers to show how she "counted on" by using her fingers. The third student might represent his thinking with equations: "3 + 3 = 6, so 3 + 4 = 7." Representations are usually written or drawn on paper, but sometimes students create representations, such as arrays, out of physical objects to model their thinking.

Students' representations do not always match the strategies and tools they use to solve problems. This often occurs when students do not know how to represent their thinking on paper. For example, if the student who solves the fish problem by using doubles plus one does not know how to record his strategy with equations, he may draw pictures instead. If he does, his sophisticated thinking may go unnoticed. You can help students accurately represent their thinking by modeling clear and succinct ways to represent different strategies and tools during whole-class discussions, by creating strategy charts with clear representations, and by helping students translate their thinking to paper as you observe students at work.

Examples of student work

As you look at students' representations of their thinking, try to figure out what strategies and tools students used. Also, think about what their work tells you about what they understand and do not yet understand about numbers and operations. Finally, think of a question you might ask each student to learn more about his/her thinking.

Early subtraction

Problem: Ten dogs were at the park. Then 4 dogs went home. How many dogs were still at the park?

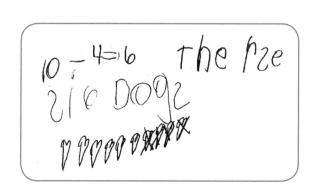

This student's classroom has heart-shaped counters. This student used them as a tool to solve the problem. He used a counting-all-and-removing strategy. He counted out 10 counters, removed 4, and then counted the 6 remaining counters. He represented a strategy with a picture. He also wrote an accurate equation. What might you ask this student to find out more about his thinking?

This student used pictures as a tool to solve the problem. Her representation shows that she grouped the 10 dogs in two sets of 5. Her class has done considerable work with ten-frames, and she may have developed a mental image of 10 as two rows of 5. It is not clear what strategy she used to count the dogs. Did she count all 10 dogs by ones, or did she draw 5 dogs and another 5 dogs and know that was 10? When she crossed off the 4 dogs, did she count them by ones or know that two rows of 2 was 4? Finally, after she had crossed off the 4 dogs, did she need to count the remaining dogs by ones, or could she just see (subitize) that 6 dogs were left? Her paper does show some inconsistencies. She correctly represented the subtraction situation as $10 - 4$ but wrote 5 as the difference. Her sentence at the bottom also states that 6 dogs "went home" instead of 6 dogs "stayed at the park." What might you ask to find out more about her strategy and thinking?

This student used a math rack as a tool to solve the problem. Her representation shows 10 beads with 4 crossed out. Her strategy is unclear because we do not know how she counted the beads. Because one row of a math rack has 10 beads, she may not have counted the original 10 beads. She may just have known that 10 were on the row. Also, the structure of the math rack (two sets of five beads in different colors on each row) may have helped her to recognize the remaining beads as 6 without counting them individually. She also represents the problem with an equation and with a picture of dogs. What could you ask to find out more about her thinking?

This student's work reveals no information about how she solved the problem. She wrote an accurate equation and drew a picture of the 6 dogs left at the park. Students often draw a picture of the answer to a problem without representing how they solved the problem. What could you ask this student to find out more about her thinking? What could you say or do to help this student accurately represent her strategy?

Moving from Elaborate Drawings to Simpler Representations

When students are asked to show their work, many initially create detailed drawings of the objects in story problems. Although this is typical, it is not ideal. Drawing elaborate pictures can take students' minds off the math in the problems. It can also take time away from solving other problems. You can help your students create simpler representations by discussing this issue with them.

Tell students that you are noticing that some students are making detailed drawings to show their solutions to problems. Explain that showing how they solved problems is helpful. However, also explain that math class is about learning math and that when students draw detailed pictures, they do not have as much time and energy to think about math. Then pose a story problem and ask students how they could use simpler pictures to represent their thinking. Students will often suggest drawing circles, squares, or lines instead of detailed objects.

Before sending students off to work, remind them that you would like them to use simple pictures to record their thinking. As you circulate and observe students at work, notice which students are recording their thinking in simple ways that do not take a lot of time, and have a few of those students share their work during the class discussion. Focus the class discussion on those representations, and ask questions such as "How did Carlos solve the problem? How do you know? Do you think this is a quick and simple way to show his strategy? Why?"

Early division

Problem: The ferry can hold 8 cars. How many trips will the ferry have to make to carry 25 cars across the river?

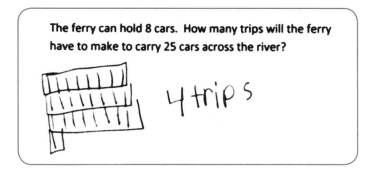

This student solved the problem by drawing lines in groups of 8 until she had drawn 25 lines. Her strategy seems to be repeated addition. How she kept track of the cars after drawing the first 8 is unclear. Did she know that three groups of eight is 24? Did she count the first 8, and then count on to 25, keeping track by placing sets of 8 tallies directly under the first set of 8? To find out, we could ask, "What did you do first? What did you do next?" Her tool was a drawing, which also served as her representation. This solution shows an understanding of the problem. She realized that although the problem had only one extra car, 4 trips were required.

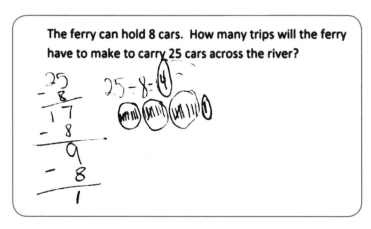

This student used a strategy of repeated subtraction. She used a series of subtraction equations as tools. She drew an additional representation with tally marks that show the four trips the ferry would need to make. Her division equation is not completely accurate. However, her solution shows an understanding of the problem.

The ferry can hold 8 cars. How many trips will the ferry have to make to carry 25 cars across the river?

The ferry will take ④ trips because 8X3=24 So 1 more trip for the last one.

This student's strategy was to start with a multiplication fact that she knew and then reason that the 25th car would require one more trip. She used a fact she knew as a tool. She represented her thinking with both an equation and a written explanation of her reasoning. Her solution indicates that she understood the problem and that she knows some multiplication combinations and can use multiplication to solve a division problem.

The ferry can hold 8 cars. How many trips will the ferry have to make to carry 25 cars across the river?

you cant get the answer because you would get 24.

This student used a picture as a tool. He solved the problem by drawing lines in groups of 8, similar to the first student. Again, we do not know how the student kept track of the cars after drawing the first 8 lines. The explanation about this student's work is most interesting. This student clearly understands that this problem requires thinking about equal groups. However, he seems unable to imagine a fourth ferry trip that does not include a whole group of 8 cars.

Early division of fractions

Problem: Renee is baking cupcakes. If each cupcake requires $^2/_3$ cup of frosting and Renee has only 8 cups of frosting, how many cupcakes can she make?

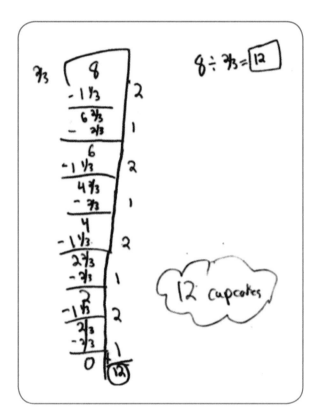

This student used repeated subtraction as a strategy. She subtracted either one or two groups of $^2/_3$ at a time until she got to 0. She kept track of the number of groups of $^2/_3$ that she had subtracted on the right. She wrote a division equation to represent the problem, and her recording looks somewhat like the recording for the division algorithm. Her recording system is her tool and her representation. What questions could you ask this student to learn more about her thinking? Can you think of a more efficient way to subtract groups of $^2/_3$?

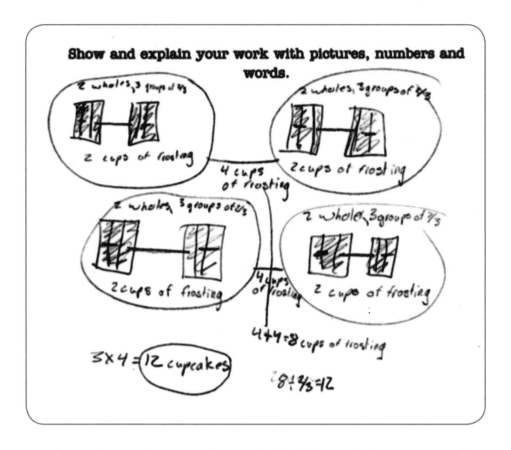

This student used pictures of rectangles divided into thirds to represent the fractions in the problem. These pictures also served as her tools. Each rectangle represents one whole, or one cup of frosting. She has circled groups of two wholes and labeled them in three different ways ("2 wholes," "3 groups of $^2/_3$," "2 cups of frosting"). Her pictures show the three groups of $^2/_3$ in each set of two wholes (look at the horizontal lines). Her strategy was to repeatedly add $^2/_3$. She noticed that 3 groups of $^2/_3$ made 2 wholes. Because she has four groups of 2 wholes, she multiplied 3 times 4 to figure out how many cupcakes she could frost. She also wrote a division equation to represent the problem.

This student seems to have figured out in his head that 2 cups of frosting would frost 3 cupcakes. He then uses this ratio to figure out how many cupcakes he can frost. He knows $2 \times 4 = 8$ (4 sets of 2 cups of frosting is 8 cups of frosting). He then multiplies 3×4 to get 12 (4 sets of 3 cupcakes is 12 cupcakes). He labels the 8 and the 12 to show that he knows what the numbers refer to. His only error is that he misuses the equals sign: 2 cups of frosting does not equal 3 cupcakes.

Moving Students to More Efficient Strategies

In general, the more students understand about a concept or operation and the more flexible students are in working with numbers, the more efficient and sophisticated their strategies will be. When students use less efficient strategies to solve problems, such as strategies that involve a lot of drawing or counting of individual objects, consider what they still need to learn. Ask yourself, "What would these students need to know or understand to solve the problem with a more sophisticated and efficient strategy?" Often, moving students from less efficient strategies to more efficient strategies involves working to help them understand concepts (such as place value) and models (such as arrays).

Sometimes, students are capable of developing efficient strategies but stick with unsophisticated and inefficient strategies because they find them safe and reliable. If you think this is the case, point out to the student that you have noticed that he or she usually _____ (counts on, draws pictures) to solve problems but that you believe he or she is ready to try other strategies. Then ask the student to choose a new strategy (from your class strategy chart) and suggest that the student use his or her favorite strategy to check the answers.

TEACH STUDENTS TO ASSESS THEIR OWN WORK AND THINKING

Students learn better when they monitor their own thinking and assess their work. Some students will enter your classroom with these habits, but most students will need to learn them. Fortunately, students can learn to be metacognitive, and doing so can affect their learning profoundly. Students can learn to assess their problem solving, understanding of new information and ideas, written work, and work habits.

Teaching students to monitor their problem solving and understanding

In monitoring and assessing their problem solving, students should ask themselves questions from the metacognitive problem-solving routine (see chapter 6): What is this problem about? What do I need to find out? What do I know that can help me solve the problem? Does my answer make sense?

Students should engage in this kind of self-monitoring throughout math class, as they work on problems, discuss them with partners, and engage in whole-class discussions with their peers. The routines chapter explained how to introduce the metacognitive problem-solving routine. In the lesson enactment chapter, Ms. Ellis reinforced the use of that routine with her students. The discourse chapter explained how to use discourse to help students evaluate their own thinking and that of their peers. Still, teaching students to be aware of their thinking and to ask themselves these questions is ongoing work, even for experienced teachers.

Students can also learn to monitor and assess their understanding of new information and ideas. They should ask themselves questions such as these: Do I understand what my partner just said? Does it make sense to me? Do I understand the representation that my teacher just drew on the board, or do I need to ask a question about it?

Learning to attend to one's own thinking occurs primarily through engagement in a classroom community that models and reinforces such thinking. You can help your students internalize these questions by modeling with think-alouds and through your questioning. If you regularly ask your students questions from the problem-solving routine, you will help them internalize the routine and become more metacognitive about their problem solving. If you regularly check in with students during whole-class discussions and ask them whether they understand what someone has just said or whether they have a question, you will help your students learn to monitor their understanding.

Teaching students to monitor and assess the quality of their written work

Students can learn to monitor and assess the quality of their written work. This means asking themselves questions such as these: Did I show all my work and thinking? Is it clear and organized so that I can check it and others will understand it? Is what I wrote actually the way that I solved the problem?

Have students clearly show or explain their thinking when solving math problems—even if the city or state assessments that your students take are multiple choice. It teaches students to become more aware of their thinking and gives you important assessment information.

Students' written work should be detailed enough to give you an accurate picture of how they solved the problem—but not so detailed that recording the work is cumbersome for students or takes significant time away from solving other problems. For most problems, students can show their thinking with a picture, equations, or a model (such as an array or number line). Students should also write an equation for the problem (if they have learned to do this) and label their answer. Sometimes students need to solve a problem before they can think of an equation.

If you model how to record strategies during class discussions and create charts of strategies that the class has discussed, students will have references for how to clearly and succinctly show their work. However, modeling is not enough to ensure that students will accurately and clearly show their work or explain their thinking. To further communicate your expectations, periodically show examples of student work (without names) on an overhead projector or document camera. Begin by showing only examples of clear and complete written work, asking the class to explain what makes the piece of work clear and complete. Have students analyze and discuss one or two examples of exemplary work at the beginning of class and send students off to work with that image fresh in their minds.

Once students have a clear idea of the criteria for exemplary written work, create examples of work that is not exemplary. Ask students what they notice about the work, and remind them to do so respectfully. Then ask, "How could we make this work more clear or complete?" Take suggestions from students, and record a more clear and complete version of the work. You can follow such a discussion by returning papers to students and asking them to check over their work and make any necessary improvements.

You can also teach students to assess their work by asking them to find their own mistakes. Instead of marking a problem wrong, tell a student that you found an error on his paper and you would like him to find it and correct it. This approach reinforces the expectation that students check their work to make sure that it makes sense. Of course, sometimes students will not be able to recognize and correct their own errors, which might indicate a misconception.

Teaching students to monitor and assess their work habits

Students can learn to monitor and assess their work habits. This means asking themselves questions such as these: Did I get to work right away? Did I put in my best effort? Did I demonstrate the problem-solving dispositions? Did I support my partner in doing his or her best thinking?

Chapter 5 explained how to establish norms for your learning community, teach students about the five dispositions of effective problem solvers, and reinforce the norms and dispositions. That chapter also suggested that you periodically ask students to assess their problem-solving dispositions after they have done class work. Similarly, you can ask students to assess other work habits such as getting to work quickly and demonstrating their best effort. You can ask students to identify work habits and dispositions that they showed that day in class. You can also ask them to identify a work habit or disposition that they can improve or further develop. Finally, you can help them identify ways to improve.

GIVE DESCRIPTIVE FEEDBACK

Timely and descriptive feedback communicates to students what they have done well and what you would like them to work on. Such feedback can improve students' performance. If you are clear about your learning goals and expectations and you observe and assess your students, you can give meaningful feedback directly connected to those goals and expectations. For example, if one goal is to move students from using repeated addition to solve multiplication problems to using arrays, you might say to a student who has just tried using arrays for the first time, "Wow. I see that you use arrays to solve this problem instead of repeated addition. That seems more efficient. Keep up the good work!" Or, if the student has not yet tried using arrays, you might say, "I noticed that you used repeated addition to solve these problems. That seems to be a reliable strategy for you. But I want you to learn how to use arrays because they will help you solve multiplication problems more efficiently. How could you solve this problem by using arrays? How might you start?"

Here are other examples of descriptive feedback that communicates both what you notice about the work and what goals or expectations you have for the student or the class:

- "I noticed that you wrote lots of interesting multiplication equations for Today's Number. Next time, include some division equations."

- "This is such clear work. I can understand exactly how you thought about each problem."

- "I noticed that you showed your reasoning carefully for the first problem but not for the second problem. How can you show your reasoning for the second problem?"

Such comments can be written or spoken. They communicate to students what you see as the strengths of their work and what you would like them to do differently. This feedback is more meaningful to students than a smiley face or check mark because it shows you attended to the student's work and thinking. Such comments are more likely to improve students' work and advance students' thinking because they explicitly state the improvements and advancements that you want.

Writing descriptive comments on student papers takes time. But you can learn to be specific, clear, and brief. You need not write descriptive comments on every paper. When you take the time to do so, give students time in class to read the comments and make any improvements. Otherwise, many students are unlikely to read or respond to your feedback.

Although many teachers believe that poor grades motivate students to do better, they rarely do. Poor grades often discourage students and can lead students to put in less effort. Struggling students often do not know what they should work on to improve their performance, and they may not know how to study for tests. These students would benefit from conferences in which the two of you review an assessment or piece of work to see what the student did well, set a few manageable goals to work on, and make a clear plan to reach those goals.

CONCLUSION

Following the guidelines in this chapter will help you and your students become clearer about your goals and expectations. Your students will get better at monitoring and assessing their own work and thinking, and you will get better at helping your students chart a path toward greater understanding and proficiency in mathematics.

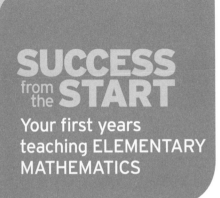

SUCCESS
from the START
Your first years
teaching ELEMENTARY
MATHEMATICS

chapter **fourteen**

Differentiation: Meeting the Needs of Diverse Learners

Guiding Principles

LEARNING IS MAXIMIZED WHEN STUDENTS—

>> interact in a safe, supportive learning community;

>> activate and build on prior knowledge;

>> process information both visually and linguistically;

>> solve problems with meaningful contexts;

>> engage in reflection, self-monitoring, and metacognition; and

>> engage in complex thinking.

Teachers who practice equity share a core belief that all students, including struggling learners and English language learners (ELLs), can make sense of mathematics by using their own ideas and strategies to solve problems. Struggling learners and ELLs should not be relegated to learning mathematics through rote procedures, drill and practice, and "supports" that do the thinking for them. Instead, they deserve the same opportunity as other students to grapple with rich and meaningful mathematical problems. Differentiating math instruction should give all students tasks that support and advance development of mathematical thinking.

Let's think about differentiating for sense making through the lens of Max, the ELL you met in the fourth-grade class. Max had difficulty solving the division problem about the Mayan referee arranging 56 balls in 4 rows for a pok-a-tok game (see chapter 10). Ms. Kramer elicited his thinking with questions that enabled him to discover his mistake, make sense of the problem, and figure out what tools and strategies he needed to solve it. Instead of funneling information (see chapter 11) and doing the thinking for him, Ms. Kramer asked questions to scaffold the development of his mathematical thinking and problem solving: What does this answer mean? Does your answer make sense? What do you know that can help you solve it? As a result, Max made sense of the problem and solved it on his own.

Teachers who practice equity also recognize that students have diverse backgrounds, experiences, learning needs, math knowledge, and levels of readiness. To ensure equity, they differentiate instruction to offer all students access to rich, meaningful mathematics learning.

Many teachers think that differentiating mathematics instruction means developing twenty-five different lesson plans. This goal is both unrealistic and unnecessary. Another way of thinking about differentiation is to consider instructional practices that offer multiple access points for a range of students. Therefore, a more appropriate goal focuses on giving tasks with multiple entry points to engage a diverse group of students in the math content within the same lesson.

Mathematics learning, like all learning, is mediated through language. Students construct connected mathematical knowledge through problem solving and interactions with their teachers and peers. When students engage in discourse and written communication about their ideas and solutions, mathematical ideas are explored, clarified, and solidified. To develop their thinking, all students need access to the language used to discuss mathematical ideas.

To access, explore, and build on mathematical ideas, all students must develop proficiency in the academic vocabulary associated with mathematics. This includes both domain-specific vocabulary (such as *addition, sum, minus, factor, multiple, denominator*) and general academic vocabulary (such as *represent, show, explain, sequence, same, different*). To connect related mathematical ideas and concepts, students must have the mathematics vocabulary and the general academic vocabulary to mediate those connections. Development of academic language is essential not only for ELLs and struggling learners but also for all students.

Differentiating math instruction for ELLs therefore challenges teachers. ELLs have various degrees of English language proficiency. ELLs with a limited understanding of English will have difficulty accessing the interactions and experiences essential to developing an understanding of math. Other ELLs, like Max, have oral expressive and receptive abilities but have difficulty reading and interpreting math tasks. Therefore, the challenge for teachers of ELLs is to both teach mathematics content and develop English language proficiency.

This chapter presents ideas about how to implement lessons with multiple access points that engage students in learning math at their levels of readiness. Although most of the ideas maximize math learning for all students, they are essential for struggling students and ELLs. This chapter also addresses how to differentiate tasks for students at different levels of readiness so that they are operating at their appropriate level of challenge. As chapter 2 described, determining where students are on the landscape of learning—what they know and understand and where they need to go next—helps you determine what tasks will appropriately challenge them.

Essential Practices

>> Explore principles and strategies to differentiate mathematics instruction.

>> Differentiate tasks and math games (including for students who need extension).

>> Develop strategies to manage differentiated lessons.

>> Design a professional development action plan.

DIFFERENTIATING MATHEMATICS INSTRUCTION: PRINCIPLES

The following principles are central to differentiating mathematics instruction for all:

- Create a supportive learning environment.
- Supply comprehensible input.
- Engage students in all forms of language production.
- Identify content and language goals.
- Assess before, during, and after instruction.
- Activate and build prior knowledge.
- Give problems with multiple entry points.
- Use flexible grouping effectively.

Create a supportive learning environment

A safe, supportive environment is essential to student learning. Chapter 5 introduced a guiding rule for such environments: "We will help each other do our best thinking, work, and problem solving." If you have established norms of safe, respectful behavior with students, they will appreciate that everyone's brain is different and that people learn in different ways and at different rates. Discuss with students their responsibility to communicate their math ideas and solutions so that everyone can understand them. You can then introduce the following math class norms to support diversity in math discourse:

- Slow down your math talk so that everyone has time to think about what you say.
- Use precise language.
- Use visuals such as equations, pictures, and models to show your math thinking.

Supply comprehensible input

Comprehensible input means that all students understand the content and language that you or peers present (Krashen, 1981). Be intentional about making information accessible to all students. Use clear, accessible language accompanied by nonlinguistic supports such as visuals, models, manipulatives, and gestures.

Dual coding—giving linguistic and nonlinguistic input at the same time—increases the neural connections among related types of knowledge. This makes it more likely that information will be processed, transformed into knowledge, and remembered. Supplying linguistic and nonlinguistic input not only advances the learning of all students but is essential to making the language and content comprehensible to struggling students and ELLs. See "Differentiating Mathematics Instruction: Strategies" later in this chapter.

Engage students in oral and written language production

Because mathematics learning is mediated through language, all students must have frequent opportunities to discuss and write about their mathematical ideas and solutions. This means calling on students even if they are slow in explaining their thinking or if you think they may be incorrect. As they get practice using math talk and representing their solutions in writing, students not only increase their language proficiency but also develop their mathematical reasoning. You can use the talk moves in chapter 12 to engage students in talking about their math ideas. However, if the language in your instruction is not comprehensible to students, the classroom discourse and written communication will also not be accessible to them.

Identify content and language goals

As you plan each math lesson, be clear about the lesson goals, which include the math content and vocabulary that you want students to learn. First identify the content goals, the mathematics you want students to learn. Then identify the academic vocabulary, the math vocabulary related to the lesson that you want students to learn and use in their writing and discourse. Next, identify the general academic vocabulary your students might need to access the task, interact with their peers, and participate in class discussions. General academic vocabulary includes words used often across domains of learning. Finally, identify the language goals for students, which include both academic vocabulary and general academic vocabulary. Look at an example of content goals, academic vocabulary, general academic vocabulary, and language goals for a lesson:

- Content goal (lesson goal): students solve addition problems with two two-digit numbers in a variety of ways

- Math vocabulary: *add, sum, numbers, digit, two-digit number*

- General academic vocabulary: *strategy, tools, different, solution, answer, solve*

- Language goals: students will accurately use the terms *add*, *sum*, *tools*, and *strategy*

In general, teachers are aware of the need to teach math vocabulary. However, teachers often mistakenly assume that students know general academic vocabulary. Assess the general academic vocabulary your students know and understand. For young students, struggling learners, and ELLs, developing general academic vocabulary must be intentionally supported.

Assess before, during, and after instruction

To differentiate instruction, preassess to find out what your students know and understand about the content and vocabulary associated with a new unit of study. Using multiple assessments, such as observations of students at work, interviews, and student work samples, is best. Your assessments should determine where your students are on the landscape of learning. From there you can plan lessons with tasks that appropriately challenge students to develop their understanding of math ideas.

Teachers who effectively differentiate instruction continually assess students' understanding and adjust their teaching to scaffold students' mathematical thinking and problem solving.

Activate and build prior knowledge

Activate students' prior knowledge and experience so they can connect what they know to new learning in the lesson. Sometimes you will need to introduce new information to make a task accessible. This is called frontloading. Frontloading can occur during or before the lesson launch and can include preteaching vocabulary and previewing text. Previewing problems before launching the lesson can give ELLs and struggling students the language and content knowledge they need to engage in the launch and access the task. When Ms. Ellis reflected on the division lesson, she decided that in future lessons she would preview problems with Max and other ELLs to build the language and content background necessary for them to understand problems so they could solve them on their own. Preview problems to make them comprehensible, but avoid giving students tips on how to solve problems.

Give problems with multiple entry points

Tasks with multiple entry points give students choice in how they solve problems. They give students choice of tools and strategies. When you assign tasks with multiple entry points, students will solve problems by using a variety of tools and strategies, depending on their level of readiness and mathematical sophistication. When students have a choice of tools and strategies, they self-differentiate.

Use flexible grouping effectively

Depending on their needs, your students will require different instructional groupings at different times to support their math learning. For example, you may need to offer focused support to an individual student or to a small group of students who need to strengthen or extend their understanding. While you work with an individual or small group, the rest of the class may work in pairs or individually. All students will benefit from opportunities to work in a variety of groupings—whole class, small group, or individually—as long as the instruction of the groupings advances them along the landscape of learning.

DIFFERENTIATING MATHEMATICS INSTRUCTION: STRATEGIES

All these strategies engage students in language production and give students comprehensible input. Earlier chapters discussed and highlighted many of these strategies. Consider how these strategies are essential for struggling students and ELLs. When students process information both linguistically and nonlinguistically, they construct more complex networks of connected knowledge. As you think about the following strategies, consider how you might integrate visual aids, verbal explanations, hand gestures, and dramatizations to increase your students' access to the language and content in your math lessons.

Create contextualized charts of words, strategies, and tools

As you introduce new math vocabulary, write the words on a class chart with pictures to represent them, if possible. You can also contextualize words in ways such as this:

$$3 \times 4 = 12$$
$$\text{factor} \times \text{factor} = \text{product}$$

As you explore and name strategies for adding, subtracting, multiplying, or dividing, add them to strategy charts with visual representations. You can create a similar chart for math tools. If these charts are prominently displayed in your room, students can readily access them in their discussions and problem solving. In class discussions, you can use hand gestures to point to specific vocabulary words, tools, or strategies as they are used in conversation, modeling how to use the charts and helping students connect oral and written math language.

Use choral response and repetition

As you introduce and write new vocabulary words, engage students in a choral reading of the words. In this way, students get practice reading, speaking, and hearing new vocabulary. This practice gives them confidence in their ability to use new words in their math talk. In addition to choral reading and repetition, repeat instructions and explanations so that students can more readily process them.

Make the math talk visual

As students explain their strategies and ideas, make the math talk visual by charting their thinking and solution paths with appropriate drawings, equations, and models. Doing so makes it possible for students to connect the math talk to math representations. It also models for students how they can represent their own solutions in writing.

Offer a variety of manipulatives and models

By giving students a variety of tools (such as number lines, ten-frames, hundred charts, and arrays) to choose from as they solve problems, you create opportunities for students to self-differentiate. For example, in Ms. Ellis's class, students used tiles, drawings, arrays, and equations to solve the division problem.

Model games, activities, and routines

Introduce new games, activities, or routines through demonstration. As you explain each step, model it with actions. You can also record each step in a flowchart with accompanying pictures. The game "Double Peace" (chapter 6) is an example of integrating verbal, kinesthetic, and visual inputs during such modeling.

Elicit nonverbal responses

Nonverbal responses such as a thumbs-up or thumbs-down enable all students to give you instant feedback. For example, you can ask students to signal a thumbs up, down, or in the middle if they agree, disagree, or are confused, respectively, about an idea or solution.

Engage students in partner talk

Students develop language proficiency and mathematical thinking as they discuss their ideas and strategies with each other. When you prompt students' thinking and engage them in partner talk, you increase their opportunities to think aloud about their mathematical ideas. When you want all students to think more deeply about important ideas or connections, engage them in partner talk so that everyone, not just a few, will benefit from the math thinking and talk. You can prompt students to use one or two vocabulary words from your class word chart during partner talk to help them develop their proficiency in math discourse.

Give wait time

Wait time allows students time to process questions and think about responses. This idea is especially important for struggling learners and ELLs. Wait time also tells students that (1) you expect everyone to think deeply about mathematical ideas and (2) success in mathematics is not about getting quick answers.

Use comprehensible teacher talk

To ensure that all students understand you, speak slowly, use concise and precise language, and articulate clearly. Not only does your teacher talk need to be easy to hear and understand, your message needs to be clear and focused. Teachers can unwittingly talk too much and get off track in their instruction. Unnecessary and extraneous language makes deciphering information difficult. Wordy, convoluted explanations pose substantial challenges to struggling students and ELLs. Reduce the amount of teacher talk, and make every word count.

Revoice and paraphrase

To ensure that all students understand important mathematical ideas and strategies as they are shared, sometimes you will need to revoice, or paraphrase, a student's thinking or strategy in clear, precise language that stresses an important idea.

Develop sequencing skills

You can elicit students' mathematical thinking with the prompt "How did you figure that out?" But this question can overwhelm some struggling learners and ELLs because organizing and then verbalizing the many thoughts in their problem-solving process is hard for them. In such cases, prompt students to break the process into manageable chunks by asking them to sequence their actions (for example, "What did you do first? Then what did you do? What did you do next?" and so on). Asking students to recall the sequence of their thinking and problem solving helps them access and organize their thinking.

Use a similar questioning protocol to help students make sense of story problems. Ask students to sequence the actions in story problems to help them understand what the problems are about, what they have to find out, and what information might be unnecessary (for example, "What happened first? Then what happened? What happened next?" and so on). You can use role play or words, pictures, and numbers to illustrate the sequence of actions in story problems. In chapter 1, Ms. Davis used this questioning to help her students understand an addition problem. She recorded the sequence of actions in a flowchart to give both linguistic and nonlinguistic support for students.

Model and engage students in think-alouds

When you prompt students to think aloud as they solve problems, they develop language and math proficiency by verbalizing ideas, procedures, or metacognitive processes. As students articulate their solutions, you can assess any difficulties or misconceptions they have. Thinking aloud is a process you can teach students through modeling. When teaching students how to play a math game, you can model your thinking as you play: "First, I have to roll these two dice [*rolls 5 and 4*]. Next, I have to find the total. Let's see, 5 and 4 is 9. I can add 4 onto the 5 . . . 5, 6, 7, 8, 9. I wonder whether I can use 4 + 4 to help me check?"

Develop metacognitive problem-solving skills

When students are made aware of thinking about their thinking and what to do as they engage in the four stages of problem solving (see chapters 2 and 6), they have far greater access to problems and can learn more as they monitor their own thinking and work. Teaching the metacognitive problem-solving routine gives all students, including ELLs and struggling learners, the tools and confidence to work autonomously on problems.

Use familiar contexts, visuals, and real objects

To make tasks and story problems comprehensible, use supports such as real objects, pictures, and visuals. When you embed story problems in familiar contexts, students tend to engage and stay grounded in the context of the problems throughout the problem-solving process. This attentiveness helps students engage more deeply in problems, enabling them to explore and make sense of the problems' structures. For ELLs and struggling students, familiar contexts also make discussing problems and their solutions easier.

* * *

The strategies described so far advance the learning of all students. The following strategies are primarily for struggling students or ELLs.

Rewrite story problems and activities in simpler terms

Sometimes story problems and activities include too much rich language for ELLs and struggling students to understand. To make story problems and activities more comprehensible, rewrite them in simpler language and with shorter sentences. For some ELLs, eliminating pronouns and unnecessary adjectives can make language more comprehensible. Compare three versions of the same problem:

1 Calvin and his sister Serena wanted to earn some money recycling bottles and cans. Their mother told them that they could get 5 cents for each clean bottle and can they brought to the recycle center. At the end of the week, they collected 76 cans and 33 bottles and brought them to the recycle center. How much money did they get?

2 Calvin and Serena collected 76 cans and 33 bottles. They took them to the recycle center. They got 5 cents for each can and bottle. How much money did they get?

3 Calvin and Serena collected 76 cans and 33 bottles. They got 5 cents for each can and bottle. How much money did they get?

Use sentence frames

Sentence frames support ELLs and struggling learners to enter, solve, and communicate solutions to problems. They can also increase opportunities for mathematical thinking by reducing the linguistic demands of a task. In the example below, students playing the game "Circles and Stars" (Burns, 1991) are asked to write a phrase using the words *groups of* and *equals* to represent each picture. They are also asked to write a multiplication equation representing the picture. The sentence frame in this example supports students:

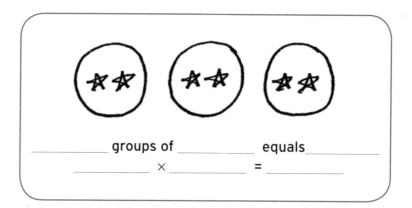

Use cognates

Cognates are words in two languages with similar pronunciation, spelling, and meaning. Cognates can sometimes serve as a bridge to English for ELLs, making content and language more comprehensible. If you have ELLs in your class who learned math in their native language, find out whether you can use any math cognates to make your math lessons and discourse more accessible. Thirty to forty percent of all English words have Spanish cognates. Here are some examples:

- product: el producto
- problem: el problema
- digit: el digito
- equal: igual
- equal groups: grupos iguales
- numerator: el numerador
- denominator: el denominador
- difference: la diferencia

So far, this chapter has explored principles and strategies central to differentiating mathematics instruction. They are central to exemplary teaching in general but essential to teaching ELLs and struggling students. Enacting them takes time and practice. Start by examining your strengths and needs to determine which principles to develop. Then create an action plan, implementing improvements gradually. The end of the chapter suggests ways to get started.

HOW TO DIFFERENTIATE TASKS AND GAMES

To ensure that all your students are learning math with understanding, assign tasks that are just the right challenge for learning to occur. As Ms. Ellis's division lesson showed, giving students the same problem with multiple entry points enables them to self-differentiate. However, sometimes you will have to further differentiate math tasks to help students develop their understanding of big ideas, strategies, and models along the landscape of learning. Although it takes some practice, differentiating tasks need not be complicated or overwhelming. This section draws on the work of Small (2009), which recommends an efficient and manageable way to differentiate math lessons: engage the whole class in learning about the same mathematical ideas but with problems of various levels of complexity.

Differentiating tasks

Two types of problems enable you to differentiate math lessons: open tasks and parallel tasks. Both types have multiple entry points. Chapter 8 introduced the two types of open tasks, open-routed tasks and open-ended tasks. Here we focus on parallel tasks. Parallel tasks are sets of two or three problems of various levels of complexity designed with the same problem structure and underlying mathematical idea. Offering parallel tasks enables all students to engage in a class discussion about the underlying mathematical ideas regardless of which problem they solve. Often, designing parallel tasks involves differentiating numbers in problems to accommodate different levels of math proficiency. Below is an example of parallel tasks designed to engage students in exploring constant difference, an important idea in subtraction. Although some problems use smaller numbers than others, each problem shares the same structure.

> *Mathematical idea:* constant difference (the difference between two numbers remains the same when you add the same value to both numbers). Possible parallel tasks include—

> *Easy:* Is the following number sentence true or false? Show your work and thinking.
> $$75 - 29 = 76 - 30$$

> *Moderate:* Is the following number sentence true or false? Show your work and thinking.
> $$142 - 99 = 143 - 100$$

> *Advanced:* Is the following number sentence true or false? Show your work and thinking.
> $$463 - 198 = 465 - 200$$

> Possible extension problem sets include—

> *Moderate:*
> $$\underline{\hspace{1.5cm}} - 45 = 80 - 60$$
> $$63 - \underline{\hspace{1.5cm}} = 70 - 57$$
> $$99 - 23 = 79 - \underline{\hspace{1.5cm}}$$

Advanced:

$$132 - 47 = \underline{\hspace{1cm}} - 51$$
$$\underline{\hspace{1cm}} - 220 = 324 - 295$$
$$264 - \underline{\hspace{1cm}} = 286 - 109$$

Questions for class discussion:

Start with the easiest problem (75 − 29 = 76 − 30).

1 Was the number sentence true or false? How did you figure that out?

2 What do you notice about the numbers in the number sentence?

3 How did the numbers change from the left of the equals sign to the right?

4 What might these two differences (75 − 29 and 76 − 30) look like on an open number line? (You can ask students to guide you in constructing an accurate representation. Doing so gives students a visual model that can clearly show constant difference.)

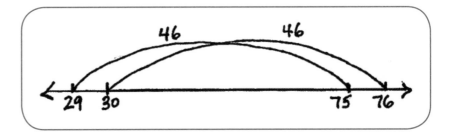

Repeat the first three questions with the second problem. Then ask questions that support students in making and proving a generalization about constant difference:

5 What happens to the difference between two numbers when you increase each number by the same value?

6 Will this always work? Why or why not?

7 What rule can you make about the difference between two numbers?

When you use parallel tasks, all students can engage in all parts of the lesson, including the class discussion. When tasks are appropriately challenging and when you make the task and the discussion comprehensible, all students have access to the questions you pose and the discussion that follows, which can deepen their thinking about mathematical ideas.

Differentiating tasks for students needing extension

Sometimes students who have completed tasks with multiple entry points need extension. There are several strategies you can use to differentiate tasks for these students. The first is to give extension problems related to problems they worked on in the lesson (such as in the parallel task above). Another way is to give students open-ended problems that have multiple answers (see chapter 8). For problems with a finite number of possible answers, ask students to find all possible answers and prove that they found them all. Students who finish problems early should prove their answers are correct by solving them a different way, if they have not done so already. Challenge them to make connections among the various solutions.

Differentiating math games

Many math programs have engaging games that support students' development of mathematical ideas and proficiency. Most games come with suggestions for intervention or extension. If not, you can modify games yourself. For example, in the game "Double Peace" (chapter 6), students find the sums of numbers 0–10 by using a deck of playing cards. For struggling learners, you can differentiate the game by using decks of 0–5 cards. (However, you will need 48 cards, so you will need to assemble a 0–5 deck from two decks.) Students needing extension can play "Triple Peace," finding the sums of three cards. Be clear about the math learning that games support, and use your ongoing assessment of students to determine which games will appropriately challenge them.

You can assign students to play differentiated versions of the same game, such as the example with "Double Peace." You can also assign students to play different games that target strategies and big ideas in content areas that students need to develop. For example, some fourth graders might play a game on comparing and ordering fractions, whereas others might play a game on adding and subtracting fractions.

Games can be differentiated by type, level of complexity, or both. Struggling learners may benefit from playing games from earlier grades. These games may have familiar contexts and models that enable students to access the big ideas and strategies you want them to learn.

MANAGING DIFFERENTIATED LESSONS: STRATEGIES

If your math lessons consist of a launch, work time, and class discussion, the work time offers the most opportunities for differentiating instruction.

Flexible grouping

During work time, flexible grouping can meet diverse learning needs. You may decide to engage the whole group in a task with multiple entry points, as Ms. Ellis did in her division lesson. As students work, you can walk the room, observing, assessing, questioning, and prompting to probe and support students' learning. At other work times, a small group of students may need strengthening or extending of a particular math idea, so you can give a minilesson tailored to their needs. You may also provide focused, individual instruction to a student who needs extension or more support. How can you give your attention to a small group or to a succession of individual students if other students need your support in completing their work?

Anchor activities

One way to offer differentiated instruction to groups or individuals without interruption is to give the rest of the class anchor activities, math tasks that students can engage in without teacher support. You can also use anchor activities when you want to introduce a new math game or activity to only half the class at a time. Anchor activities challenge students to practice math facts, develop computational fluency, or solidify math ideas. To work independently on anchor activities, students must already have learned and practiced the activity and be clear about their expectations for work and behavior. If you model the routine of working on anchor activities, students can engage with them independently while you instruct small groups or individuals.

Effective Anchor Activities

Example anchor activities include math games, ongoing assignments, computer games and activities (chapter 15), and number-of-the-day problems (chapter 7). Effective anchor activities—

- give students meaningful mathematics that connects to the content and instruction;

- reinforce proficiency and solidify understanding;

- give students choice; and

- enable you to offer focused instruction to individuals or small groups without interruption.

For students to get the most learning from anchor activities during work time, the activities must be neatly organized, labeled, and stored for easy access. In well-managed classrooms, students independently choose and work on anchor activities. In math classes that support students in taking responsibility for their own learning, students routinely choose and work on anchor activities independently after finishing their work. Flexible grouping that enables you to differentiate math instruction is effective only if you have a well-managed classroom with accessible anchor tasks, clear expectations, and practiced routines.

GETTING STARTED: DESIGN A PROFESSIONAL DEVELOPMENT ACTION PLAN

As you begin to learn about differentiating instruction, start with small moves. Review principles of differentiated math instruction, and then reflect on those you know and can implement—and those you need to develop. Initially, focus on one or two principles to develop; then choose actions you can take to improve your teaching.

When you identify actions for improvement, enlist your colleagues for help. For example, if assessment before instruction is a principle you need to develop, work with colleagues to plan a preassessment for a unit. If you need help giving problems with multiple entry points, work with colleagues to rewrite problems to give students choice in the tools and strategies they use. If you want to increase comprehensible input by using linguistic and nonlinguistic representations, start by developing with your students class charts of tools, strategies, and vocabulary that incorporate pictures and symbols. Visit colleagues' classrooms to get ideas about how they use nonlinguistic representations in their charts. If you identify language production as a goal, increase students' purposeful math talk by modeling concise and precise math talk and using think-turn-talk moves. Ask a colleague to observe your launch or class discussion to give you feedback on use of language. If a colleague is not available, run a tape recorder so you can listen later and analyze your math talk. You can start to improve your ability to differentiate math instruction in many ways.

CONCLUSION

As a fundamental matter of equity, all students must have access to rich mathematics that engages them in problem solving and sense making. You can offer rich mathematics instruction for all students, including ELLs and struggling learners, by implementing principles and strategies for differentiation that benefit all students.

In the context of this chapter's ideas, revisit your thinking about lesson planning. What ideas might you incorporate in your lesson planning to differentiate for the diverse needs of your students? Who are your students, and what teaching practices might advance their understanding of mathematics? Learning to differentiate instruction takes time. A first step is awareness of what is important to think about. Then assess your needs, as well as those of your students, and plan actions that will best serve your students.

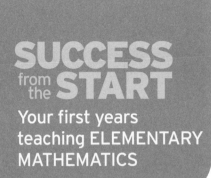

chapter fifteen

Homework

Guiding Principles

LEARNING IS MAXIMIZED WHEN STUDENTS—

>> interact in a safe, supportive learning community;

>> activate and build on prior knowledge;

>> process information both visually and linguistically;

>> solve problems with meaningful contexts;

>> engage in reflection, self-monitoring, and metacognition; and

>> engage in complex thinking.

Homework is an extension of your teaching; like your teaching, it should be purposeful. For students, homework should deepen understanding and solidify skills learned in class. Students can also learn to work independently and gain confidence in their math ability. For parents, homework communicates what students are learning. Homework can also serve as a vehicle for parents to help their children develop independent learning habits.

Finally, for teachers, homework gives feedback about students' learning that guides decisions about what math instruction students need.

Conflicting research exists about the benefits of homework and how much time students should spend on it. In general, the total number of minutes students should spend on homework is their grade level times ten. Time should serve as a guideline, not as an absolute. For example, if a first grader happily plays a math game with her family for twenty minutes, the homework accomplished two important outcomes: strengthening math skills and strengthening family bonds.

Whether you have a mandatory school homework policy or if you can set your own guidelines, your homework must purposefully advance student learning. You must be clear about how the home-

See More4U's Family Engagement chapter and the Math Orientation Workshop for suggestions to families about helping students with homework.

work supports student learning and what you expect students to learn from doing it. To maximize student learning, homework must be well designed.

The following are hallmarks of well-designed math homework:

- Tasks develop or solidify important mathematical ideas. Homework that supports math learning is purposeful.

- Students know the purpose of the homework. When students understand why they are doing homework and see its purpose in advancing their learning, they are more likely to invest in doing it.

- Instructions and expectations are clear. When students know what to do and what to expect, they can enter the task confidently and independently. Give written homework directions so students and their parents can read them. (If parents do not read English, have directions translated or explained in the native language.)

- Tasks are appropriately challenging. When tasks are accessible and challenge students appropriately, students are more likely to engage with homework and learn.

Essential Practices

>> **Know the different types of math homework and their purposes.**

>> **Make homework materials accessible.**

>> **Differentiate homework.**

>> **Give and receive feedback.**

DIFFERENT TYPES OF MATH HOMEWORK AND THEIR PURPOSES

Math homework generally falls into two categories: (1) practice and (2) preparation or elaboration.

Practice homework

Practice homework lets students practice skills and deepen understanding of important ideas learned in school. Homework should consist of math that students are familiar with. Usually, students need a week to become familiar with new ideas before you give them homework related to that content. If you assign homework with content that students are unfamiliar with or have just been introduced to, they probably will not know how to complete it independently. This sets up potential stress for families, who may feel compelled to teach their children. If they do so in ways inconsistent with those of the school, conflict arises. Families are not responsible for teaching students how to do the math; families support students' independent work habits and problem solving.

Problems

Homework problems give students practice in using tools and strategies learned in class. It is better for students to solve fewer problems in greater depth. Homework problems should require students to show their work and thinking so that students can more deeply engage in problem solving. When students have been taught the metacognitive problem-solving routine, they can practice how to think and monitor their work as they solve homework problems. They also get practice representing their work with clarity and precision.

Cumulative review problems give students continued practice with skills and concepts learned earlier in the year. Sustained practice enhances retention of knowledge and skills. Give students in grades 3–5 cumulative review problems every week. Many teachers give students cumulative review problems on Mondays and collect them on Fridays. This sustained practice enables students to more readily access and connect prior knowledge to new mathematical ideas introduced.

Math games

Many math programs include games that deepen students' understanding of number and operations and strengthen computation skills. If you consistently assign such games for homework, students get repeated practice that helps them learn their basic number facts and develop computational fluency. Games also give students and families a chance to engage in the math together. Playing games with their children lets parents see and experience the math their children learn in school. Build a large repertoire of games with increasing levels of challenge so that students do not get bored. Games that give grades K–3 students practice in number and operations and computation can be given for homework as cumulative review when they are studying other topics, such as geometry.

Sometimes family members or caregivers are not available to play math games assigned for homework. You can teach students how to play math games alone or with an imaginary partner. A second grader once reported the results of playing "Double Peace" with his imaginary partner: "I won the first game and Harry won the second. But when I won, I had 38 cards, and when Harry won, he had only 30!"

Focused fact practice

Before memorizing number facts, students should have a conceptual understanding of the numbers and operations underlying the facts. Some students learn their basic number facts through repeated practice with games that support development of computational fluency. Other students, however, need more focused and repeated practice to learn the number facts.

Students who need focused practice can use customized flash cards to support their learning of the number facts. For facts they do not know, ask students to identify and construct "helper problems"—facts that they know that can help them solve facts that they do not know—on the back of the cards. An example of a helper problem for $8 + 7$ is $(7 + 7) + 1$ (the strategy "doubles plus or minus 1"). An example of a helper problem for 8×7 is $(8 \times 5) + (8 \times 2)$ (using the distributive property). When students use these cards to practice their facts for homework, parents can appreciate that their students are learning their facts in a focused way. When parents see students using facts that they know to solve facts that they do not know, parents can appreciate how students make sense of mathematics to solve problems.

Preparation and elaboration homework

Preparation homework prepares students to study new content. Elaboration homework is for students to elaborate on information already introduced in class.

Preparing for multiplication

Before launching his multiplication unit of study, a third-grade teacher wants his students to have a meaningful context for understanding things that come in groups. For homework, he asks his students to brainstorm with family members things that come in groups of three, four, five . . . up to twelve. This activity not only engages family members in creative brainstorming but also supplies data for the next day's math class activity: constructing poster charts of things that come in groups.

Elaborating on multiplication

For homework, the third-grade teacher asks his students to choose one of the examples of things that come in groups and write and illustrate a multiplication story problem about it.

Preparing for decimals

Before launching her unit on decimals, a fourth-grade teacher assigns students to find and list decimals that they notice in their community and at home. They share their findings the next day, serving as a context for a discussion about decimals.

Elaborating on decimals

After a week of studying decimals, the fourth-grade teacher assigns students to write what they know about decimals by using words, numbers, and representations. Students are not expected to have a complete knowledge of decimals; her purpose is to assess what they know and understand at this point.

MAKE HOMEWORK MATERIALS ACCESSIBLE

To engage in the homework you assign, students must have access to the materials needed to complete their work.

Math boxes are simply boxes kept at home and serve as a place to store math games, manipulatives, and models that students need to complete homework. You can enlist families' help in getting shoeboxes or shoebox-sized bins to serve as math boxes.

Math games that students have learned in school can be sent home in plastic bags with instructions and game pieces. You can make game boards more durable by backing them on cardboard or laminating them. Game pieces need not be expensive manipulatives from your classroom. Inexpensive decks of ordinary playing cards can substitute for the more expensive numeral cards that often come with math programs. Families can remove the jokers and face cards and designate one set of face cards as the numeral zero.

Manipulatives are often necessary for primary students to support their developing understanding of number and operations, and these tools should be included in a math box. Pennies or other objects can be substituted for Unifix cubes or counters. Math boxes should also include models such as ten-frames, hundred charts, number lines, arrays, fraction clocks, and fraction strips. Some models, such as ten-frames and hundred charts, may also serve as game boards. However, students may use these models to help them solve other problems in their homework.

Sometimes struggling learners benefit from using the same manipulatives for homework that they use in the classroom. Use your own discretion as you consider what materials will best support students in completing homework. If you differentiate math instruction to meet the diverse needs of students, the homework should also be differentiated (see the next section). Therefore, the games and items in students' math boxes may vary.

The Family Engagement chapter (available on More4U) suggests that you engage families as partners by inviting them to volunteer in your math class. Enlist their help in assembling games and materials for math boxes. Such a collaborative effort offers many benefits. Families who volunteer become more familiar with your math curriculum. They will most likely feel valued because their efforts make a significant contribution to students' success in math. Engaging families in this way builds relationships essential to productive family-school partnership. Finally, having parents help you assemble games and materials gives you more time to attend to your math teaching.

DIFFERENTIATE HOMEWORK

Just as you differentiate tasks in math class to challenge students to develop their understanding of math along the landscape of learning, you should also differentiate homework. Two efficient ways to differentiate math homework are to differentiate games and to give students choice of problems.

Differentiate games

Chapter 14 suggested ways to modify math games to include variations that offer different levels of cognitive challenge. For a homework assignment, you can give all students the same game to play—at whatever level most appropriately challenges them. Another way to differentiate homework is to assign students to play different games, depending on the concepts and skills that students are developing. Another option is to give students a menu of games to choose from. Be clear about the mathematics you want students to develop and solidify as you assign games for homework.

Give students choice of problems

Another efficient way to differentiate homework is to give students problems at different levels of complexity and ask them to choose a given number of problems to solve. For example, if you give students homework with eight problems, ask students to choose four or five problems to solve. In this way, students self-differentiate. If any students choose problems that are too easy, talk to them privately, reaffirming your expectations that they choose appropriately challenging problems.

GIVE AND RECEIVE FEEDBACK

Review student homework so you can assess understandings or misconceptions. If students have misconceptions or do not understand the work, find out what they do know and where their understanding breaks down. In this way, the feedback you get from homework guides your instructional decisions. Depending on the assignment, you may choose to write descriptive feedback such as "You did a great job of showing all your steps and thinking" or "You did well to double-check by using a different strategy. Which do you think is most efficient?" However, it is not necessary, to write such detailed comments on every homework assignment.

Mr. Marcus, a fifth-grade teacher, devised an effective system for involving his students in giving and receiving feedback. He developed a rating scale with his students to indicate whether homework was too challenging (TC), just right (JR), or not challenging (NC) enough:

After they complete their homework, his students draw a scale (without the initials) at the top of the homework page to indicate the level of challenge:

Some students just use the initials: TC, JR or NC.

By engaging students in giving feedback on their work, Mr. Marcus invites them to take responsibility for their learning. From the students' point of view, this makes homework more purposeful. Also, Mr. Marcus explicitly describes to his students how he gives feedback and keeps track of their homework. After he reviews their homework, he marks each with a check. If students need help or more challenge, he checks in with them and asks, "What was challenging?" or "Why was this too easy?" He keeps track of students' homework completion in a record book, which he has shown to them. Students know that they are accountable for completing their homework, and Mr. Marcus is accountable for checking their work and responding to their feedback.

Think creatively about how you can engage your students in giving you purposeful feedback about homework.

CONCLUSION

As you plan homework assignments, remember that students may have different levels of support and resources at home. The homework you assign should strengthen and solidify students' mathematical ideas without putting undue pressure on families. To plan for successful student learning and family participation in homework, ensure the following:

- The homework is purposeful in strengthening or solidifying students' mathematical ideas.

- You explicitly state the purpose of the homework to students.

- The math ideas and procedures of tasks are familiar to students.

- Homework directions are clear and concise.

- Students have access to materials that enable them to complete the homework.

References

Boaler, Jo. *What's Math Got To Do With It? How parents and teachers can help children learn to love their least favorite subject.* New York: Penguin Books, 2008.

Bransford, John D., Ann L. Brown, and Rodney R. Cocking, eds. *How People Learn: Brain, Mind Experience, and School.* Expanded edition. Washington, D. C.: National Academy Press, 2000.

Bresser, Rusty, Kathy Melanese, and Christine Sphar. *Supporting English Language Learners in Math Class: Grades K-2.* Sausalito, CA: Math Solutions Publications, 2009.

————. *Supporting English Language Learners in Math Class: Grades 3-5.* Sausalito, CA: Math Solutions Publications, 2009.

Brewster, Cori, and Jennifer Fager. "Increasing Student Engagement and Motivation: From Time-on-Task to Homework." Northwest Regional Education Laboratory, 2000.

Brodesky, Amy, Fred Gross, Anna McTigue, and Cornelia Tierney. "Planning Strategies for Students with Special Needs: A Professional Development Activity". *Teaching Children Mathematics* 11 no.3 (Oct. 2004): 146-154.

Brophy, J. *Motivating Students to Learn.* Boston: McGraw-Hill, 1998.

Burns, Marilyn. *Math by All Means: Multiplication Grade 3.* Sausalito, CA: Math Solutions Publications, 1991.

Cai, Jinfa, and Frank Lester. "Why Is Teaching with Problem Solving Important to Student Learning?" *NCTM Research Brief* (2010).

Caine, Geoffrey, and Renate Nummela Caine. *Making Connections: Teaching and the Human Brain.* Alexandria, VA: ASCD, 1991.

Carpenter, Thomas P., Elizabeth Fennema, Megan Loef Franke, Linda Levi, and Susan B. Empson. *Children's Mathematics: Cognitively Guided Instruction.* Portsmouth, NH: Heinemann, 1999.

Chapin, Suzanne H., Catherine O'Connor, and Nancy Canavan Anderson. *Classroom Discussions: Using Math Talk to Help Students Learn, Grades 1-6.* Sausalito, CA: Math Solutions Publications, 2003.

Clements, Douglas H. "Computers in Early Childhood Mathematics." *Contemporary Issues in Early Childhood* 3, no. 2 (2002): 22.

Clements, D. H., and Sarama, J. (1998). *Building blocks—foundations for mathematical thinking, pre- kindergarten to grade 2: Research-based materials development* [National Science Foundation, grant number ESI-9730804; see www.Gse.Buffalo.Edu/org/buildingblocks/]. Buffalo, NY: State University of New York at Buffalo.

Coggins, Debra, Drew Kravin, Grace Davila Coates, and Maria Dreux Carroll. *English Language Learners in the Mathematics Classroom.* Thousand Oakes, CA: Corwin Press, 2007.

Danielson, Charlotte. *Enhancing Professional Practice.* Alexandria, VA: ASCD, 1996.

Darling-Hammond, Linda. *The Flat World and Education: How America's Commitment to Equity Will Determine Our Future.* New York: Teachers College Press, 2010.

Darling-Hammond, Linda. *The Right to Learn: A Blueprint for Creating Schools that Work.* San Francisco, CA: Jossey-Bass, 1997.

Delpit, Lisa D. *Other People's Children: Cultural Conflict in the Classroom* (Rev. ed.). New York: The New Press, 2006.

Donovan, Suzanne M. and John D. Bransford, eds. *How Students Learn: Mathematics in the Classroom.* Washington D. C.: The National Academies Press, 2005.

Dreambox Learning®. "Numbers to One Hundred on the Math Rack." http://www.dreambox.com/teachertools.

Dweck, C. S. *Mindset: The New Psychology of Success.* New York: Random House, 2006.

Empson, Susan B., and Linda Levi. *Extending Children's Mathematics: Fractions and Decimals: Innovations in Cognitively Guided Instruction.* Portsmouth, NH: Heinemann, 2011.

Epstein, Joyce L. *School, Family, and Community Partnerships.* Boulder, CO: Westview Press, 2011.

Ernst, Kathy. "Coaching and Supervising Reflective Practice". In *Student Successes with Thinking Maps®: School-Based Research, Results, and Models for Achievement Using Visual Tools* (2nd ed.) edited by David N. Hyerle and Larry Alper,178-191.Thousand Oaks, CA: Corwin Press, 2011.

Fisher, Douglas, and Nancy Frey. *Better Learning through Structured Teaching.* Alexandria, VA: ASCD, 2008.

Fosnot, Catherine Twomey, and Maarten Dolk. *Young Mathematicians at Work: Constructing Number Sense, Addition and Subtraction.* Portsmouth, NH: Heinemann, 2001.

———. *Young Mathematicians at Work: Constructing Multiplication and Division.* Portsmouth, NH: Heinemann, 2001.

———. *Young Mathematicians at Work: Constructing Fractions, Decimals, and Percents.* Portsmouth, NH: Heinemann, 2002.

Franke, M., H. Ghousseini, E Kazemi, and M. Lampert. "Supporting Teachers to Learn the Practice of Ambitious Mathematics Teaching." Presentation at the Teachers Development Conference, Portland, OR, February 16-19, 2011.

Fuson, Karen C., Douglas H. Clements, and Sybilla Beckman. *Focus in Grade 2: Teaching with Curriculum Focal Points.* Reston, VA: NCTM, 2011.

Goleman, Daniel. *Emotional Intelligence.* New York: Bantam Books, 1995.

Good, T.L. and J.E. Brophy. *Looking in Classrooms* (8th ed.). New York: Longman, 2000.

Harvard Family Research Project. www.finenetwork.org.

Herbal-Eisenmann, Beth A., and Lynn M. Breyfogle. "Questioning Our Patterns of Questioning." *Mathematics Teaching in the Middle School* 10, no. 9 (2005).

Hiebert, James, Thomas P. Carpenter, Elizabeth Fennema, Karen C. Fuson, Diana Wearne, Hanlie Murray, Alwyn Olivier, and Piet Human. *Making Sense : Teaching and Learning Mathematics with Understanding.* Portsmouth, NH: Heinemann, 1997.

Hyerle, David, and Chris Yeager. *Thinking Maps®: A Language for Learning.* Cary, N.C.: Thinking Maps, Inc., 2007.

Hyerle, David. *Visual Tools for Transforming Information into Knowledge* (2nd ed.). Thousand Oaks, CA: Corwin Press, 2009.

Jensen, Eric P. *Teaching with the Brain in Mind* (2nd ed.). Alexandria, VA: ASCD, 2005.

———. "A Fresh Look at Brain-Based Education." *Phi Delta Kappan* 89, no. 6 (2008): 408-17.

Jesse, Dan. "Increasing Parental Involvement: A Key to Student Achievement." http://www.mcrel.org/PDF/noteworthy/Learners_Learning_Schooling/danj.asp.

Kallick, Bena, and Ross Brewer. *How to Assess Problem-Solving Skills in Math.* New York: Scholastic Professional Books, 1997.

Kamii, C., and A. Dominick. "The Harmful Affects of Algorithms in Grades 1-4." In *Teaching and Learning of Algorithms in School Mathematics*, 130-40. Reston, VA: NCTM, 1998.

Kilpatrick, Jeremy, Jane Swafford, and Bradford Findell, eds. Adding It Up: Helping Children Learn Mathematics. Washington, D.C.: National Academies Press, 2001.

Krashen, Stephen D. "Second Language Acquisition and Second Language Learning." Pergamon Press Inc., 1981. http://www.sdkrashen.com/SL_Acquisition_and_Learning/index.html

Lambdin, D. V. "Benefits of Teaching through Problem Solving." In *Teaching Mathematics through Problem Solving: Prekindergarten-Grade 6*, edited by Frank K. Lester Jr. and R. I. Charles, 3-13. Reston, VA: National Council of Teachers of Mathematics, 2003.

Lampert, Magdalene, and Filippo Graziani. "Instructional Activities as a Tool for Teachers' and Teacher Educators' Learning." *The Elementary School Journal* 109, no. 5 (2009): 491-509.

Leinwand, Steven. *Accessible Mathematics: 10 Instructional Shifts That Raise Student Achievement.* Portsmouth, NH: Heinemann, 2009.

Martin, Tami S. *Mathematics Teaching Today: Improving Practice, Improving Student Learning.* Reston, VA: National Council of Teachers of Mathematics, 2007.

MacAnallen, Rachel R., "Examining Mathematics Anxiety in Elementary Classroom Teachers" (January 1, 2010). *Dissertations Collection for University of Connecticut.* Paper AAI3464333.

Marzano, Robert J. ed. *On Excellence In Teaching.* Bloomington, IN: Solution Tree Press, 2010.

Marzano, Robert J. *Transforming Classroom Grading.* Alexandria, VA: Association for Supervision and Curriculum Development, 2000.

Marzano, Robert J., Debra J. Pickering, and Jane E. Pollock. *Classroom Instruction That Works.* Alexandria, VA: ASCD, 2001.

Lovin, Lou, Maggie Kyger, and David Allsopp. "Differentiation for Special Needs Learners". *Teaching Children Mathematics* 11 no.3 (Oct. 2004): 158-167.

Mokros, Jan, Susan Jo Russell, and Karen Economopoulos. Beyond Arithmetic: Changing Mathematics in the Elementary Classroom: Dale Seymour Publications, 1996.

National Coalition for Parent Involvement in Education. www.ncpie.org.

National Council of Teachers of Mathematics. "Family Resources." www.nctm.org/resources/families.aspx.

————. *Curriculum and Evaluation Standards for School Mathematics.* Reston, Va.: Author, 1989.

————. *Principles and Standards for School Mathematics.* Reston, VA: National Council of Teachers of Mathematics, 1989.

————. *Principles and Standards for School Mathematics.* Reston, VA: National Council of Teachers of Mathematics, 2000.

———— . "Pan Balance - Shapes." http://illuminations.nctm.org/ActivityDetail. aspx?ID=33.

———— . "Fraction Feud." http://calculationnation.nctm.org/Games/.

———— . "How Many under the Shell." http://illuminations.nctm.org/ActivityDetail. aspx?ID=198.

———— . *Professional Standards for Teaching Mathematics*. Reston, VA: The Council, 1991.

National Network of Partnership Schools. www.csos.jhu.edu.

Northwest Regional Educational Laboratory. "Homework and Practice." http://www. netc.org/focus/strategies/home.php.

Office of Communication and Outreach. "Helping Your Child with Homework." edited by U.S. Department of Communication. Washington, D.C., 2005.

Pappano, Laura. "Differentiated Instruction Reexamined". *Harvard Education Letter*, 27 no.3 May/June (2011).

Polly, Drew. "Technology to Develop Algebraic Reasoning." *Teaching Children Mathematics* (2011).

Polya, G. *How to Solve It: A New Aspect of Mathematical Method*. Princeton, N.J.: Princeton University Press, 1985.

Ramirez, A.Y. "Fred" and Ivannia Soto-Hinman. "A Place for All Families". *Educational Leadership*, 66 no.7 April (2009): 79-82.

Restak, Richard. *The Secret Life of the Brain*. Washington, D.C.: National Academies Press, 2001.

Russell, Susan Jo. (May, 2000). Developing Computational Fluency with Whole Numbers in the Elementary Grades. In Ferrucci, Beverly J. and Heid, M. Kathleen (eds). Millenium Focus Issue: Perspectives on Principles and Standards. *The New England Math Journal*. Volume XXXII, Number 2. Keene, NH: Association of Teachers of Mathematics in New England. Pages 40-54.

Russell, Susan Jo, Deborah Schifter, Virginia Bastable. *Connecting Arithmetic to Algebra: Strategies for Building Algebraic Thinking in the Elementary Grades*. Portsmouth, NH: Heinemann, 2011.

Schmoker, Mike. "When Pedagogic Fads Trump Priorities." *Education Week* 30 no.5 (2010): 22-23.

Schön, Donald A. *The Reflective Practitioner*. New York: Basic Books, 1983.

Schoenfeld, Alan H. "Learning to Think Mathematically: Problem Solving, Metacognition, and Sense-Making in Mathematics." In *Handbook for Research on Mathematics Teaching and Learning*, edited by Douglas A. Grouws, 334-70. New York: MacMillan, 1992.

Schuster, Lainie, and Nancy Canavan Anderson. *Good Questions for Math Teaching: Why Ask Them and What to Ask, Grades 5-8*. Sausalito, CA: Math Solutions Publications, 2005.

Sergiovanni, T. *Building Community in Schools*. San Francisco, CA: Jossey-Bass, 1994.

Small, Marian. *Good Questions: Great Ways to Differentiate Mathematics Instruction*. New York: Teachers College Press, 2009.

Smith, M. S., E. K. Hughes, R. A. Engle, and M. K. Stein. "Orchestrating Discussions." *Mathematics Teaching in the Middle School* 14, no. 9 (2009): 548-56.

Smith, Margaret S., and Mary Kay Stein. *5 Practices for Orchestrating Productive Mathematics Discussions*. Reston, VA: NCTM, 2011.

Smith, M. S., M. K. Stein, F. Arbaugh, C. A. Brown, and J. Mossgrove. "Characterizing the Cognitive Demands of Mathematical Tasks." In *Professional Development Guidebook (a Supplement to the National Council of Teachers of Mathematics 2004 Yearbook).* Reston, VA: National Council of Teachers of Mathematics, 2004.

Sousa, David. *How the Brain Learns Mathematics.* Thousand Oaks, CA: Corwin Press, 2008.

Sousa, David A. and Carol Ann Tomlinson. *Differentiation and the Brain: How Neuroscience Supports the Learner-Friendly Classroom.* Bloomington, IN: Solution Tree Press, 2011.

Southwest Educational Development Laboratory (SEDL). "National Center for Family and Community Connections with Schools." www.sedl.org/connections.

Stein, M. K., M. S. Smith, M. A. Henningsen, and E. A. Silver. *Implementing Standards-Based Mathematics Instruction: A Casebook for Professional Development.* Second ed. Reston, VA: NCTM, 2009.

Sylwester, Robert. *A Celebration of Neurons: An Educator's Guide to the Human Brain.* Alexandria, VA: ASCD, 1995.

TERC. 2008. *Investigations in Number, Data, and Space*, 2nd Edition. Cambridge, MA: Pearson Education, Inc.

Tierney, Cornelia, and Susan Jo Russell. *Ten Minute Math.* Parsippany, N.J.: Dale Seymour Productions, 2001.

Tomlinson, Carol Ann. http://www.caroltomlinson.com

Van de Walle, John A., and S. Folk. *Elementary and Middle School Mathematics: Teaching Developmentally.* Second Canadian Edition ed. Toronto, ON: Pearson Education Canada, 2008.

Van de Walle, John A., and LouAnn H. Lovin. *Teaching Student Centered Mathematics: Grades K-3.* Vol. One, The Van de Walle Professional Mathematics Series. Boston: Pearson, 2006.

——— . *Teaching Student-Centered Mathematics: Grades 3-5.* Vol. Two, The Van de Walle Professional Mathematics Series, Boston: Pearson, 2006.

Weiss, Heather B., Suzanne M. Bouffard, Beatrice L. Bridglall, and Edmund W. Gordon. "Reframing Family Involvement in Education: Supporting Families to Support Educational Equity." In *Equity Matters: Research Review No 5*: Columbia University, 2009.

West, Lucy, and Fritz C. Staub. *Content Focused Coaching: Transforming Mathematics Lessons.* Portsmouth, NH: Heinemann, 2003.

Wiliam, Dylan. "Metacognition." http://www.journeytoexcellence.org.uk/videos/expertspeakers/metacognitiondylanwiliam.asp.

Willingham, Daniel T. *Why Don't Students Like School?* San Francisco: Jossey-Bass, 2009.

Wolfe, Pat. *Brain Matters: Translating the Research into Classroom Practice.* Alexandria, VA: ASCD, 2001.

Wolfe, Pat, and Ron Brandt. "What Do We Know from Brain Research?" *Educational Leadership* 56 no. 3 (1998).

INDEX

Accessibility, of homework materials, 254–255

Accuracy, as component of computational fluency, 21, 91

Action planning

 in lesson reflection, 172–173, 186–190

 professional development, for diverse learners, 248–249

Activities, rewriting for diverse learners, 243

Amygdala hijacks, 22

Anchor activities, for diverse learners, 248

Anxiety, inhibition of complex thinking by, 22–24, 53

Assessment, 217–232

 as basis for planning instruction, 24–25

 determining method for, 176–177

 of diverse learners, 239

 examples of student work and, 222–229

 goals and anticipated solutions to focus, 217

 observation and questioning for, 219–220

 observations of students at work to inform, 177–180

 preassessment for each unit and, 218–219

 teaching students to assess their own work and thinking and, 230–232

 of written work, 177–180, 220–222

Attitudes, of teachers, about mathematics, 54

Audiotaping, to get feedback on teaching, 191

Back-to-school night, 40–42

Beliefs, of teachers, about mathematics, 54

Brain

 engaging in learning with understanding, 22–31, 32

 exploring reasons for brains to do best thinking and problem solving and, 61–64

 transformation of information into knowledge by, 18–19

CCSSM (Common Core State Standards for Mathematics), vii

Charts

 contextualized, for diverse learners, 140

 strategy, 27

 wall space for, 51–52

Checking answers, learning with understanding and, 124

Choral Counting outline, 103–105

Choral response, for diverse learners, 140

Class discussion

 fostering, 208–212

 planning, 146–149

 whole-class, meeting areas for, 47–48

Class norms

 engaging students in constructing, 64

 feedback about enacting, 73

Classroom setup, 45–52

Cognates, for diverse learners, 244

Cognitive dissonance, 18

Colleagues

 best as resources, 37–38

 feedback on teaching from, 191

 ongoing support from, 36–38

 teaching at previous grade level, as resource, 36

Common Core State Standards for Mathematics (CCSSM), vii

Communicating

 with families, 40–43

 of thinking, 8–9

Complex thinking

 barriers to, 22–24, 53

 engaging students in, 30–31

Comprehensible input, for diverse learners, 238, 241

Computational fluency, 91

 definition of, 91

 essential practices for, 92

 flexibility and, 91, 93–94

 importance of, 21–22

 instructional routines supporting, 96–110

 making generalizations explicit to develop, 110–111

 models supporting development of, 94–96

Computers, space for, 50

Connections, looking for, 8–9

Content, for diverse learners, 238–239

Contexts

 adding, modifying, or creating, learning with understanding and, 123

 familiar, for diverse learners, 243

 meaningful. *See* Meaningful contexts

Contextualized charts, for diverse learners, 140

Curriculum materials, familiarizing yourself with, 38–39

Desk arrangements, for individual, partner, and small-group work, 48–50

Discussion. *See* Class discussion

Dispositions, problem-solving. *See* Problem-solving dispositions

Diverse learners, 235–249

 designing a professional development action plan for, 248–249

 managing differentiated lessons for, 247–248

 methods for differentiating tasks and games for, 244–247

 principles of differentiating mathematics instruction for, 237–240

strategies for differentiating mathematics instruction for, 240–244
Division lessons
lesson planning for, 132–149
lesson reflection on, 173–191
"Double Peace," 79–81
Dual coding, for diverse learners, 238
Dual-coding theory, 26

Efficiency, as component of computational fluency, 21, 91, 93–94
ELLs (English language learners). See Diverse learners
Embarrassment, inhibition of complex thinking by, 22–24
Emotional safety, to maximize learning by understanding, 22–24
Emotions. See also Supportive learning environment
role in learning, 53
English language learners (ELLs). See Diverse learners
Entry points, multiple, for diverse learners, 239
Errors, diagnosing and responding to, 218
Estimating, learning with understanding and, 123
Evidence review, in lesson reflection, 170–171, 173–186
Expectations
clarity and explicitness of, 23
for communicating one's thinking, 217
for learning, high, establishing, 56–59

Families, developing positive relationships with, 40–43
Fear, inhibition of complex thinking by, 22–24, 53
Feedback
descriptive, giving, 232–233
about developing problem-solving dispositions and enacting class norms, 73
homework and, 256–257
on teaching, methods for getting, 191
Flexibility, as component of computational fluency, 21–22, 91
Flexible grouping, for diverse learners, 247–248
Fluency, computational. See Computational fluency
Focused fact practice, as homework, 253–254
Funneling discourse pattern, 197, 198

Games
building math talk into, 213
differentiating, 255–256
for diverse learners, 247
as homework, 253
learning with understanding and, 122
routines to manage, 78–81

Generalizations
engaging students in complex thinking through, 31
making explicit to develop computational fluency, 110–111
Gestures, for diverse learners, 238
Grouping, instructional. See Instructional grouping
Grouping, instructional, for diverse learners, 247–248
Group norms
engaging class in reflecting on, 72
engaging students in reflecting on, monitoring, and assessing performance in carrying out, 72

Homework, 251–257
differentiating, 255–256
essential practices for, 252
families and, 41–42
giving and receiving feedback and, 256–257
making materials accessible and, 254–255
practice, 252–254
preparation and elaboration, 254
How Many Days Have We Been in School routine, 97–99

Individual work, desk arrangement for, 48–50
Information
processing through multiple senses, 26
transformation into knowledge by brain, 18–19
Initiate-respond-evaluate (IRE) discourse pattern, 197–198
Instructional grouping
for diverse learners, 239–240, 247–248
selecting children for, 25
Instructional routines, supporting computational fluency, 96–110
Investigations, learning with understanding and, 121
IRE (initiate-respond-evaluate) discourse pattern, 197–198

"Key words," problem with teaching, 120
Knowledge, transformation of into by brain, 18–19

Language
goals for, for diverse learners, 238–239
oral and written, for diverse learners, 238
Launching lessons
activating prior knowledge and, 152–155
difficulty with, lesson planning and, 130–131
evidence review and, 174–176
planning, 142–145
Learning
opportunities for, treating mistakes as, 23
role of emotions in, 53
rote, learning with understanding vs., 19–21

routines to support. *See* Routines to support mathematics learning

Learning environment, supportive. *See* Supportive learning environment

Learning goals
    for communicating one's thinking, 217
    to focus assessment and questioning, 217
    identifying and communicating, 216–217
    lesson planning and, 133–134, 136–137, 140–141

Learning with understanding, 115–127
    brain-engaging practices to maximize, 22–31, 32
    characteristics of tasks promoting, 116–119
    essential practices for, 115
    meaningful contexts and, 120–127
    rote learning vs., 19–21

Lesson analysis, in lesson reflection, 171, 186

Lesson enactment, 151–167
    activating prior knowledge and, 152–155
    sharing of strategies and, 161–167
    student approaches to problem and, 155
    student reasoning and, 156–161

Lesson planning, 129–149
    difficulty launching lessons and, 130–131
    difficulty maintaining focus on learning of class and, 131
    for division lessons, 132–149
    framework for, 131–132
    preparing to observe and support mathematical thinking and, 130

Lesson reflection, 169–194
    action planning and, 172–173, 186–190
    on division lesson, 173–191
    evidence review and, 170–171, 173–186
    framework for, 170
    lesson analysis and, 171, 186

Lessons, introducing, 5–7

Manipulatives, for diverse learners, 238, 241

Math anxiety
    reducing, 23–24
    in teachers, 54

Mathematical discourse, 195–214
    asking questions eliciting student thinking and, 198–204
    developing productive discourse patterns for, 197–198
    essential practices for, 197
    fostering broad participation and rich discussion and, 208–212
    making mathematical thinking visual and, 204–208
    methods of support of student learning by, 195–196

teaching explicit behaviors and language for, 212–214

Mathematical models, for diverse learners, 238

Mathematical thinking
    making visual, 204–208
    preparing to observe and support, 130

Math games, 53. *See* Games

Math materials
    accessible to students, 51
    care, use, and storage of, 81–82
    needed by students, 50
    routines to manage, 78–82

Math orientation workshops, 42

Math programs, contents of, 39

Math vocabulary walls, 27

Meaningful contexts
    learning with understanding and, 120–127
    for problem solving, 28–29

Meeting areas, for whole-class discussions, 47–48

Metacognition, engaging students in, 29–30

Mistakes, treating as learning opportunities, 23

Models
    for diverse learners, 238, 241
    supporting development computational fluency, 94–96
    visual. *See* Visual models

NCTM Process Standards, vii, 8–9, 32
    teaching with, 19–20

Neocortex Story, 62–63

Nonverbal responses, eliciting with diverse learners, 241

Norms, class. *See* Class norms

Number of the Day routine, 99–100

Number Strings routine, 105–110

Observations
    to assess and build on students' knowledge, 219–220
    of students at work, to inform assessment of written work, 177–180

Open-ended tasks, learning with understanding and, 125

Open tasks, 245

Parallel tasks, for diverse learners, 245–246

Paraphrasing, for diverse learners, 242

Partnerships, selecting children for, 25

Partner talk, with diverse learners, 241

Partner work, desk arrangement for, 48–50

Practice homework, 252–254

Preassessment, 218–219

Preparation and elaboration homework, 254

Prior experience, related to routine, activating, 76

Prior knowledge, activating and building, 25–26, 152–155
    for diverse learners, 239
Problems
    homework, 253
    sequence of actions in, 6–7
Problem solving, 8–9
    developing computational fluency through, 92–94
    meaningful contexts for, 28–29
    metacognition and, 29–30
    metacognitive routine for, teaching, 82–88
    metacognitive skills for, developing in diverse
        learners, 242
    minimizing directions for, learning with under-
        standing and, 122–123
    teaching students to monitor, 230
Problem-solving dispositions, vii–viii
    engaging students in monitoring and assessing
        development and transfer of, 73–74
    feedback about developing, 73
    guiding students in examining, 59–61
    teaching, 61
Professional development action plan, for diverse learners,
    248–249
Prompting students, class discussion and, 210

Questioning
    to assess and build on students' knowledge, 219–220
    to elicit student thinking, 198–204
Quick Images routine, 100–103

Readiness levels, grouping children and, 25
Real objects, for diverse learners, 243
Reasoning, 8–9
    class discussion and, 210
Repetition, for diverse learners, 140
Representations
    assessing, 221, 222
    simple, moving from elaborate drawings to, 234–235
    visual, mathematical thinking and, 204–208
Representing thinking on paper, 8–9
Restatement, class discussion and, 210
Revoicing
    class discussion and, 209
    for diverse learners, 242
Rote learning, learning with understanding vs., 19–21
Routines to support mathematics learning, 75–89
    activating students' prior experience related to, 76
    essential practices for supporting, 76
    following a general protocol to establish, 77–78

    math games and math materials management and,
        78–82
    problem-solving, metacognitive, teaching, 82–88
    purposeful, explicit, and consistently implemented,
        76–77

Scaffolding
    grouping students and, 25
    of model use, 27
Sentence frames, for diverse learners, 243–244
Sequencing skills, developing in diverse learners, 242
Showing work, learning with understanding and, 123
Small-group work, desk arrangement for, 48–50
Solutions, student, sharing with whole group, 10–15
Story problems
    learning with understanding and, 120–121
    rewriting for diverse learners, 243
Strategies
    assessing, 221, 222
    more efficient, moving students to, 229
Strategy charts, 27
Stress, inhibition of complex thinking by, 22–24, 53
Struggling learners. See Diverse learners
Students having difficulty, supporting, 9–10
Student solutions, sharing with whole group, 10–15
Supportive learning environment, 53–73
    building and sustaining, 70–72
    dispositions of problem solvers and, 59–61
    for diverse learners, 237
    engaging students in constructing class norms and,
        64–70
    essential practices for, 55
    examining one's beliefs and attitudes about math-
        ematics and, 54
    exploring reasons for brains to do best thinking and
        problem solving and, 61–64
    high expectations for learning and, 56–59
    laying groundwork for, 56–70
    to maximize learning with understanding, 22–24
    picturing, 54–56

Tasks
    for diverse learners, 244–247
    lesson planning and, 133–134, 137–140
Teachers. See also Colleagues
    examination of beliefs and attitudes about mathematics
        by, 54
Teaching
    of "key words," problem with, 120
    of metacognitive routine for problem solving, 82–88

Think-alouds, for diverse learners, 242
Thinking
 communicating, 8–9
 complex. *See* Complex thinking
 expectations for, 217
 explaining, learning with understanding and, 123
 mathematical. *See* Mathematical thinking
 questions eliciting, 198–204
 representing on paper, 8–9
Today's Number routine, 205–208
Tools, assessing, 221, 222

Understanding, learning with. *See* Learning with understanding

Videotaping, to get feedback on teaching, 191
Visual learning, 26–28
Visual models, 27
 for diverse learners, 240–241
 wall space for, 51–52
Visual representations, mathematical thinking and, 204–208
Visuals, for diverse learners, 238, 243

Wait time, 23
 class discussion and, 209
 for diverse learners, 241
Wall space, for visual models and charts, 51–52
Whole-class discussions, meeting areas for, 47–48
Work habits, teaching students to monitor, 231–232
Work time
 evidence review and, 176–186
 planning, 146
Written work
 analyzing, 220–222
 teaching students to monitor, 230–231